INFORMATION SOURCES
FOR RESEARCH AND DEVELOPMENT

THE USE OF
ECONOMICS LITERATURE

**INFORMATION SOURCES
FOR RESEARCH AND DEVELOPMENT**

A series under the General Editorship of

R. T. BOTTLE,
B.Sc, PhD, FRIC MIINFSCI

and

D. J. FOSKETT,
MA, FLA

THE USE OF
ECONOMICS LITERATURE

Edited by
JOHN FLETCHER
B.A. (Econ.), A.L.A.

Economics Librarian, University of Warwick

LONDON
BUTTERWORTHS

THE BUTTERWORTH GROUP

ENGLAND
Butterworth & Co. (Publishers) Ltd
London: 88 Kingsway WC2B 6AB

AUSTRALIA
Butterworth & Co. (Australia) Ltd
Sydney: 20 Loftus Street
Melbourne: 343 Little Collins Street
Brisbane: 240 Queen Street

CANADA
Butterworth & Co (Canada) Ltd
Toronto: 14 Curity Avenue, 374

NEW ZEALAND
Butterworth & Co (New Zealand) Ltd
Wellington: 49/51 Ballance Street
Auckland: 35 High Street

SOUTH AFRICA
Butterworth & Co (South Africa) (Pty) Ltd
Durban: 33/35 Beach Grove

First published 1971

© Butterworth & Co (Publishers) Ltd, 1971

Suggested UDC No. 002:33

ISBN 0 408 70171 4

Printed in England by Northumberland Press Limited
Gateshead

FOREWORD

Libraries do not consist of books any more than the national income consists of the stock of capital. It is the flow of services from the stock which counts and in maximising the value of the flow of services, the highly-skilled labour of the graduate Librarian specialising in a particular subject, can do more than anything else. It follows that a book about books organised by a possessor of this skill and including a number of direct beneficiaries of it, among the contributors, adds to the stock of books in a specially valuable way. To know where to look and how to look for what has been written in particular fields is a prerequisite of effective academic activity; both in teaching and research. It can help particularly with the productive choice of a field for research, as the earlier chapters stress; and not only the inexperienced postgraduate who has to make the choice, but also members of the academic staff whose advice is sought and often inadequately given. But the latter can also gain directly for themselves in overcoming the inertia of specialisation into which they often feel locked by sheer unfamiliarity with the literature of other fields. With better guidance from books such as this, they can break free, and we may hope to see more economists relieved of the risk of barrenness in fresh fields. The general economist may be doomed to extinction; all the more important to replace him with others who have many irons in the fire.

So both those who seek and those who have found where they want to work in economics should be the particular beneficiaries of this book. But it also serves the wider purposes of demonstrating the proposition that the indispensable complement to having books is knowing how to use them.

University of Warwick   J. R. SARGENT

CONTENTS

vii

THE USE OF ECONOMICS LITERATURE

Note on Alterations to Government Economic Departments and Publications following the UK General Election in 1970

Since the manuscript of this book was written there has been a change of government in Great Britain, and a major reorganisation of many of the government departments mentioned in the text. The following is a brief list of the more important changes affecting the contents of Chapters 7 and 10.

The Board of Trade was amalgamated with the Ministry of Technology in the Department of Trade and Industry (DTI). The new Department takes on all the responsibilities of the Board plus responsibility for monopolies and mergers from the Department of Employment and Productivity (renamed the Department of Employment).

The Monopolies Commission is to be strengthened, and the National Board for Prices and Incomes abolished. The latter will be replaced by three review bodies to deal with the pay of certain groups for whom no negotiating machinery is appropriate. The work of these bodies will be coordinated by an independent Office of Manpower Economics, and the Commission for Industry and Manpower will not, therefore, be set up.

A Consultative Document and an Industrial Relations Bill have been published to replace the proposals in *In Place of Strife* (Cmnd. 3888).

The Industrial Reorganisation Corporation is to be wound up.

From the issue of October 21st, the *Board of Trade Journal* is renamed *Trade and Industry*.

Regional industrial development is under the Department of Trade and Industry, but the planning aspects of regional policy remain the responsibility of the Ministry of Housing and Local Government, which is subsumed into the new Department of the Environment.

J.F.   December 1970

CONTRIBUTORS

GEORGE S. BAIN, M.A., D.PHIL., Deputy Director, Industrial Relations Research Unit of the SSRC, University of Warwick

R. D. COLLISON BLACK, B.COMM., M.A., PH.D., Professor of Economics, Queen's University, Belfast

ERIC C. BLAKE, B.A., A.L.A., Chief, Government Publications Department, British Library of Political and Economic Science

JOHN R. CABLE, B.A., M.A. (ECON.), Lecturer in Economics, University of Warwick

JEREMY E. K. CORBETT, B.A., Research Assistant, University of Warwick

DAVID R. CROOME, B.A., M.A., Lecturer in Economics, Queen Mary College, University of London

CHARLES A. CROSSLEY, F.L.A., Senior Assistant Librarian, Readers' Services, University of Bradford

SUSAN EDGE, B.A., Library Clerk, House of Commons Library

L. FISHMAN, B.A., PH.D., Professor of Economics, University of Keele

JOHN FLETCHER, B.A. (ECON.), A.L.A., Assistant Librarian, Economics and Business Studies, University of Warwick

A. G. FORD, M.A., D.PHIL., Professor of Economics, University of Warwick

A. F. HEATH, B.A., Jesus College, Oxford

D. C. L. HOLLAND, M.A., Librarian, House of Commons Library

K. E. HUNT, M.A., DIP.AGRIC.SCI., University Lecturer in Agricultural Economics, Institute for Agricultural Economics, Oxford

C. E. V. LESER, DR. PHIL., M.SC. (ECON.), Professor of Econometrics, University of Leeds

S. K. NATH, B.SC. (ECON.), PH.D., Senior Lecturer in Economics, University of Warwick

F. GRAHAM PYATT, B.A. (ECON.), A.M., M.A., PH.D., Professor of Mathematical Economics, University of Warwick

MICHAEL SHAFE, B.SC. (ECON.), A.L.A., Sub-Librarian, University of York; temporarily at University of Wisconsin

G. N. VON TUNZELMAN, B.A., M.A., St. John's College, Cambridge

ALAN H. WILLIAMS, B.COMM., Professor of Economic Policy, University of York

GEOFFREY E. WOOD, M.A., Lecturer in Economics, University of Warwick

GILLIAN B. WOOLVEN, B.A., A.L.A., formerly Assistant Librarian, Nuffield College, Oxford, and Research Fellow, University of Manchester Institute of Science and Technology

CHAPTER ONE

INTRODUCTION

JOHN FLETCHER

The literature of economics is currently growing at a compound rate of about five and a half per cent a year. New journals devoted to specific aspects of economics are born each year, and due to the consistently large supply of journal articles the mortality rate of economics journals is abnormally low. The delay in publication has given rise to the 'working paper' (*see* pp. 68–70). Doctoral dissertations completed in American universities and listed in *American Economic Review* annually have increased sevenfold from 1928 to 1969. Book publication in economics is increasing too, but probably not at such a high rate. Allied to this growth in the literature is the growth in the number of practising economists: for example, membership of the American Economic Association has almost doubled in the last ten years. With the established academic principle of 'publish or perish' this gives rise to an even greater supply of publishable material: a vicious spiral of new publications.

The complexity of the literature used by the researcher in economics and the inevitable problems of handling it in libraries are also increasing. One only needs to scan the range of types of literature cited by economists to see the breadth of their subject interests: statistics, theory, mathematics, government documents, statutes, international agreements, unpublished working papers and theses are now commonly used alongside the traditional monographs, conference papers and journal articles.

The study of economics, like that of most subjects, has become more specialised: the 'general economist' is a rare bird nowadays, and the least specialised are interested in a group of narrow, but related, subjects. At first sight specialisation appears to help the researcher: by narrowing his field of vision, he reduces the quantity of newly published literature he must scan to keep up to date with developments in his specialist subject. There is, for example,

1

less new material on British incomes policy than on labour economics or wages.

Unfortunately, specialisation also entails a degree of blinkering, and the recent developments in economics make an economist with literary tunnel vision an inefficient researcher. Techniques are being developed in one specialised area which are also valuable to workers in another: the development economist, for example, cannot afford to ignore new methods and analysis being used in public finance, international trade, industrial economics, monetary policy or consumer behaviour, to note just a few related subjects.

Interdisciplinary subjects are also growing up, and these too must be watched carefully for new developments which may influence the work being done in economics. Industrial law, industrial psychology, economic sociology, and operational research all have repercussions on economics, as do the more traditional subjects of mathematics, especially statistical mathematics, politics, law, sociology, and education.

The net result is the bewilderment of the researcher, but a few aids are being created to help him: bibliographical tools designed to speed up the economists' scanning of bushels of chaff to find the occasional ear of wheat. The *Journal of Economic Literature* began in 1969 as a restyled and completely changed version of *Journal of Economic Abstracts*. This is providing an excellent service in giving a rapid, and fairly comprehensive view of the economics literature organised in such a way that the specialist can scan the *Journal* quickly and efficiently, and feel reasonably certain that he will have found references to most of the main published items of interest to him. This current awareness or alerting service is invaluable, and for retrospective searching the economist has the *International Bibliography of Economics* and the *Index of Economic Journals* (now *Index of Economic Articles*).

The present book is the first joint attempt by librarians and economists to view the literature of the subject, and provide a guide to it. It is aimed at advanced undergraduate, and postgraduate students, and especially those embarking on research projects in subjects partially divorced from their previous experience. More experienced economists too will find its contents of value in indicating recent trends and titles in subjects allied to their own specialisation. The book falls broadly into three parts: libraries, materials and subjects, and there is inevitably some overlap between them. First is a chapter on the British and American libraries which are strong in economics material, and on the best way of tackling a literature search on a new research topic. Following this is a chapter on how libraries are organised, with special reference to economics collections. This chapter is aimed to assist researchers to make the best use of existing library resources.

Next is a group of seven chapters on the various kinds of material most used by economists, including bibliographical tools, periodicals, unpublished papers and theses, British and United States government publications, official publications of international organisations, and economic statistics from the U.K., U.S. and some supra-national sources.

Lastly, the fourteen chapters on different subject areas within economics are written by experienced and practising economists, and are aimed to give a brief guide to the material available in each subject. These are not intended to be comprehensive reviews of the subject, or surveys of the literature, but rather to reflect the author's personal view of that literature, and note the sources of information and bibliographical tools which he has found most useful. No attempt has been made to impose uniformity on these authors, since the literature of the different fields of study within economics varies widely: in some, like labour economics, journals are more important than books, whilst the reverse may be true of another subject such as international economics. Uniformity is thus impossible, and in any case, undesirable.

What this book attempts to do, then, is to give economists, and would-be economists, a guide to three things: (a) what material there is on the various branches of the subject, what is important and valuable, and what level it best serves; (b) what tools are available to assist the researcher in making a more extensive and intensive survey of the literature of his specialised field, and (c) where the material can be found. We hope too that it will be found useful as a reference tool, as a source of information on statistics sources, bibliographical tools, periodicals, economics libraries and above all, on economics books.

CHAPTER TWO

LIBRARIES AND MAKING A LITERATURE SEARCH

JOHN FLETCHER

By the time he graduates, the economics student will have used several different types and sizes of library, from the school library or the private collection of a favourite schoolmaster, through the local public library, to the large university library. Later in his career he may do research and need to use other university libraries, or archives collections, or he may enter industry or commerce and use the small special library of his firm or the industrial research organisation.

All these libraries with their varying size and subject coverage, have one aim in common: the dissemination of information. Slowly the image of the library as a prison for books, with the librarian as warder, is giving way to the concept of the store of information in many different forms, with the librarian as the guide through the complexities of a large warehouse. In Chapter 3 the organisation of the library is examined and advice given on how to make the best use of the collection. This chapter surveys the different kinds of library, their aims, contents and clienteles, and looks in more detail at a few of the libraries specialising in economics literature.

In most countries a law of copyright exists which defines the conditions under which published material may be reproduced. The same law usually decrees that anyone publishing anything (in Great Britain the law includes anything from encyclopaedias to beer bottle labels) must deposit one copy in the national library. These are known as 'deposit libraries' and in Great Britain the British Museum is the national library, in the United States of America it is the Library of Congress. In addition, organisations such as the government publisher, or the United Nations, may designate other libraries as deposit libraries for their own publications. The British Library of Political and Economic Science at the London School of Economics is a depository for United

4

States government publications, Leeds City Libraries for UNESCO documents. In the United States of America there are many deposit libraries for government and international organisations' publications.

Basically there are four kinds of library, and this chapter will consider each in turn: national, academic, public, and special. There are differences of size, content, availability, and above all, users.

National Libraries

These are the great libraries, the really large collections of material from books, through pamphlets, periodicals, manuscripts and maps to the new media such as microfilms, photographs, slides and films, and now sound and video tapes. The **British Museum** began book collecting when the Sir Hans Sloane collection was given to the nation in 1753. Four years later George II gave the Royal Library, and with it came the copyright deposit. The collection really came alive under Anthony Panizzi, principal librarian from 1851 to 1866: he reorganised the stock, and enforced the copyright law deposit clause.

Nowadays the British Museum does not attempt to be comprehensive internationally but collects most books in the English language, and a high percentage of foreign books in 'humanistic' subjects. Like most deposit libraries it is not allowed by law to lend its stock which is available for reference only. Admission is restricted, and researchers must apply for permission to use the library. There are now over six million volumes in the Department of Printed Books.

National Library of Scotland, Edinburgh
National Library of Wales, Aberystwyth

These two large regional collections are also copyright deposit libraries in that they may request a copy of any book published in Great Britain. Both are strong in regional archival and printed material, and old-established: the Scottish library grew out of the Advocates Library founded in 1682. Admission to use the collections is restricted in a similar way to the British Museum.

Both Libraries are in the 2–2½ million volume range, with extensive manuscripts and special collections. Regional material and humanistic subjects predominate, and there is a wealth of historical raw material.

5

Library of Congress

This is possibly the world's largest library with about forty million items, of which about thirteen million are books. The strongest subjects are law, history and the social sciences, with many special collections.

Academic Libraries

This term can be applied to a wide range of libraries from the large collections of Cambridge University Library and the Bodleian Library at Oxford (both deposit libraries on demand) to the small specialised libraries of colleges of education. Here, however, the main concern is with university libraries. The university libraries of Oxford, Cambridge and London apart (*see* pp. 8–9), British university libraries fall into three broad groups by size and age. First come the old-established provincial universities with about 700 000 volumes: Birmingham, Manchester, Glasgow and Edinburgh Universities, for example. The provincial universities founded just before and after the second world war, such as Nottingham, Keele, Bristol and Hull, are the second group with about 300 000 volumes. Last is the group of 'new' universities and technological universities which received their charters in the 1960s: Warwick, Lancaster, Essex, Bradford, Surrey and Salford are in the 100 000 to 150 000 volume group, most aiming for a quarter of a million volumes by the end of the decade.

These statistics are not impressive when compared with American and European universities, although they look better when the relative sizes of student populations are taken into account. Harvard University Library's seven and a half million books, Yale's four and a half million, and California (Berkeley) with three million are examples of the largest American academic libraries. The state universities tend to have around three quarters of a million volumes though many of the smaller universities have less.

These libraries' bookstocks will reflect the emphases of the teaching programme in the institution they serve. The position the library holds in the pecking order for limited funds will govern its ability to meet the ever-increasing demands made on its services. The quality of these services will depend in turn on the finance being available, and the personalities of the chief librarian and his staff.

6

Public Libraries

The free public library movement got under way in Great Britain in the 1850s in the larger cities such as Birmingham (1850) and Manchester (1854). In the United States the movement began about the same time with Boston (1854), Cincinnati (1856) and Chicago (1873), but in both countries the main development came in the 1930s. All are financed from public funds collected locally and are thus to a large extent dependent upon local interest and support for finance and the services offered. Most of the larger libraries have a departmental system with separate collections in different subject areas. One of these is usually economics, though often under the more acceptable title of 'business' or 'commercial' library. Most academics dismiss the public library as a source of economics material, but many contain excellent collections of economic and commercial information, and are very useful sources for the economist, especially the economic historian.

Special Libraries

This is an amorphous group comprising the much smaller libraries (sometimes called information services) found in firms or research organisations. They are usually small, very specialised collections of a few thousand books or pamphlets in a narrow subject area. They are geared to provide a rapid and detailed information service to their restricted clientele, but many will allow genuine researchers from outside the organisation to use their resources if these are unique and necessary to the research project.

Guides to Libraries

With such a welter of libraries, guides to special collections of material are necessary. For Great Britain there is the *Aslib Directory* (2 vols, Aslib, 1968–70) which enumerates libraries geographically, and provides a subject index. Lee Ash and Denis Lorenz: *Subject Collections* (Bowker, 1967) does a similar job for the United States and Canada, listing libraries under alphabetically-arranged subject headings. The arrangement of Richard C. Lewanski: *Subject Collections in European Libraries* (Bowker, 1965) is a classified one using the Dewey Decimal Classification. All these guides give varying amounts of detail about the size of the collection, its strengths, and its availability to researchers.

7

Economics Libraries

There is not room here to list all the libraries which have specialist collections in economics, but a few are so important that they warrant special mention.

British Library of Political and Economic Science

This is the Library of the London School of Economics and Political Science in the University of London. Founded in 1896 by Sidney Webb and public subscription it grew rapidly between the wars, and is now the best specialised library in this subject area in Great Britain. The half a million volumes are particularly strong in international affairs, labour economics and history, official publications, and economic theory, with specialist collections in transport, trade unions and the book trade. It has daunting physical problems of space, and is not normally open to other readers except during vacations.

Goldsmiths' Library, University of London

This is the first of three libraries based on the private collections of Professor Foxwell. His first collection of 30 000 volumes of early economics was bought by the Goldsmiths' Company and given to the University of London in 1903. This laid the foundation of the present collection of 70 000 volumes of books and manuscripts from the sixteenth century to 1850: later special material is collected by the British Library of Political and Economic Science. Like this library, Goldsmiths' Library is available to other researchers during vacations, with the permission of the librarian.

Marshall Library, University of Cambridge

This small library of 65 000 volumes is probably the best purely economics library in Great Britain. Established in 1925, it is based on the departmental library collected by Alfred Marshall and to which his own library was bequeathed in 1924. Other important collections include the Pryme Library (of early political economy) and the libraries of Lord Keynes and Professor Pigou. Although small and heavily used by staff and students the collection is open to other researchers on prior application to the librarian.

8

Institute of Economics and Statistics, University of Oxford

Another small library of about 60 000 volumes: the special strength of this collection lies in its excellent coverage of current economic conditions and problems of developing countries. It houses an excellent collection of economic statistics from all over the world.

Other British Libraries

Most libraries in universities teaching economics have collections of current literature, and some of the older established libraries such as that at St. Andrews, have valuable earlier material. Useful archival material on local industries and families are in the university libraries of Nottingham and Leeds, and Aberdeen has a collection on Scottish trade unions and on transport. Edinburgh University Library has a collection of over a thousand late eighteenth- and early nineteenth-century books on economic theory, including some of Adam Smith's library. Hull has a good working library in economics with particular strength in banking and finance, especially relating to south-east Asia. Bristol has a collection of business and trade union histories, and Reading's interest in agriculture has given rise to an interesting collection of historical farm records. Russian and East European studies and the West African Centre at Birmingham University have created good collections on these subjects, whilst Southampton University has the Ford Collection of parliamentary papers. A few other special collections are mentioned in the sections by Professor Black and Mr Hunt on pp. 190–191 and 277.

The public libraries of large cities contain valuable local collections of economic and industrial material, and especially worth noting is the Guildhall Library in London, with its collection of business and commercial histories. The commercial reference room is now in separate premises, and called the City Business Library. The Board of Trade Statistics and Market Intelligence Library is the largest easily accessible collection of current economic statistics in Great Britain, with over 3000 titles. With the aid of a grant from the Nuffield Foundation and invaluable assistance from the Board of Trade the library of the University of Warwick is building up a comprehensive collection of historical and current economic statistics from all over the world. It is hoped that by 1971 it will be organised and available for use by industrial and academic researchers.

9

United States Libraries

There are many large and comprehensive collections of economics books in American academic libraries, and only a few can be noted here. Pride of place must go, of course, to the Baker Library at Harvard University. Professor Foxwell having disposed of his first library to the Goldsmiths' Company, began collecting again, and sold the second library to form the foundation of the Baker Library. This has developed as the library for economics and business studies at Harvard, and now has about 400 000 volumes. It is especially strong in business and industrial history, with large collections of manuscripts and documentary material.

The Seligman Library at Columbia University is the third library based on the book-buying activities of Professor Foxwell: the special collection of early economic material is excellent. Yale University has two smaller specialised collections of current economics material: the libraries of the Economics Growth Center and the Cowles Foundation for Research in Economics, whilst the Pliny Fisk Library of Economics and Finance at Princeton University has a good collection of material on corporations. The University of California Institute of Industrial Relations Library is strong on labour economics and trade unions, and the Harvard University Industrial Relations Library should also be mentioned in this context. Wayne State University Library although not large in total, has a special Labor History Archives Collection, and Syracuse University Library a useful economic history collection.

Many public libraries in the United States also have special collections of interest to economists, including Detroit, Minneapolis, Brooklyn, New York and Cleveland. Some special libraries who may make their collections available to genuine researchers are the Federal Reserve Banks, Department of Agriculture, Department of Labor, and the Bureau of the Census.

Making a Literature Search

Most research workers beginning a new project, or extending their present one, feel the need for a complete list of what has been, or is about to be written on their subject. Their ability to produce one quickly and efficiently usually depends upon the extent to which their University Librarian has pursued a policy of teaching undergraduates. Depressingly few undergraduates are given a thorough training in the use of the Library and of the literature of their subject, and it is at the stage of beginning some original research that the researcher appreciates this lack of training.

This book is a survey of the basic literature which an economist needs to know of, whilst this chapter is a series of brief notes on the steps he should take to produce a reasonably complete picture of the published and unpublished material on his chosen topic, without unnecessary duplication of effort, and without omitting any vital stage.

The first, and most important, step is the careful definition of the subject. Librarians are all too familiar with the inquirer who pitches his question too high, who asks for 'your books on American industry' when he wants to know the number of employees of General Motors, or who asks for 'Russian economic theory' when he wants the Liberman controversy. The definition of the subject can be a salutary task: the careful delineation of the subject matter, and the decision on where the project shall begin and end, can make or mar the result. The subject should also be related mentally to the wider subjects which embrace it, for books on the more general subject will include valuable material on its parts.

'Definition of the subject' should also include a decision on the period through which the search is to be made, the type of material to be included, and the completeness of the finished list desired. The first is often dictated by the subject, or the researcher's time available; the second may be decided by the researcher's knowledge that the subject has only been written about in a certain form, although this is a dangerous assumption, and it is normally preferable to attempt coverage of all types of material; the degree of completeness is again a function of the time available.

An ancillary, and useful, side issue of the decision on subject definition is the compilation of a list of terms used in connection with the topic which may be used in subject indexes. This list, if used correctly, and added to as the search proceeds, will ensure that no entries are missed because they are made under unusual terms. Synonyms and possible transatlantic variations in terminology should be noted.

The researcher's 'home' library catalogue, together with any special indexes which the library staff may compile, should be tackled first (see pp. 22–26), then Besterman's *World Bibliography of Bibliographies,* and *Bibliographic Index* (pp. 33–34) to ensure that there is no recent bibliography of the subject. Review articles (pp. 54 and 183) will be found later in the normal course of checking for journal articles in abstracting and indexing services.

Assume now that no bibliography has been found which would

make it unnecessary to continue the search, and that the personal literature search must be begun. As they are found, references to books and articles should be reproduced accurately, and with a note of the source of the reference. It is best to make the bibliography on cards to facilitate checking, rearrangement, and constant addition. The minimum correct bibliographical reference laid down in British Standard BSS 1629 is as follows: for books: author, title, year of publication (librarians welcome the inclusion of the name of the publisher, and this can be of some value to the researcher as a guide to the country of origin, and the standard of scholarship of the work); for periodical articles: author, title (of the article), periodical title, volume number, issue number, date of issue, and page numbers of the article. Where more appropriate the first two items may be transposed. It is advisable to add the source in which the reference was found in order to enable a recheck to be made in case of later difficulties in tracing the work.

The subject catalogue of the library is the first step (*see* pp. 25–26), and this should be checked very carefully under all possible headings. The importance of the general bibliographies will depend upon the size and quality of the library catalogue already checked: the larger the library, the less likely that the standard national bibliographies will yield much new material. The time needed, however, to check these for normal purposes is so small as to make it a worth-while operation since even the most efficient library cannot afford to buy everything published. The following national bibliographies should therefore be searched.

British National Bibliography (p. 36) and *Cumulative Book Index* (p. 37) for English-language material, and the relevant national bibliographies (pp. 36–38) if other countries' publications are needed. For older publications and those issued in unexpected places the subject catalogue of the Library of Congress (pp. 35–36) and especially the *London Bibliography of the Social Sciences* (p. 39) are essential. Government publications and those of supranational organisations should be included in most literature searches and these can be found by checking the tools noted in Chapters 7, 8 and 9, and in the *PAIS Bulletin* (pp. 42 and 184).

Periodical articles can now be added to the bibliography by using the abstracting and indexing services most appropriate to the subject. *Index Bibliographicus,* vol. 2 (4th edn Fédération Internationale de Documentation, 1964) is the best guide to specialised services, but most economists would be satisfied with *Index of Economic Journals* (p. 185), *International Bibliography of Economics* (pp. 185–186) and *Economic Abstracts*.

The *Journal of Economic Literature*, now vastly improved,

should be used finally to bring the list of references as up to date as possible.

Unpublished theses are then added by checking the tools noted in Chapter 6, especially *Dissertation Abstracts International* and *Index to Theses*. . . . The list of doctoral dissertations in the September issue of *American Economic Review*, or in other journals (*see* p. 73) will bring the list up to date. There is, as yet, no current listing of the working papers discussed in Chapter 6, so the researcher must be satisfied with those collected by his own library (found usually through the library catalogue). The tools mentioned on pp. 67–68 will add not references, but information on who is currently working on the same or allied problems. This list of other workers in the field may also help in tracking down unpublished working papers circulated in advance of publication.

This completes the preparation of the bibliography. New references will be added as the books and articles are read and citations followed up. Keeping the list up to date is essential, and relatively simple: new issues of the current bibliographies, abstracting and indexing services, and above all *Journal of Economic Literature* should be scanned. Some periodicals will have proved particularly fruitful sources of articles on the specific topic, and new issues of these should be checked as they arrive in the library. For journals not in the 'home' library the contents pages of over 120 journals are reproduced in each issue of *Economic Journal*. The Department of Trade and Industrial Central Library is to publish a weekly *Contents of Recent Economic Journals* from January 1971, covering (initially) 143 titles.

The time taken to complete this search will vary with the comprehensiveness sought, and the nature of the subject, but should not be more than two or three days. This is time well spent at the beginning of a new project, for many researchers have completed several months' hard work, only to discover that it had already been published, or written up elsewhere.

CHAPTER THREE

USING THE ECONOMICS LIBRARY

CHARLES A. CROSSLEY

No seeker of information can proceed far without using a library. All libraries vary in pattern of provision, although information is the common coinage. No attempt will be made here to describe a typical library and its methods and services: guidance will be offered instead which is designed to help any reader searching for information in a library with economics or its application in mind.

The first thing to note about a library is that it is a storehouse of knowledge, wherein the record of that knowledge may be contained in a very wide variety of physical forms. These range from the traditional book, through periodicals, newspapers, leaflets and memoranda, reports, maps, financial statements, statistical data, graphs, charts, microfilm, microcard or microfiche, film, magnetic tape or wire, or gramophone records. With the realisation of this wide range comes ready acceptance of the first maxim for library users: don't expect to find all you seek in one place! Physical considerations alone require separate storage of diverse items such as those outlined. In addition, convenient usage normally demands that reference works be housed separately from the main book stock and probably near the entrance to the library or, at least, adjacent to service points and catalogues. The nature of periodical files likewise frequently results in these being shelved away from the books which deal with the same subject. Nevertheless, because some readers prefer to have their books and journals near to each other, certain libraries make this provision.

The ways in which the various categories of material are stored will be outlined so as to give the reader an indication of the practices he may meet with when using a library, particularly if it is one with which he is unfamiliar.

The book stock will normally be arranged on the shelves in a systematic order and the various possibilities will be described in detail later.

Periodicals will frequently be dealt with by providing immediate access to the latest issue and often to recent issues. They may be arranged alphabetically by title or in some way by subject. In a specialised library where almost all the periodicals relate to one subject, the arrangement is likely to be by title. Newspapers may well be filed along with the periodicals: there is real sense in juxtaposing the *Financial Times* with *Investor's Chronicle* for example.

Pamphlet material is frequently housed in boxes, shelved sometimes with the books on the same subject but sometimes on the bottom shelf of each book-case. Another method which may be encountered is to store them in folders in filing cabinets. All other library material which is similarly or even more flimsy is probably to be found in such cabinets.

Maps, charts, plans and other similar geographical material are frequently stored flat in special planchests in order to avoid damage or deterioration. For like reasons microfilm, microcard, microfiche (a hybrid form of sheet film now becoming increasingly common) and all film media are to be found housed in cabinets wherein the temperatures and humidity may be controlled. Gramophone records and tapes will also require separate storage.

Finally it should be noted that many academic libraries possess special collections of books and other materials which have been deposited as gifts, bequests or loans and that these are normally housed apart from the main stock of the library. Faced with this bewildering array of separate 'stores' of published sources of information the reader must be quickly reassured that a key to such varied treasure chests exists: the catalogue. Before the catalogue is described, the means of arrangement must be considered in more detail.

Classification

Any collection of books requires an arrangement. So much is self-evident and it is hardly less so that the large library needs a well-organised and detailed systematic scheme of arrangement if readers are going to be able to find their way around its collections easily and effectively.

During the past hundred years a small number of schemes has been developed which today are in widespread use and the economist in his search for information in libraries is almost certain to encounter one or other of them.

15

Dewey Decimal Classification

The classification of knowledge has been practised for many hundreds of years: for long it was the prerogative of the philosophers to draw up schemes whereby knowledge could be comparted and the relations between subjects could be comprehended. It was an American librarian, Melvil Dewey, less than a hundred years ago, who added a further ingredient which converted a theoretical classification of knowledge into a practical library arrangement which provided for existing knowledge, as represented in books. To his scheme of classification he allotted symbols which, by their very nature, allowed for interpolation and expansion: arabic numerals, used as decimal fractions. The symbols were attached to *subjects*, and not to books or shelves, as in earlier schemes, thus ensuring absolute flexibility, with the place of a subject in the scheme related always to other subjects by the notation of arabic numerals. The field of knowledge was divided into ten main classes, representing nine major subject areas and a tenth miscellaneous, general class, as follows: *

000	Generalities
100	Philosophy and Related Disciplines
200	Religion
300	The Social Sciences
400	Language
500	Pure Sciences
600	Technology (Applied Sciences)
700	The Arts
800	Literature and Rhetoric
900	General Geography, History, etc.

Each of these is divided into its traditional classes and each is given an individual number, e.g.

300	Social sciences
310	Statistical method and statistics
320	Political science
330	Economics
340	Law
350	Public administration
360	Welfare and association

* (The terminology is taken from the latest (17th) edition of the Dewey Classification.)

16

370 Education
380 Commerce
390 Custom and folk-lore

The relationships of economics and the other social science subjects are clearly seen. The content of the Economics class is as follows:

330 Economics
331 Labour
332 Lucrative capital
333 Land (Natural resources)
334 Co-operative systems
335 Collectivist systems and schools
336 Public finance
337 (No longer used)
338 Production
339 Distribution and consumption

Further subdivision proceeds in the same way, but at this stage a decimal point is introduced. Thus in the Dewey Decimal Scheme all classification numbers have a minimum of three figures and, if further specification is required, the number bears a point after the third figure, e.g. Keynesianism is represented by 330·156. The method is illustrated by examination of the 331 Labour class:

331 Labour
331·1 Industrial relations
331·2 Wages
331·3–331·6 Special classes of workers
331·3 Specified age groups
331·4 Women
331·5 Sub-standard wage earners
331·6 Other groups
331·7 Labour by occupation
331·8 Other topics

The 'Other Topics' class here exemplifies a common feature in the classification. Dewey ensured exhaustive division of each class by providing in this way for what seemed, at the time, to be less important subdivisions, e.g. 331·88 Labour organisations (Trade unions).

Although there has been a deliberate attempt to restrict the length of these numbers to about the size illustrated above, the

17

user of a library may frequently be puzzled, or even annoyed, by some which are very much longer. These arise because the classification schemes makes provision for specifying in great detail by such things as country, profession, industry, etc., and this facility is nowhere more apparent than in the Social Sciences class; for example, Working hours in nursing: 331·818161073. Geographical specification results in classification numbers such as: Wages in France: 331·2944.

Readers must be warned of certain peculiarities: that Trade and Commerce, Transport economics and Communications are to be found in class 380, separated from Economics by the whole of the Law, Public Administration, Welfare and Education classes; and Management, Advertising, Office Organisation and Transport Administration are part of the Technology class and are all to be found in class 650. When these anomalies have been recognised, the reader will be able to find his way around the scheme to discover the material he requires without much trouble.

If some of the seemingly strange juxtapositions and separations are noted and borne in mind, the reader will find considerable advantage in gaining a working knowledge of the scheme, for, and this is the Dewey Decimal Classification's trump card, he will find it in use in nearly every public library he enters, in a large number of university and college libraries, and in many other libraries with specialist collections such as the economist will need.

Universal Decimal Classification

The Universal Decimal Classification (UDC) grew out of the need for a classification scheme with much greater detail, designed to deal with micro-knowledge as opposed to the macro-knowledge of the larger unit; an obvious example is the periodical article. The scheme's originators based it firmly on the Dewey Decimal scheme, recognising the international character of its arabic numeral notation and the enormous flexibility of the decimal fraction idea. Thus the ten main classes of the scheme are identical, even though the terminology differs slightly. The content of the Economics class, 33, likewise corresponds closely with the Dewey class 330. The correlation even persists down to the division of subjects as limited as, say, 333 Land. Comparison shows an almost identical set of divisions, albeit with changes in terminology once again (e.g. 333·8, Subsurface (Mineral resources)—DC; Mines and mineral resources —UDC).

In UDC, the classification number for economics is 33, rather than Dewey's 330. In this scheme the numbers are shorn of super-fluous zeros, those at the end of a number, and this can even mean a single-figure class number, e.g. 3 for Social Sciences. The point is used simply as a separating device to break up lengthy numbers into groups of three digits or less; its most frequent position is after the first three figures and each subsequent group of three (e.g. Market research surveys 380·132·3).

Full and abridged versions of the Economics (33), Commerce and Trade (38), Accounting and Management (657/658) sections are available.

The UDC also displays very obviously the enhanced flexibility its originators sought and specialist libraries have exploited this advantage in varying degrees. This is not the place to provide a full exposition of the features of the scheme which give the flexibility, but a few examples will illustrate the results and familiarise the reader with the kind of practice he may encounter in his library.

38	Trade and commerce
38(43)	Trade and commerce in Germany
38 : 669·1	Iron trade
38 : 669·1(43)	Iron trade in Germany
38 "18"	Trade and commerce in the 19th century

The use of these (and a few other) punctuation symbols to link parts of classification numbers permits the building up of shelf numbers to cater for almost any aspect of a subject. The price paid is the sacrifice of simplicity.

Library of Congress Classification

This scheme was devised at the turn of the century for the already vast and rapidly-growing collections of the library of the national legislative body of the United States. Its basis was empirical rather than philosophical and it has appealed to an increasing number of large and academic libraries inside and outside the United States. Notable British users include the British Library of Political and Economic Science at the London School of Economics.

The arrangement is of 21 large general classes (allocated to letters of the alphabet), of which H is the class of immediate interest, covering as it does the Social Sciences. The first half of the class contains Economics subjects and Sociology occupies the remainder. Divisions are indicated by lettered divisions, as:

19

HA	Statistics	HF	Commerce (including Business organisation and administration)
HB	Economic theory		
HC	National production and Economic conditions		
HD	Agriculture. Industry.	HG	Finance
HE	Transportation. Communication	HJ	Public finance

Each of these is very fully subdivided, and enumeration of subjects is as exhaustive as a major national library with particular interest in economics, industry, trade, agriculture, etc., has found necessary. Numbers are used arithmetically to denote these subjects; i.e. the figures are filed in ascending order, rather than as decimal fractions: 7, 8, 9 precede 10, 11, 12, 13 ...; 99 precedes 112, etc.

Each section is divided in such a way as to give general, reference and introductory works at the beginning of the sequence, followed by historical and theoretical treatments of the subject, before proceeding to the applications and 'special' aspects of the subject in question. Thus the divisions of HG Private Finance, include:

HG	1	Periodicals—United States and Canada
	11	—Great Britain
	61	Annuals
	171	History
	173	Treatises
	201–1486	Money
e.g.	321–329	Mints
	325	Assaying
	393	Decimal system
	1501–3540	Banking
	3701–3781	Credit
	3811–4000	Exchange
	4501–6270	Investments
e.g.	4551	Stock exchanges
	8011–9970	Insurance

The detail in the scheme is enormous, as shown by the range of numbers available for each subject in the example, and even beyond this there is provision for geographical subdivision where necessary. The only drawback for the British library is the emphasis given to American needs, which is obviously unavoidable but not a serious problem.

Bliss' Bibliographic Classification

In this classification the economist will find that a separate class (T) has been allocated to his subject. This appears at the end of a section dealing with Applied Social Sciences (following R, Political Science and S, Jurisprudence and Law), and is succeeded by U, Useful and Industrial Arts and Technology. Perhaps few economists would deny the aptness of the juxtaposition of industry and its management with technology's 'Useful and Industrial Arts'.

Subjects with which Economics has links are reasonably collocated, although a basic subject of increasing consequence nowadays, Mathematics, in Class A, is about as remote as it could be. The organisation of the class is as follows:

T	Economics	TL	Corporation in Business
TA	General economics	TM	Exchange, Economic;
TB	Social economics		Commerce and Finance
TC	Land and capital	TN	Transportation
TD	Industry	TO	Accountancy
TG	Labor and Laboring classes	TP	Finance
		TQ	Credit
TH	Organisation, etc., of Labor	TR	Banks
		TS	Insurance
TI	Machine Industry; Manufacture	TT	State Economics
		TU	Taxation
TJ	Business	TV	Public Service
(TK	Advertising)	TW	National Economy
		TY	Special Business

Two points are immediately obvious: firstly, a system of roman letters is used not only to represent a main subject, but also for its subdivisions; secondly, the Economics class is self-contained, including as it does the traditional topics, and also finding room for Commerce (TM), Business (TJ), and all aspects of Management. Another feature is the provision for geographical specification: TW may be divided on a national basis to give, say, TWe for the British Economy, TWb for the Economic condition of the United States, etc. Each may be divided by topic, e.g. TWe, E British Public Debt.

A notable feature of the Bliss scheme is the extreme brevity of the class marks allocated to all subjects, even minor ones: three or four letters is often the maximum length. Examples are: THR Trade Unions; TRV Foreign Exchange.

It is likely that the economist, in common with his fellow workers in social science fields, will prefer an arrangement which is not too detailed. If this is so, the Bliss Classification may earn his commendation.

Other Classification Schemes

Many libraries have been arranged by classifications devised specially as tailor-made systems. Such libraries will normally provide some guidance for readers, in the form of leaflets or plans, to enable them to find their way round the shelves and the subject arrangement. Occasionally the schemes are published and therefore may be used elsewhere. An example is the *Classification of Business Literature* of the Baker Library of the Harvard University Graduate School of Business Administration (rev. edn, Shoestring Press, 1961).

The Catalogue

At its simplest a catalogue is a mere inventory of stock. A library catalogue serves many other purposes, however, and it will repay examination to discover how it can help the reader. The librarian is guided in his work of producing a catalogue by paying attention to the needs of his readers: what is their approach when they use the library? Do they seek works by a particular author? with a particular title? or one on a particular subject? This last approach, by subject, has been found to be the dominant one. Accordingly in almost all libraries which the economist is likely to use, some form of subject catalogue exists. In this the user will be able to locate books, etc., on the particular subject he is interested in.

This subject catalogue will always be supplemented by an author catalogue in which the reader can discover whether the library has a book of which he knows the author's name and title, or which books by a given author are stocked by the library. The author catalogue may or may not be separate from the subject catalogue: in many libraries authors' names are interfiled with subject names. Search under titles is not always, perhaps not often, possible in a library catalogue. Further guidance on the problems of title approach will be given later.

Physically the catalogue can take several different forms. It may be a printed catalogue in book form. Because they are always out-of-date as a record of a library's stock, printed catalogues gave way during the present century to card catalogues and sheaf catalogues. In each of these one card or manilla slip is used to record details about one publication and all cards or slips are filed together in drawers or binders. It should be noted that the book form of catalogue is beginning to reappear as the computer proves itself capable of printing out details of books in libraries in much the same way as it can produce warehouse stock lists or workers' pay rolls.

Scrutiny of the content of the catalogue entry for a book will always be profitable because it will identify a book uniquely and will provide information to assist in selection of the most suitable book. A typical entry appears below:

SEARLE-BARNES, Robert Griffith
    Pay and productivity bargaining: a study of the effect of national wage agreements in the Nottingham coalfield, by R. G. Searle-Barnes. Manchester, Manchester U.P., 1969. xxv, 190 p.; illus., form., 23 cm. index.

                                        331·282233094252

The author's surname appears as a heading (in this case a hyphenated name), followed by the forenames. Next comes the full title, including the sub-title. The name of the place where the book was published is given next, followed by the name of the publisher (in this case the name of a university press is abbreviated), and the date of publication. The existence of a second or subsequent edition of the book would be indicated by an abbreviation such as '3rd edn', appearing before the name of the place of publication. The next line contains information regarding the physical characteristics of the book. The number of pages, of introductory matter as well as of text, is given (in this case) as so many in roman figures and so many numbered consecutively in arabic numerals. The book is illustrated, contains formulae and an index, and is 23 cm high. Other features of a book which may be listed include the presence of a bibliography.

Lastly, this sample quotes the classification number by which the book would be shelved.

Forms of authorship other than personal are common. The 'author' may be a corporate body such as National Institute of Economic and Social Research, Imperial Chemical Industries Limited, Board of Trade, European Economic Community, and libraries will make entry under headings such as these.

The organisations listed include a society, a private firm, a government department and an intergovernmental body. The trend in libraries nowadays is towards simplifying their practice with regard to headings they adopt on their catalogue entries, encouraged by the publication of a new code of rules which will gain increasing acceptance in English-speaking countries, but for some time yet the reader will encounter differences in procedure which may result in his finding organisations of various kinds entered, not under their names, but under the place where they are situated, followed by the name of the body.

Government publications have long caused difficulties for users of library catalogues but there are signs that some acceptable and comprehensible uniformity is on the way. It should be borne in mind that where such publications are issued by a body which has legislative, judicial or executive functions, as in the case of ministries and departments, they will be found collected under the name of the sovereign state: GREAT BRITAIN, UNITED STATES, etc., with a sub-heading consisting of the name of the body. This applies equally at central and regional or local government levels.

e.g. GREAT BRITAIN. Board of Trade
UNITED STATES. Department of Labor
but
NATIONAL BOARD FOR PRICES AND INCOMES
COMMITTEE OF ENQUIRY ON PRESSURE VESSELS

Meetings variously designated as Conference, Congress, Symposium, Workshop, Study Group, Colloquium, also create problems for the catalogue user when he seeks the published proceedings. Such gatherings are frequently organised or sponsored by a society, in which case there will usually be an entry under the name of the organisation. Almost without exception such meetings are known by a distinguishing name, such as Conference on Investment in Human Beings, National Conference on Company Mergers and Acquisitions. Libraries will invariably make an entry under these names, but the reader should exercise care and check his references before searching. Was it the 'Conference on . . .' or the 'International Conference on . . .'? Was it 'Congress' or 'Symposium'? If such conferences occur at intervals they may contain an ordinal number in their name, e.g. 'Third International Congress on . . .'. The library catalogue will relegate the number to the end of the heading and make an entry such as:

INTERNATIONAL CONFERENCE ON INPUT-OUTPUT TECHNIQUES, 3rd, Geneva, 1961.

In cases where the name of the editor of the proceedings is

24

known, the library catalogue will probably contain an extra entry, i.e. an 'added' entry, under his name. Indeed it is usual to find an entry under editor for all works produced under editorial direction.

If the library possesses a separate subject catalogue arranged by the classification scheme, a duplicate of the entry under author will appear there, usually with the classification number given at the top of the entry, to facilitate filing. Such a catalogue is called a 'Classified Catalogue' and is much favoured in Great Britain. It has the advantage of listing the books which are on loan from the library as well as those which can be found on a shelf at any given moment *in the same order*.

It is also usual to place extra, i.e. 'added', entries in the classified catalogue to draw attention to minor subjects treated in a book or to other aspects of the subject which are covered in it. The reader is thereby led to other parts of the library where useful information may be found. The classified catalogue also collects together in one place information about all relevant books on a subject, even though the books themselves have to be scattered in the library by reason of physical characteristics, such as oversize books, pamphlets, microfilms, etc.

Such a catalogue must be supplemented, of course, by an alphabetical index of subjects. This index is the key to the classified arrangement of the shelves or to the catalogue itself. The index entry for the subject of the book cited in the sample might be as follows:

Nottinghamshire: Coal mining: Wages: Economics.
331.282233094252

Many libraries have a different form of catalogue entirely: in one sequence are filed entries for books under the names of their authors, under the names of their subjects and even, sometimes, under the words of their titles. Such a catalogue is known as a 'Dictionary Catalogue'. Many readers find this arrangement particularly helpful, because access to entries under a subject is direct, there is no necessity to use first a subject index and then go to a separate classified catalogue, and the entries are filed under the names of the subjects rather than under unfamiliar sets of symbols: the classification numbers of the scheme used. Thus the book by Searle-Barnes may appear under the heading 'Wages'.

The dictionary catalogue contains an elaborate and essential scheme of cross references whereby the user is led from headings not used to those under which books will be entered (e.g. Remuneration *See* Wages) and from headings used to related head-

25

ings (e.g. Wage*s See also* Incentive bonus schemes). These cross-references should be followed up because they enable the reader to exploit fully the catalogue and the stock it represents.

The word filing system of a catalogue is obviously important. The arrangement is alphabetical, but the words may be filed in either of two common ways: letter by letter or word by word. The example illustrates the resulting differences in sequence:

Letter by Letter	*Word by Word*
NEW, Peter	NEW, Peter
NEWARK	NEW HAMPSHIRE
NEWBURY	NEW men in new suits
NEWCASTLE	NEW SOUTH WALES
NEW HAMPSHIRE	NEW YORK
NEWMAN, John	NEWARK
NEW men in new suits	NEWBURY
NEW SOUTH WALES	NEWCASTLE
NEWTON, Isaac	NEWMAN, John
NEW YORK	NEWTON, Isaac

In the first column the existence of separate words is ignored, and thus filing order is determined letter by letter, disregarding spaces. In the second column, each word is treated separately: entries beginning with the word NEW are all filed before those where the entry word merely *begins* NEW ..., e.g. NEWARK, NEWBURY.

This brief survey of the various cataloguing practices should enable the reader to find his way through the entries of most library catalogues if he will adapt the foregoing to allow for local variations.

Interlibrary Loans

One of the most important services offered by a library is the facility whereby an item wanted by a reader can be borrowed from another library if his own has not got it in stock. No library can be self-sufficient and all-comprehensive in coverage, not even the largest of those described in Chapter 2. The National Lending Library for Science and Technology has for the past few years been extending its subject coverage far beyond the natural, physical and applied sciences into the social sciences, and beyond, into the humanities, with the result that every journal the economist is likely to require is to be found in its stocks, available on demand

and only a postal delivery away. Future developments at national level await implementation by the Government, with or without emendation, of the recommendations of the recent report of the Dainton Committee on National Libraries (National Libraries Committee. Report (Chairman : F. S. Dainton). HMSO, 1969).

Other inter-lending systems also operate whereby libraries within some loosely-knit scheme of co-operation provide a service for each other. These may be city-based or may operate on a county basis. All are designed to provide for a reader that which his own library does not possess. Sufficient has now been said to make the moral self-evident: access to the world's literature is offered, and it is incumbent on the reader to use the services provided.

Photocopy Service

Libraries have an undoubted duty to attempt to provide information for their clients in a convenient and acceptable form. Modern developments in technology have brought new techniques whereby this end may be more easily achieved, and photocopying processes and microphotography are amongst the most significant. Libraries now face a greatly increased demand for the reproduction of pages from books, periodicals and almost any other printed matter.

The research worker or student is urged to avail himself of the facilities offered, but to bear in mind the present restrictions imposed by the Copyright Act of 1956, under which libraries are empowered to make copies subject to certain provisions. The conditions laid down are legal requirements and the library user should respect these, particularly because they serve to protect the interests (i.e., the copyright protection), of the author.

Inquiry Service

One of the most positive ways in which libraries, nowadays, manifest their oft declared belief that they must offer a dynamic service lies in their provision of an inquiry service. This can and does take many forms, and operates at several levels: at its simplest it may entail answering a question about foreign exchange rates, which may be asked in person or by telephone (or telex); on the other hand, a postal enquiry about movements of commodity prices may necessitate consultation of library files and indexes. Or a university lecturer may require a bibliography of recent work on welfare economics. In this chapter no attempt will be made to

27

offer suggestions about how the economist or student can set about finding the answers for himself, because the remainder of this book is directed towards this end, and Chapter 2 in particular gives guidance on search methods which might be employed.

It is sufficient here to draw the reader's attention to the existence of inquiry services as such, and to urge that he avail himself of the facilities. The librarian does not claim omniscience, but he does acquire expertise in knowledge of and use of sources of information, and this proficiency extends frequently over many subject fields.

Subject Specialists

A library may range widely over many subject fields or its collections may be narrowly concerned with one specific subject, such as commerce or business management. In the latter case the librarian will, *ipso facto,* be rightly regarded as a subject expert, in that, even if he has not had formal academic or practical training in the discipline concerned, he will have become experienced in the literature and sources of information covering that subject. Lately the larger libraries which the economist may have occasion to use, casually or regularly (and these notably include the university libraries) have recognised the need for subject specialists to be responsible for all library matters within a specified subject area. For the library user these librarians form the link with the stock and all the information contained therein. They will have prime responsibility for ensuring that the book selection and acquisition processes result in a suitable, balanced collection; they will act as a point of contact for the reader; they will be responsible for help, guidance and even tuition for their specialist users, whether student, lecturer, government official or lay public.

Other Services

In an attempt to guide readers through the admittedly bewildering maze of publications such as categorised in this chapter and exemplified elsewhere in the book, many libraries produce guides of one kind or another. Of obvious utility are leaflets or booklets on 'How to use the Library' and most good libraries offer such a publication.

Apart from such guides many libraries publish lists of reference works, abstracts journals, periodicals held, or catalogues of their special collections. These are frequently available free of charge, but, because of the relatively high cost of producing them, especially detailed catalogues of the type mentioned, many are offered for sale.

It should be noted that all libraries welcome suggestions for additions to stock, and many provide special forms on which the necessary details can be given. It is very usual for the library to undertake to notify the reader when the book he has suggested becomes available.

If, on the other hand, the library already owns a copy of a book which a reader requires and it is out on loan to another reader, the normal practice is for the reader to fill in some form of reservation card on which particulars of the book are given, together with the name and address of the reader. When the book is returned it is then a simple matter to send notification that it has been reserved for collection.

Libraries are constantly-developing organisms and librarians in the latter half of the twentieth century are striving more than ever to give a better service. All readers should therefore watch for new developments. In addition, their librarian will welcome, and need, their suggestions about improvements.

CHAPTER FOUR

REFERENCE AND BIBLIOGRAPHICAL TOOLS

MICHAEL SHAFE

It is now a truism to mention the information explosion in the social sciences. The defence systems devised to cope with this continuous explosion are private and public, national and international. Because of the controversial and political aspects of much of the information, the non-partisan work of such international bodies as UNESCO and OECD in the bibliographical field are of the greatest importance.

Partly because of the possible controversial uses to which social science information can be put, and partly because it can be quicker, the authoritative general reference source should not be ignored when searching for economic information.

Unlike subjects such as the natural sciences, literature, or history, there are few guides to the literature of economics alone. The economist must learn the basic tools for searching his literature, which might at first glance include some which were too wide in their scope and therefore irrelevant.

The only guide to the literature of economics rather than the social sciences in general, is Maltby's *Economics and Commerce: the Sources of Information and their Organisation,* which was written primarily for library school students; Mallaber in the *Library Association Record,* vol. 70, No. 8, 1968, criticised this book for the traditional division by type rather than by how the literature was used by the specialist. The division used in this chapter could be criticised for the same reason, but I make no apologies. Here I am covering only the general works, and they must be divided by type; that is the way the literature is. At this level of generality the inquirer has to follow the bibliographical form. It is at the next stage in the chain of information searching that the practitioner's approach should be reflected in the layout of guides.

Once an inquiry has been delineated and its level established, the use of general reference works can be determined. Factual inquiries obviously lend themselves more to the general treatment than literature searches, but even small libraries with a few standard yearbooks can supply a great deal of apparently obscure information, without holding the official statistics of even the largest countries. A literature search in depth on a specific aspect of economics may require general reference works only as a preliminary introduction or not at all. But if the specialist works are not available or up to date enough, the general works may bridge the gap.

The relationship between the librarian and the economist in a search of information is an important one. Too often the 'old boy network', mentioned in Graham Mackenzie's article in *Aslib Proceedings*, July 1969, on reader instruction, is the first source of information and the library is thought of only as a secondary source. That net is full of holes: not only are members of the network relying on one another's undoubted specialist and up to date knowledge, but they can also perpetuate errors and leave unknown areas still unexplored. Librarians can help to reduce the size of the holes in the net; as specialists get more specialised and their reading gets narrower, the librarian can indicate peripheral areas, often ignored by or unknown to the specialist, which contain valuable material. Time is money, and as specialists' browsing time dwindles, the librarian can help to increase the economists' productivity and effectiveness. More economists could adopt J. K. Galbraith's dictum: 'One of the greatest pieces of economic wisdom is to know what you do not know'.

Guides to Reference Works, and the Literature of the Social Sciences and Economics

A guide to the literature is more than a bibliography of bibliographies. It gives examples of sources in its chosen field, drawing on all types of material, and it discusses the sources, evaluates them, and shows how one can compensate for the deficiencies in another. It can guide the user to other sources of information not necessarily in published form, such as specialised libraries, international, governmental or non-governmental organisations, report literature. Some guides to the literature are discursive, others have introductory sections followed by lists of works and possibly short annotations. But for the specialist inquirer they should cover the literature as it is used.

How to Find Out: a Guide to Sources of Information for All

Arranged by the Dewey Decimal Classification, by G. Chandler (3rd rev. edn, Pergamon, 1967); and *Facts and How to Find Them: a Guide to Sources of Information,* by W. A. Bagley (7th edn, Pitman, 1964) are just two of many introductory guides of a fairly simple nature, covering all subjects. More important as introductions to reference material are: *Handbuch der Bibliographischen Nachschlagewerke,* by W. Totok, R. Weitzel, K. H. Weimann (3rd edn, Klostermann, 1966); *Les Sources du Travail Biblographique,* by L.-N. Malclès (3 vols, Droz, 1950–58); *Guide to Reference Material,* by A. J. Walford (2nd edn, Vol. 2: Philosophy and Psychology, Religion, Social Sciences, Geography, Biography and History; Library Association, 1968); *Guide to Reference Books,* by C. M. Winchell (8th edn and supplements, American Library Association, 1967–). These major guides are bibliographical rather than discursive, classified, with bibliographical details and critical annotations. Two lists of reference works particularly useful for librarians are *New Reference Tools for Librarians,* 1966-67 (Robert Maxwell & Co., 1969); and *Social and Comparative Studies: a Bibliography of Reference Material held by the Library,* by B. J. C. Wintour (University of Essex Library, 1969). These are classified with some bibliographical details, and the Essex volume has a few short annotations.

Guides to the literature of the social sciences are of the greatest importance in preliminary literature searching for economics, for the simple reason that there are so few guides to economics literature. The three major guides are: *Literature of the Social Sciences: an Introductory Survey and Guide,* by P. R. Lewis (Library Association, 1960), which is still a most useful introduction, set out as the literature is used by the specialist, with a slight bias towards British and Commonwealth material. There is much needed emphasis on the interdependence of the several branches of the social sciences. As has been stated many times before, a new edition is sorely needed. *A Reader's Guide to the Social Sciences,* ed. by B. F. Hoselitz (Free P., 1959) has lengthy descriptions of the literature and, like Lewis, is now seriously out of date. *Sources of Information in the Social Sciences: a Guide to the Literature,* by C. M. White and others (Bedminster P., 1964) is a work by ten specialist contributors, and specialist librarians have compiled bibliographies for each chapter. Both works lack subject indexes and White lacks co-ordination between the specialist chapters. However, Lewis admits that some sections in White are superior to his own.

The long out of print *Guide to the Collections of the British Library of Political and Economic Science,* 1948, being a guide to the largest specialist library for economics in this country, is still useful, but a new edition is badly needed.

The most comprehensive recent guide to economic literature is *Economics and Commerce: the Sources of Information and their Organisation*, by A. Maltby (Bingley, 1968), which was primarily intended as a textbook for library school students; however it was hoped that librarians and teachers of economics would find it useful. Mallaber's critical review of this work mentions, not only that the subject is not covered as practitioners would wish, but 'that nowhere in the book is there mentioned a single source of information except printed and published sources'. Nevertheless, as the only up to date guide to the subject, if its arrangement is accepted, it is most useful.

Sources of commercial information can be traced by using one of the following guides: *Sources of Business Information*, by E. T. Coman (2nd rev. edn, California U.P., 1964), or *Commercial Information: a Source Handbook*, by D. E. Davinson (Pergamon, 1965). Davinson is an excellent condensed guide indispensable in a commercial library and containing much general material of use to the economist. The latest example is: *Encyclopedia of Business Information Sources: a Detailed Subject Listing of Primary Areas of Interest to Managerial Personnel*, ..., comp. by P. Wasserman (2 vols, Gale Research, due 1970). The first edition was called *Executive Guide to Information Sources*, and the work has now been expanded to cater for more general users.

Bibliographies of Bibliographies

The foremost general bibliography of bibliographies is: *World Bibliography of Bibliographies and Bibliographical Catalogues, Calendars, Abstracts, Digests, Indexes and the like*, by T. Besterman (4th edn, 5 vols, Societas Bibliographicus, 1965–66). The arrangement is alphabetical by subject with the fifth volume as an author index. There are no annotations, and this latest edition covers the period up to 1963; the 3rd edition stopped at 1953. Alternatives which can be used to update Besterman are: *Index Bibliographicus* (4th edn, vol. 2: Social Sciences: F.I.D., 1964), which is classified by the Universal Decimal Classification; and *Bibliographic Index: a Cumulative Bibliography of Bibliographies* (Wilson, 1938–), which appears twice a year, with annual and multi-annual cumulations. The arrangement is the normal Wilson dictionary arrangement. Coverage is of bibliographies in books, periodicals and pamphlets, mostly in the English language.

As the international aspects of the social sciences increase, so does the need for international bibliographical information. In the past decade there has been increasing bibliographical activity in most countries of the world and the problem arose of tracing the sources in little-known countries.

The UNESCO periodical *Bibliography, Documentation, Terminology,* regularly describes, country by country, the existing bibliographical services, official and unofficial. *Bibliographical Services Throughout the World,* 1960–1964, by P. Avicenne (UNESCO 1969) follows similar works by Malclès (for 1951–53) and Collison (for 1950–59). This most recent work describes the bibliographical position of eighty-three countries. *Serial Bibliographies in the Humanities and Social Sciences,* comp. by R. A. Gray (Pierian P., 1969) lists those bibliographies intended to be issued more or less regularly, including concealed bibliographies appearing in journals. The arrangement follows Dewey's Decimal Classification, but excludes general serial bibliographies such as *Bibliographic Index. Bibliographie Wirtschafts—und Sozialwissenschaftlicher Bibliographien Zugänge der Bibliothek des Instituts für Weltwirtschaft, Kiel, in den Jahren 1962 bis 1967,* comp. by F. Otto (Inst. f. Weltwirtschaft, 1968) is an alphabetical listing of nearly 3000 bibliographies received in the Institute's Library.

For bibliographies of individual authors from all sources, including periodical articles, Festschriften, biographical dictionaries, the major work is *Internationale Personalbibliographie,* 1800–1959, by M. Arnim (2nd edn, 3 vols, Hiersemann, 1952–63). There is a German emphasis here, but the scope is international. The first two volumes cover the years 1800 to 1943, the third volume is a supplement to the first two and extends the period covered to 1959. A new edition or further extension is needed.

National and General Bibliographies

RETROSPECTIVE

The catalogues of the major libraries of the world such as the Library of Congress, the British Museum and the Bibliothèque Nationale, contain records of most of the world's bibliographical output, and are used by all scholars. In addition there are national bibliographies of most countries of the world, recording the current output. Most national libraries produce author catalogues with subject index volumes. The national bibliographies tend to be classified catalogues. All cover, more or less comprehensively, commercial, official and non-governmental material. For the subject specialist the subject approach is probably the first consideration, but the total output by a person or organisation is covered by the author approach.

It should be made clear that these bibliographies concern themselves with monographs, series, pamphlets, etc., and not with periodical articles. *British Museum. General Catalogue of Printed Books* (Photolithographic edn to 1955, 263 vols, Trustees of the B.M., 1959–66), and its *Ten Year Supplement, 1956–65,* (50 vols, 1968), is the author index, whilst *The British Museum Subject Index of Modern Books acquired since 1881* is a comprehensive alphabetical subject catalogue of the works added to the British Museum collections. Personal names are not used as subject headings, as these are covered in the *General Catalogue,* but biographies are listed under the relevant subject heading.

Library of Congress. Catalog of Books Represented by Library of Congress Printed Cards Issued to 1942, July 31, (167 vols, Edwards, 1942–46), has supplements for 1942–47, 1948–52, 1953–57, 1958–62 and 1963–67 (the last three being entitled *National Union Catalog ...*). The *National Union Catalog* also appears as a monthly list with quarterly and annual, as well as five-yearly cumulations, and can therefore be used as a source for current material. From 1948 these catalogues represent titles received in the Library of Congress and about 400 other major American libraries.

In recent years a number of reprints have appeared of the Library of Congress and National Union Catalogue author catalogues, e.g. *Library of Congress and National Union Catalog Author lists, 1942–62: a Master Cumulation* (152 vols, Gale Research, 1969–). but the most important new arrival on the national bibliographical scene in recent years is the publication of *National Union Catalog: Pre–1956 Imprints,* (c.610 vols, Mansell, 1968–), and the *12 Year Supplement, 1956–67,* (c.120 vols, 1970–). This is a record, with locations and a book numbering system, of the holdings of all the important research libraries of North America, and it cumulates and supersedes the five earlier Library of Congress/National Union Catalog catalogues. When completed it will be the largest book catalogue in the history of printing, with 12 million entries in the main work alone. It should be complete by 1979.

The Library of Congress, like the British Museum, produces a parallel set of subject catalogues, but covers the years 1945– only. These appear quarterly with annual and five-yearly cumulations. Compared with the *British Museum Subject Index,* the Library of

Congress volumes have more specific subject headings, and are more up to date. The arrangement is alphabetical, and personal names are used as headings.

A complete list of national and general bibliographies is available in most guides to reference works, but here is a select list of some important ones:

Australia: *Australian National Bibliography* (1961–).

Canada: *Canadiana* (1951–); *Ontario New Universities Library Project: Author-title Catalogue—Final Cumulation, 1964–67* (5 vols, 1967). (There is also a three volume subject catalogue.) This is a union catalogue of five newly formed university libraries, each with the same basic collection of 34 600 in-print monographs.

France: *Bibliothèque Nationale: Catalogue Général des Livres Imprimés de la Bibliothèque Nationale: Auteurs* (1897–). *Bibliothèque Nationale: Catalogue Général des Livres Imprimés: Auteurs, Collectivités Auteurs, Anonymes, 1960–64* (1965–). *Biblio: Catalogue des Ouvrages Parus en Langue Française dans le Monde Entier* (monthly, 1934–).

Germany: *Deutsche Nationalbibliographie* (1931–) produced now in East Germany, is in two parts, one covering commercial book production in German speaking countries, the other covering items not available through the book trade: theses, some government publications, institutional publications. *Deutsche Bibliographie* (1953–) also claims to cover all German language publications, and also cumulates half-yearly, annually and five-yearly.

Great Britain: *British National Bibliography* (1950–). This is a classified bibliography based on books deposited at the Copyright Office of the British Museum, and has a single alphabetical index of authors, titles, subjects and series. Appearing weekly it cumulates monthly, quarterly, half-yearly, nine-monthly and annually, with five-yearly cumulations of the indexes. There are also five-yearly cumulations of the subject catalogue starting in 1951. The five-yearly cumulations extend to 1964, but in 1970 three-yearly cumulations of the indexes were issued, covering 1965-67.

Italy: *Bibliografia Nazionale Italiana* (1958–) is the continuation of *Bolletino delle Publicazioni Italiane,* which started in 1886, and now appears monthly in classified order, with annual cumulations. *Pagliaini's Catalogo Generale della Libreria Italiana,* which appeared, with supplements, in fourteen volumes, covers the years 1847–1940.

Russia: *Ezhegodnik Knigi SSSR* (1927–31, 1935, 1941–) is an annual, published in two parts (Humanities and Science), listing all monographs published in Russia.

Spain: *Bibliografía Española* (1958–) is the Spanish equivalent of British National Bibliography. Early attempts at national bibliographies were *Bibliografía Española* (1901–22), *Bibliografía Hispánica* (1942–57) which is now continued as *El Libro Español* (1958–).

CURRENT

One disadvantage of many general and national bibliographies is that they are not sufficiently up to date, and to a researcher, this can be a serious drawback. Most countries now attempt to produce current lists of the latest publications, some more successfully than others. Those national bibliographies listed above which are issued weekly or monthly can equally well be used as current bibliographies, but the items so listed can still appear several weeks or even months after publication date.

What follows is a list of those bibliographies which are intended primarily as current bibliographies. The items mentioned above, although very useful in their most frequent parts as current bibliographies, are above all recording and building up national, retrospective lists.

Cumulative Book Index: World List of Books in the English Language (Wilson, 1898–), is basically monthly with many cumulations up to five years, and has a dictionary arrangement with one sequence of authors, titles, subjects (sometimes with subheadings), editors, translators, and series; publishers are listed, with addresses. In the early cumulations books published in countries other than the United States, Great Britain and Canada, in English, are listed separately by country. Government publications are only covered selectively. *The Bookseller* (published by Whitaker) is issued weekly, and contains an alphabetical list of new British books, including some government publications. Until December 1969 the last issue of each month contained a monthly cumulated list, but from January 1970 the monthly cumulation is issued separately. *Whitaker's Cumulative Book List* (1924–) cumulates quarterly and annually the *Bookseller* weekly lists in a classified sequence.

Novye Knigi SSSR (1956–) appears weekly in two parts: books of the week, and forthcoming books, with short annotations. *Library of Congress. Monthly List of Russian Accessions* (1948–58), and from 1958–69 entitled *Monthly Index of Russian Accessions,* was a useful English-language subject index of Russian books and journals.

37

Bibliographie de la France (1811–) appears weekly in three parts: copyright material (with occasional supplements for such categories as maps, theses and music), book trade information, and publishers' announcements (entitled *Livres de la Semaine* which cumulates into *Livres du Mois, du Trimestre, du Semestre* and *de l'Année*).

Publishers often produce current bibliographies which are of more than commercial interest, and which include books published by other firms: for example Nijhoff distribute *Nijhoff Information: Books and Periodicals from the Netherlands in Foreign Languages,* and Harrassowitz produce *German Book Digest: a Selective List of Recent German Books. The Review-Service for New German Books* (monthly) gives page-long annotations of new German books, and *Das Deutsche Buch* is a bi-monthly selection from the weekly *Deutsche Bibliographie* with short annotations.

'BOOKS IN PRINT' AND FORTHCOMING BOOKS ANNOUNCEMENTS

'Books in Print' volumes usually appear annually with author, title and subject approaches. Forthcoming announcements give similar information more frequently and also cover recent publications.

Books in Print (2 vols., Bowker) is annual, one volume for authors, the other for titles and publishers, and published in conjunction with *Subject Guide to Books in Print, and Publishers' Trade List Annual. British Books in Print ... the Reference Catalogue of Current Literature* (Whitaker), is now annual with the first section as an author sequence and the second a title and catchword sequence. *Paperbacks in Print* is a companion volume.

There is no German 'Books in Print', but the publishers Koehler and Volckmar produce an annual catalogue, with supplements, of their holdings of recent German books.

Le Livre Français: 1970, French Books in Print is announced for September 1970 by Paris Publishers Inc., as an annual in four volumes, one volume each for authors and titles and two volumes for subjects. *Forthcoming Books ... including New Books in Print* (Bowker), is issued six times a year with subject sections and author and title index. It is from Bowker's *Books in Print* stable and updates *Books in Print.*

Social Science and Economic Bibliographies

The retrospective international bibliography for all social scientists, whatever their speciality is: *The London Bibliography of the Social Sciences* (L.S.E., 1931–). The original four volumes and supplements up to 1936 comprised the subject catalogue of nine London specialist libraries including the British Library of Political and Economic Science (at London School of Economics), but from 1936 only the BLPES holdings were covered. The rather complicated arrangement of this work should not put off prospective users: it is too important to ignore. Subjects with numerous subdivisions are arranged alphabetically, each subject or division then consisting of works in chronological order of publication. Government publications form a separate sub-division for each subject. Cross-references abound, though the latest supplements are not repeating them. Supplements were slow to appear, but in 1970 Mansell issued the latest supplement in seven volumes bringing the coverage to 1968. This and the previous supplement are without author indexes, but a separate index of cross-references is to be published. The Library's *Monthly List of Accessions* updates the printed catalogue, for current material, and is arranged in twenty-two subject classes.

American Behavioral Scientist. The ABS Guide to Recent Publications in the Social and Behavioral Sciences (A.B.S., 1965–) covers books, periodical articles, pamphlets and government publications over the whole range of the social sciences, but is very selective. The original volume cumulated monthly bibliographies between 1957 and 1964 from the *ABS*, and annual supplements have been issued from 1966. There is broad subject arrangement, then alphabetical listing by author. A large proportion of entries are in non-English languages, but apart from this advantage over the *Bulletin of the Public Affairs Information Service* (*see* pp. 42 and 184) the latter is more comprehensive and current.

Bibliographie der Sozialwissenchaften, 1905–43, 1950– (Vandenhoeck and Ruprecht) was originally (1905–43) issued as *Bibliographie der Staats und Wirtschaftswissenschaften*, and since 1950 as a new series, is a supplement to *Jahrbuch für Sozialwissenschaft*; volumes for 1943–50 are planned for publication. The arrangement is in fifteen sections with annual author and subject indexes, but a disadvantage is that the three issues a year do not cumulate, and appear very late. It complements the *Bulletin of the Public Affairs Information Service*.

Bibliographically, economics is a young subject, and most retrospective economics bibliographies go no further back than the mid- or late eighteenth century. One that does is: *Kress Library of Business and Economics. Catalogue: covering material published through 1776 with data upon cognate items in other Harvard*

Libraries (Baker Library, Harvard Graduate School of Business Administration, 1940). Supplementary volumes cover the years 1777–1817 (1957), 1818–48 (1964) and 1473–1848 (1967). Specialist library catalogues used as subject bibliographies are an excellent source for literature searching and this is a prime example. The arrangement is chronological, then alphabetical by author, and despite the fact that the volumes vary in comprehensiveness, this is a major tool for economists.

Harvard University Press have announced two volumes of their *Widener Library Shelflist* (Nos. 23–24) to cover 65 000 economics titles and periodicals in all branches of economics. This will no doubt be a retrospective bibliography which simply cannot be ignored. Between 1966 and 1968 G. K. Hall & Co. reprinted seven catalogues of the Library of the Institut für Weltwirtschaft, covering persons, regions, subjects, titles, corporate bodies and periodicals. In all there are 207 volumes, but the price of about $16 000 will put this major compilation beyond the purse of all but the largest libraries and this is most unfortunate for a catalogue in the same league as the *London Bibliography of the Social Sciences*.

The following titles are also of interest in tracing the earlier works in economics: *Select Bibliography of Modern Economic Theory, 1870–1929*, comp. by H. E. Batson (Routledge, 1930, repr. 1967); *Bibliography of Economics, 1751–75*, by H. Higgs (British Academy, 1935); *Literature of Political Economy: a Classified Catalogue of Selected Publications*, by J. R. McCulloch (Longman, 1845, repr. Kelley, 1964); *Contemporary Printed Sources for British and Irish Economic History, 1701–50*, by L. W. Hanson (Cambridge U.P., 1963); and *A Catalogue of Pamphlets on Economic Subjects Between 1750 and 1900 and now Housed in Irish Libraries*, by R. D. C. Black (Queen's Univ., 1969).

Two items one would not expect in this survey, but which can be of use in tracing nineteenth-century material are: *The Cambridge Bibliography of English Literature*, ed. by F. W. Bateson (vol. 3: 1800–1900; Cambridge U.P., 1940), (*The New Cambridge Bibliography of English Literature* excludes economic, political and historical material); and *Select List of Books on European History, 1815–1914*, ed. by A. Bullock and A. J. P. Taylor (2nd edn, Oxford U.P., 1957). These, and other bibliographies of this period, contain references to the classic economic works of the nineteenth century and their inclusion emphasises the need for economists to look outside their immediate interest in tracing relevant material.

Bibliographie Général des Sciences Juridiques, Politiques, Economiques et Sociales de 1800 à 1925/6, by A. Grandin (3 vols,

Sirey, 1926), and supplements covering the years 1926–50 includes only books in French and is supplemented by *Bibliographie d'Economie Politique, 1945–60*, by R. Mossé (Sirey, 1963), with later supplements.

The Honours School in Philosophy, Politics and Economics, in Oxford University, produced a *Bibliography in Economics*, compiled by M. Hall and others in 1957 and 1959, which has now been revised as: Oxford University Sub-Faculty of Economics: *Bibliography for Students of Economics* (Oxford U.P., 1968). There are nine subject sections, without annotations, of the standard texts needed by those reading for degrees in economics at Oxford. *Universal Reference System: Political Science, Government and Public Policy Series* (vol. 8: Economic Regulation, Business, and Government; Pergamon, 1969) is a computerised bibliography with brief annotations, indexing in depth 2960 books, pamphlets and periodical articles, totalling 33 200 entries, with updating supplements issued to the main volumes. *Documentation Economique* (Presses Univ. de France, 1934–39, 1947–   ), is a bi-monthly service founded by Mossé, providing signed abstracts of books and periodical articles on perforated cards. International in scope, author and subject indexes are provided with each 'issue', but there are often delays of several months between publication and abstract.

A most important bibliography of current economics writings is Pittsburgh University Department of Economics: *International Economics Selections Bibliography, Series 1: New Books in Economics* (Pittsburgh University, 1964–   ). From 1954–62 (Nos. 1–35) this quarterly bibliography was issued by Johns Hopkins University as *Economics Library Selections, Series 1: New Books in Economics*. Despite an emphasis on English language works, foreign publications are covered and short evaluative annotations are provided with a coded indication of the type of library for which the book is recommended. There is a subject arrangement with author index. Series 2 of this work: *Basic Lists in Special Subjects* (1954–63) also originated by Johns Hopkins University, consists of seven retrospective bibliographies, covering such topics as international economics, statistics and econometrics, economics of development and growth, economics reference works and professional journals. This series has also been taken over by Pittsburgh University, and further numbers are planned. So far new editions of the first and last titles mentioned have been issued. In 1965 they issued an index to the Johns Hopkins issues 1954–62: *Economics Library Selections, Cumulative Bibliography Series 1 and 2, 1954–62*, comp. by Pittsburgh University, Department of

Economics (Gordon and Breach, 1965), which with the Series 2 items provide an excellent summary of the output of economics literature in the 1950s and early 1960s.

Another important bibliography, which concentrates on listing periodical articles, but also includes books is: *International Bibliography of Economics, 1952–* (UNESCO, and Tavistock Publs., *1955–*). This annual bibliography is prepared by the International Committee for Social Sciences Documentation and is part of the International Bibliography of the Social Sciences. Its two to three-year time-lag is a handicap for current interest, but its international coverage is strong. Fifteen subject sections are arranged with running numbers for each item up to about 7000 per volume, and subject and author indexes refer to the item numbers. *Bibliography on Income and Wealth, 1937/47–1957/60* (8 vols, International Association for Research in Income and Wealth, 1952–64), is an international co-operative compilation, annotating books, pamphlets and periodical articles in English, French and Spanish (works in other languages are annotated in English). The periodical *Review of Income and Wealth* includes the continuation of this bibliography.

Bibliographie Européene: Ouvrages et Documents sur les Communautés et d'Information des Communautés Européenes is a card catalogue, updated annually, of works on all aspects of European economic integration from 1940. Items are classified, subject and author index cards are supplied.

Referred to above, also described elsewhere, is the *Bulletin of the Public Affairs Information Service* (PAIS for short). It is 'a selective subject list of the latest books, pamphlets, government publications, reports of public and private agencies, and periodical articles, relating to economic and social conditions, public administration and international relations, published in English throughout the world'. First published in 1915, this service is weekly with numerous cumulations up to annual with *c.* 30 000 entries a year. This work is the foremost English language current indexing service for the social sciences in the world.

Abstracting and indexing journals are fully described elsewhere, but it should be noted that most economics periodicals with any academic standing contain authoritative reviews of new works, lists of new books received and occasional bibliographical review articles.

Bibliographies of Translations and Trade Catalogues

TRANSLATIONS

Index Translationum: Repertoire International des Traductions–International Bibliography of Translations (1–31, International Institute of Intellectual Co-operation, 1932–40; N.S. 1–, UNESCO, 1949–   ). The first series was quarterly, the New Series is annual, and arranged by country in which the translation is published, then by broad UDC subject headings. Details of the originals are given where possible, and indexes for authors, publishers and translators exist for both series. In 1940 twelve countries were covered: the number is now over seventy.

TRADE CATALOGUES

Publishers' and booksellers' catalogues are a useful source as current or retrospective subject bibliographies. What follows is a selective list of publishers, booksellers and reprint publishers who produce catalogues of economics books. Nearly all publishers and booksellers produce general catalogues often with subject divisions including economics, and these are too numerous to mention. However, most publishers and booksellers will willingly place individuals on subject specialist mailing lists for announcements and catalogues.

Some *reprint publishers* of importance to economists are: Frank Cass (U.K.); Cornmarket Press (U.K.); G. K. Hall (U.S.); Augustus M. Kelley (U.S.) (the economic reprint specialist); and Johnson Reprint (U.S.). *Booksellers issuing economics catalogues* are: B. H. Blackwell; Economists' Bookshop; Dillon's Univ. Bookshop; Parker & Son. The following *publishers* regularly issue economics lists: Allen and Unwin; Macmillan, Oxford U.P., Cambridge U.P., Pall Mall, Irwin, McGraw Hill and the larger American university presses, such as Yale, Harvard and Columbia, individually and in groups.

Encyclopaedias and Dictionaries; and Biographical Information

Encyclopaedias and dictionaries vary enormously in depth and range of information. The choice of which work should be consulted varies, not with the known or assumed expertise or intelligence of the inquirer but the accurate assessment of the depth and range of the inquiry. The large range of encyclopaedias and dictionaries (the terms are sometimes interchangeable) covers general and very specialised works, all of which can contain either short, defining articles, or long, scholarly articles in depth, or combinations of both types.

The very general encyclopaedias, e.g. *Britannica, Americana, Chambers, Brockhaus, Larousse, Espasa*, will not be discussed here, but for broad summaries they can be profitably consulted. This section will concentrate on the social science and economics encyclopaedias and dictionaries. With a good encyclopaedia it should be possible to trace the date of compilation (often quite different from publication date), long articles should be signed and contain (for specialist economic articles) diagrams and statistics, and there should be up to date, accurate, bibliographical references. Cross references are most essential.

The three most important social science encyclopaedias are: *Encyclopædia of the Social Sciences*, ed. by E. R. A. Seligman (15 vols, Macmillan, 1930–35, repr. 1951); *Handwörterbuch der Sozialwissenschaften* (13 vols, Mohr, and Fischer 1956–68); and the *International Encyclopedia of the Social Sciences*, ed. by D. Sills (17 vols, Macmillan, 1968). All three contain long signed articles, with diagrams, bibliographies and cross references. One advantage of these works over some more specific works is that the editors are better able to attract the leading scholars in their respective fields to contribute to a 'prestige' work.

A smaller one-volume work, which is really an encyclopaedic dictionary of the social sciences is: *Dictionary of the Social Sciences*, ed. by J. Gould and W. L. Kolb (Tavistock, 1964). Many social scientists contributed to this work, produced under the auspices of UNESCO. The short articles are signed, bibliographical references occur in the text, and there are many cross references. It has been criticised for giving explanations rather than definitions, but in an inexact science where practitioners are still defining and redefining concepts, this approach has its place.

The four works mentioned above are useful to the economist who requires information on the margins of economics and the other social sciences, as well as summaries of broad themes in economics. The major encyclopaedia of economics is: *Palgrave's Dictionary of Political Economy*, ed. by H. Higgs (3 vols, Macmillan, 1923–26, repr. by Kelley, 1963, and Cass, 1964). Sir R. H. I. Palgrave produced the first edition which was published in 1894–96, and its main interest now is for the historical aspects: economic theories and the great economists, but allowing for its age it is still an important encyclopaedic work on economics.

Articles are long and signed, and the now dated bibliographies excellently compiled. A more recent encyclopaedic dictionary is: *Dictionnaire des Sciences Economiques*, ed. by J. Romeuf and others (2 vols, Presses Univ. de France, 1956–58).

For up to date economic information, particularly of the definition variety, there are many examples: *Dictionary of Economic Terms*, by A. Gilpin (rev. edn, Butterworths, 1970); *McGraw-Hill Dictionary of Modern Economics: a Handbook of Terms and Organizations*, ed. by D. Greenwald (McGraw-Hill, 1965); *A Dictionary of Economics and Commerce*, by J. L. Hanson (2nd edn, Macdonald & Evans, 1967); *Everyman's Dictionary of Economics: an Alphabetical Exposition of Economic Concepts and their Applications*, comp. by A. Beldon and F. G. Pennance (Dent, 1965); *A Dictionary of Economics*, ed. by H. S. Sloan and A. J. Zurcher (4th edn, Barnes & Noble, 1961); and *A New Dictionary of Economics*, by P. A. S. Taylor (Routledge, 1966).

Multi-lingual Dictionaries

Most multi-lingual dictionaries of economic terms are intended for commercial users, businessmen and exporters, and there are examples to cover combinations of most languages used in international commerce. For the academic economist the multi-lingual dictionaries of social science terms might be more fruitful, or even the general bi-lingual dictionaries, such as 'Mansion' (*Harrap's Standard French and English Dictionary*, ed. by J. E. Mansion), some of which are richer in technical terms than many so-called technical dictionaries. *Systematic Glossary, English-French-Spanish-Russian, of Selected Economic and Social Terms*, comp. by I. Paenson (Pergamon, 1963), gives quite long definitions of terms in context. *Dictionary of Development Economics: Economic Terminology in three Languages—English, French, German*, comp. and arr. by T. Scharf (Elsevier, 1969); *Dictionnaire Commercial et Financier: français-néerlandais-anglais-allemand*, by J. V. Servotte (3rd rev. edn, Brépols, 1964); *Wirtschaftswörterbuch*, by R. von Eichborn (2 vols, Econ–Verlag, 1961, Pitman, 1963), (English–German, and German–English); and *Dizionaria Commerciale, Inglese-Italiano, Italiano-Inglese: Economica-Legge-Finanza*, by G. Motta (Signorelli, 1961) are worth noting. Several titles include up to 30 000 entries, and common features are treatment of idioms, phrases, abbreviations, weights and measures, and organisations. US usage is frequently distinguished from British.

45

Biographical Information

Both general and specialised works exist to provide biographical information about economists, historical or modern, studies in depth of theories, works published and activities, or simply date and place of birth and death, or present university appointment. Only a few can be noted here.

A bibliography of current biographical output is *Biography Index: a Cumulative Index to Biographical Material in Books and Periodicals* (Wilson, 1946–), which appears quarterly with annual and three-yearly cumulations. *Current Biography* (Wilson, 1940–), appears monthly with annual cumulations and ten-year indexes and contains medium-length articles.

Most major nations have produced (and in many cases are still, very slowly, producing) authoritative dictionaries of national biography. More aptly described as biographical encyclopaedias, these works give lengthy signed articles covering an individual's life and works in depth. The contributors are usually eminent in their subject's field. The most important works, with supplements are *The Dictionary of National Biography* (Oxford U.P., 1908–). The basic work of twenty-two volumes covers the period up to 1900, supplements and concise versions bring the work up to 1950. Signed articles by noted authorities are sometimes of great length, with bibliographies and sources: (Adam Smith 8 pages, Ricardo 3 pages, Keynes 6 pages). Corrections and additions are published in the *Bulletin of the Institute of Historical Research.* A useful supplement to *DNB* for lesser known nineteenth-century persons is *Modern English Biography*, by F. Boase (3 vols and 3 supplements, Netherton and Worth, 1892–1921; repr. 6 vols, Cass, 1965).

Dictionary of American Biography (Scribner, 1928–) is an eleven-volume American equivalent to the British *DNB* and with its supplements, covers the period to 1940. A concise edition in one volume covers the same period.

Shorter biographical entries, usually written, or checked by the biographee, form the genus 'Who's Who'. Nearly every nation has its Who's Who; some, like (the British) *Who's Who* and *Who's Who in America*, include important foreigners. For Great Britain and America there are series of 'Who Was Whos', which cumulate the deceased biographees from the 'Who's Whos', have shorter articles than the national dictionaries, but cover a large number of less important people.

Biographical information, in depth, of famous economists can also be found in such works as *Palgrave, Seligman,* the *Inter-*

national Encyclopedia of the Social Sciences, and smaller specialist encyclopaedias. Two studies of famous economists are worth noting here: *Ten Great Economists: from Marx to Keynes*, by J. A. Schumpeter (Allen and Unwin, 1952), and *The Worldly Philosophers: the Great Economic Thinkers*, by R. L. Heilbroner (3rd rev. edn, Allan Lane, 1969). This edition was first published in the United States by Simon and Schuster in 1967. The previous British edition of 1955, revised by P. Streeton, was published by Eyre and Spottiswoode with the title *The Great Economists*.

For current information on contemporary economists the following are useful sources, giving addresses, position, research interests, publications. *Handbook of the American Economic Association; American Men of Science: Social and Behavioral Sciences*, ed. by the Jaques Cattell Press (2 vols, 11th edn, Bowker, 1968); *The National Faculty Directory: an Alphabetical List, with Addresses, of 330 000 Full-time and Part-time Faculty at Junior Colleges, Colleges, and Universities in the US* (Gale Research, 1970–). This compilation is promised as an annual work, and covers over 2500 American institutions. *The Commonwealth Universities Yearbook* and *Minerva: Jahrbuch der Gelehrten Welt* list academic staff in institutions of higher education throughout the world.

Directories and Almanacs

Commercial directories exist for nearly every State in the UN, and in the most advanced of these, for every conceivable trade, industry and service. No list can compensate for a visit to a well stocked commercial library. What follows is a very selective list to show the kinds of work that are available, starting with the often ignored classified sections of telephone directories, and local town directories.

Kelly's Directory of Manufacturers and Merchants, including Industrial Services (3 vols, Kelly's Directories) is an annual alphabetical and classified list with international coverage. *The Kompass Register of Industry and Commerce*, produced for several European countries, has changed the title of its British edition to: *UK Kompass: Register of British Industry and Commerce* (3 vols, Kompass Register), and is annual, comprising three volumes: indexes to companies, products and services; classified list of products and services; company information in county and town order.

Thomas' Register of American Manufacturers (5 vols, Thomas, annual), and *McRae's Blue Book* are the standard directories for the United States.

Guide to Key British Enterprises (5th edn, Dun and Bradstreet, 1969); *Exchange Telegraph Daily Statistics Services* (*see* p. 140); *Stock Exchange Official Year-Book* (2 vols, Skinner, annual), and *Stock Exchange. Register of Defunct and Other Companies* are useful sources of financial information about British companies, whilst *Who Owns Whom* (UK and Continental edns, Roskill, annual) and *The Directory of Directors* (Skinner, annual) are self-explanatory.

Guides to Organisations and Associations

This section does not exclude information on commercial organisations, but the emphasis is on governmental, non-governmental and international bodies. The most general is: *Yearbook of International Organizations: the Encyclopaedic Dictionary of International Organizations, their Officers, their Abbreviations, 1968/9* (12th edn, Union of International Associations, 1969). *Guide to International Organisations*, comp. by the Central Office of Information, Reference Division (HMSO, 1960–) is loose-leaf, updated by replacement pages, and covers governmental and non-governmental bodies, with page-long descriptions with addresses, officers, and membership.

Two major examples of general national guides are: *Directory of British Associations, 1967/8* (2nd edn, CBD Research, 1967), which gives full details in title order, with abbreviations and subject indexes (a companion *Directory of European Associations* is due for publication in 1970), and the American equivalent: *Encyclopedia of Associations* (5th edn, 3 vols, Gale, 1969).

Factual Handbooks

A quick reference tool of current facts, needed by most people at some time or other, should be found in any library. There are numerous examples, most of them issued annually. *Whitaker's Almanack* has a British bias; *Information Please Almanac, Atlas and Yearbook* and *World Almanac and Book of Facts* have a United States bias. International coverage is provided by *The Statesman's Year-book, The International Year-book and Statesmen's Who's Who, The Europa Year-book* (not confined to Europe). Two weekly loose-leaf compilations are *Keesing's Con-*

temporary Archives: Weekly Diary of World Events, and *Facts on File: the Index of World Events*. *World Economic Survey*, comp. by the Department of Economic and Social Affairs (UN, annual) is a continuation of the *League of Nations World Economic Survey*, and the *UN World Economic Report*.

Dictionaries of Abbreviations

Abbreviations and acronyms are a part of modern life, international bodies and the social sciences seem to spawn them, and the need for dictionaries of abbreviations and acronyms has been met in the general and specific fields. *Acronyms and Initialisms Dictionary* (3rd edn, Gale Research, 1970, and annual supplements) is large with a strong American emphasis, while *Dictionary of Abbreviations and Symbols*, by E. F. Allen (Cassell, 1949) is strong in the commercial field. Further examples are: *Abbreviations Dictionary: Abbreviations, Contractions, Signs and Symbols Defined*, by R. De Sola (rev. edn, Duell, Sloan and Pearce, 1964); *Dictionary of Modern Acronyms and Abbreviations*, by M. Goldstein (Bobbs-Merrill, 1963); *Complete Dictionary of Abbreviations*, by R. J. Schwartz (Crowell, 1955; Harrap, 1957); *British Initials and Abbreviations*, comp. by I. Wilkes (2nd edn, Hill, 1966); *Cassell's Dictionary of Abbreviations*, comp. by J. W. Gurnett and C. H. J. Kyte (Cassell, 1966); *Internationales Verzeichnis von Abkürzungen von Verbanden, Behörden und Organisationen–International guide of abbreviations,* comp. by K. G. Saur (2 vols, Verlag Dokumentation, 1968).

Internationale Titelabkürzungen von Zeitschriften, Zeitungen, wichtigen Handbüchern, Wörterbüchern, Gesetzen usw., ed. by O. Leistner (Biblio-Verlag, 1967–) appears in parts (1–13 covers A–Vn), and lists periodical title abbreviations on an international scale, and *Periodical Title Abbreviations*, ed. by C. E. Hall (Gale Research, 1969) covers about 10 000 titles.

CHAPTER FIVE

PERIODICALS

JOHN FLETCHER

There are many definitions of 'periodical' or 'journal', the terms will be used synonymously in this chapter, but here the term denotes serials with a running title, published at intervals of less than a year, with no known end to the sequence, and usually containing articles by several authors in each issue.

Periodicals are a vital part of the literature of economics, probably more so than in the other social sciences, and the indications are that their importance is increasing. The present author has completed some unpublished surveys of the references made by economists in their journal articles. These indicate that in 1950, 42% of the citations were to journals, and that this had increased to 47% by 1968. In certain subject areas of economics especially those in which there is considerable research activity, and where events move rapidly, the importance of periodicals is undoubtedly greater.

The value and importance of periodicals in economics as in other subjects stems from the form: articles are short, and ideally published more quickly than books. Journal articles tend therefore to have replaced the earlier broadsheet or pamphlet as the vehicle for the first officially published results of research work, and because the discussion papers and working papers dealt with in Chapter 6 are usually restricted and not to be referred to without the author's permission, articles are the first freely-quotable publication. The size of periodical articles means also that subjects, new theories, opinions or empirical evidence on a scale too small to warrant publication of a monograph, can still be published and fairly rapidly.

Periodical publications do, however, raise problems for the librarian and for the library user. There is the range of subjects covered within one issue, which is invariably wider than that found in most monographs; periodicals must therefore be treated differently since their subject content cannot be traced through normal library subject catalogues, and abstracting and indexing services are devised to meet this need. A more recent complication is the birth of interdisciplinary journals to cater for the newly developing multi-subjects. The post-war increase in the number and size of economics periodicals has aggravated what was already a difficult problem. The Marshall Library at Cambridge now subscribes to 538 periodical titles, but this, though one of the best, is far from being a complete collection of economics journals. Finally, the problem of the increasing time-lag between the submission of a manuscript and its publication in an economics journal is diminishing one of the primary *raisons d'être* of journals. The average total delay between submission and publication is currently eight or nine months (see R. K. Coe and I. Weinstock: Editorial policies of major economics journals, in *Quarterly Journal of Economics and Business*; vol. 7, No. 4, winter 1967, pp. 37–43). With an acceptance rate as low as 9% for some of the major journals, it is unlikely that the time-lag will diminish, or that journals will cease to be a vital part of economics literature.

This Chapter is a rapid survey of the more important economics journals, and gives brief notes on the contents, value and use of most of them. In Chapters 12–24 subject specialists review the important literature of their subjects, and note the most valuable periodicals. Here an attempt is made to survey the general economics journals which cover all or most subjects of economics.

Most economists have their own views on the relative importance of individual titles, based on the sources of the key articles in their own subject area. In the notes which follow the explicit or implicit 'ranking' of journal titles is based on the author's citation analyses mentioned above. Whilst this type of analysis has disadvantages as a means of measuring importance, it is objective and the results quoted are fairly general and consistent.

Prestige Academic Periodicals

There are two outstanding prestige journals in economics, journals in which all economists seek to have their papers published: *American Economic Review* and *Economic Journal*.

AMERICAN ECONOMIC REVIEW

The most important and influential economics journal is the publication of the American Economic Association. Publication began in 1911 and there are now four issues a year, with a large supplement containing the papers and proceedings of the Association's annual meeting. Additional supplements of one longer paper, or with several authors' contributions on one subject are issued occasionally. Like most economics journals, *American Economic Review* is increasing in size: there is an increase of about 45% in the number of articles and the number of pages since 1948.

'(The *American Economic Review* aims) to supply such material as is essential to one who desires to keep up with the progress of economic thought and with the events of fundamental economic importance' (Notes on the Association, *American Economic Review*, vol. 47, No. 4, July 1957, p. viii). Subjects covered include all aspects of economic theory and applied economics. There are frequent articles on various aspects of economic policy in the United States and abroad, but few articles on economic history, history of economic thought or public finance. The subject matter of *American Economic Review* has changed with the subject matter of economics: recent volumes have contained more articles on technological change, consumer demand and investment behaviour, and fewer on foreign economic conditions, and in the industrial economics area more articles on the theoretical and empirical analysis of firms' behaviour and less on the monopoly problem and analysis of individual industries. Poverty, once considered a sociological topic, is now appearing in the *Review* as an economic problem.

Conferences of the Association after the war were joint affairs with other American professional bodies such as the Econometric Society and American Marketing Association, and there was usually a specific theme for each meeting. Latterly this policy has been abandoned, and the annual meeting of the American Economic Association is now less restricted in subject matter.

'Communications' is the term used to describe the shorter articles which appear in each issue, and these may be on new subjects which do not warrant a larger article, comments on, or replies to, other articles, or brief notes on the latest developments in a piece of research previously reported. The September issue contains a list of doctoral dissertations accepted in American universities' departments of economics, more details of which can be found in Chapter 6. Book reviews, about 200 a year, and lists of books received were included in *American Economic Review* until 1969 when they were transferred to the *Journal of Economic Literature*. There was a list of journal articles which like the books received was in broad subject groups, until 1966, when this was transferred to *Journal of Economic Abstracts*, the forerunner of *Journal of Economic Litera-*

ture. Directories of members of the American Economic Association were issued in, or as supplements to, *American Economic Review* in 1938, 1942, 1948, 1956, 1966 and 1969. As one would expect, the institutional affiliations of authors of articles published in *American Economic Review* do not show any university having the commanding position that Harvard has in the *Quarterly Journal of Economics,* or Chicago in the *Journal of Political Economy:* California, MIT and Stanford head the list for the *American Economic Review.*

American Economic Review has the highest number of manuscripts submitted, and the lowest acceptance rate of all the major economics journals: the high quality of the content tends to beget quality. It has grown more, however, in size than stature, and has probably lost ground to *Economic Journal* and especially to the *Review of Economic Studies,* but its position is still at the top, with *Economic Journal* as its only close rival.

ECONOMIC JOURNAL

Second only in importance to *American Economic Review,* and the leading British prestige economics periodical, *Economic Journal* is the organ of the Royal Economic Society, and began publication in 1891. It is a quarterly publication and there are no supplements since *Economic History* ceased publication in 1940. Unlike the American Economic Association, the Royal Economic Society does not sponsor conferences, or issue any other serial publication since the demise of its series of *Memoranda.*

The contents of *Economic Journal* like those of other periodicals has always reflected the current interests of economists and the current economic problems of the country. Thus between the wars it was strongly biased towards economic theory, especially monetary theory, currency problems and commodity markets, though surprisingly there were few articles on industry, wages and labour until 1939, and only a few articles on agriculture, imperial economic history and the history of economic thought. Post-war, however, the subject range of *Economic Journal* has widened considerably to include wages, foreign trade, industry, planning, all aspects of economic theory, industrial economics, national accounting, methodology and especially economic growth theory. There are still a few articles on the history of economic thought, but none on economic history.

The layout of the *Economic Journal* has remained virtually unchanged since 1915: seven or eight main articles, notes and memoranda, and about thirty long book reviews are followed by two very useful bibliographical lists. 'Recent periodicals' gives the contents pages of more than a hundred current issues of economics journals from all over the world. The order in which these are arranged is somewhat confusing being (apparently) geographical, but the value of having such a wide range, including the English translation of the titles of Russian and other East European journal articles is great. The 'New books' section similarly lists new monograph publications in order of the country of origin, and for most titles a few lines of notes are added.

Like most of the major economics periodicals, *Economic Journal* has an international list of contributors, though probably the majority are British or are working in British universities. The Royal Economic Society and American Economic Association have jointly commissioned a small number of review articles on the 'state of the art' in specific subject areas. This is a welcome move, and an essential one since economics lacks a regular review journal such as is found in most natural sciences.

Whilst most economists would still agree that *Economic Journal* is the most important general economics journal published in Great Britain, among the new generation of econometricians there is a feeling that it is losing its leading position. Certainly the articles seem to be aimed now more at the generally-qualified economist than the mathematical economist. This is not a criticism, for such an approach is still needed, and the mathematically-minded have *Econometrica, Review of Economics and Statistics,* and *Review of Economic Studies;* but it may mean that as economics becomes more numerate and less descriptive the *Economic Journal* may become less of a leader, and more one of a group of leaders of British economics periodicals.

Academic 'Second-line' Periodicals

These are the other major British and American journals which have no obvious subject leanings, and can be considered as dealing with 'general economics'. There are four American 'second-liners', *Quarterly Journal of Economics, Journal of Political Economy, Econometrica,* and *Review of Economics and Statistics,* and three British ones, *Economica, Oxford Economic Papers,* and *Review of Economic Studies.* The term 'second-line' in this context has no derogatory connotation, since many of these journals have published articles which are classics in their own field, but it denotes slightly less general importance than the leaders.

54

ECONOMICA

This quarterly publication of the London School of Economics and Political Science began in 1921 as a journal to cover all the social sciences, but when a new series was started in 1934, the subject range was restricted to 'economics, economic history, statistics and closely related problems'. The subject content of *Economica* has always reflected the interests and methodology of the economists working at the School. Before the war, subjects were general economic theory, with the usual prewar interest in the international monetary system, applied economics, economic history and economics as a subject. After the war, the emphasis moved towards applied economics, though economic theory still accounts for about half the articles, in contrast to most of the other major journals where applied economics predominates.

Applied economics articles in *Economica* tend to be statistical studies of economic history and conditions in small, and in some cases minute, subjects: building wages, for example. This is now one of the few major journals which includes articles on the history of economic thought. In the 1950s there were some very useful studies of statistical sources, but these have now ceased. There is a small number of long book reviews in each issue.

Economica is a steady journal, rarely brilliant, but with a high standard of quality, and will probably remain one of the more important British journals.

OXFORD ECONOMIC PAPERS

Publication by Oxford University Press began in 1937, and a new series with a change of policy began in 1949. Issued three times a year it is 'intended primarily as a channel for the publication of articles by Oxford authors' (editorial note in volume 1). This is the only British economics journal to state this criterion for acceptance of an article explicitly, though the interpretation of 'Oxford authors' is now fairly wide.

Generally speaking *Oxford Economic Papers* is probably the least mathematical of the major economics journals, and covers economic theory and applied economics, with more emphasis on the latter. There is now a distinct leaning towards industrial and labour economics, and incomes policy, and although the editorial note referred to above states that 'occasional articles on economic history and public administration' would be accepted, there have been very few such articles in recent years. Survey articles are occasionally included and the editors seem keen to include this kind of contribution. Most issues are multi-subject, but a few are devoted to one topic, such as restrictive practices.

Oxford Economic Papers has a lower than average acceptance rate for manuscripts, and a higher than average increase in size, which is some indication of the standing accorded to publication in this journal. Its quality is high, and consistent, and most articles are aimed at the postgraduate research level, though a few are useful for advanced undergraduate teaching.

JOURNAL OF POLITICAL ECONOMY

This is one of the earliest American academic economics journals, published by the University of Chicago Press since 1892, and now appearing six times a year. It has also experienced the most rapid increase in size of any economics journal, almost doubling in size from 1966 to 1968.

The full range of subjects in economics is covered by the *Journal of Political Economy* including history of economic thought, labour economics, monopoly and industrial economics, foreign trade, and even some articles on non-economic social science topics such as fertility and migration. More than any other economics periodical, however, *Journal of Political Economy* is known for its strong links with its sponsoring school of economics, and has fluctuated in popularity with that school. Contributions are accepted from all quarters, but the Chicago economists supply a larger percentage than any other institution: Pan A. Yotopoulos in his article 'Institutional affiliation of the contributors to three professional journals' (*American Economic Review*, vol. 51, No. 3, September 1961, pp. 665–670) found that 15·6% of contributors had links with the University of Chicago, which is probably the highest self-contribution rate of any major economics journal with the obvious exception of *Oxford Economic Papers* and *Yale Economic Essays*. Most issues include a wide range of subjects, but occasionally one issue is devoted to one topic, such as growth theory, with several articles on different aspects of the subject.

Journal of Political Economy has long been one of the leading academic economics periodicals. It has succeeded in keeping up with the changes in the subject content and emphasis of economics and looks set to retain its leading position. Some time ago it was able to accept only 15% of the papers submitted, but the recent increase in size should ease this situation.

QUARTERLY JOURNAL OF ECONOMICS

This is the older of the two quarterly economics journals from Harvard University Press, and began publication in 1886. It covers the whole range of economics subjects: prewar there were many articles on labour economics, labour relations, international trade and finance, and some on economic theory and the history of economic thought. In the 1940s and 1950s there was a surprising number of articles on trade union organisation and on monopoly, and later on Soviet and east European economic conditions. Now the emphasis seems to be on industrial economics, business finance and investment, taxation and international finance, although there is still a wide spread of subject interest, with an increasing emphasis on the mathematical approach to the subjects. Like most of the major general periodicals there are very few articles on economic development.

In the study by Yotopoulos (*op. cit.*) 14·6% of the contributions were found to be from writers with Harvard affiliations out of a total contribution of 49·8% from twelve American institutions. *Quarterly Journal of Economics* is the oldest English-language academic economics periodical and has retained an important place in the hierarchy. By accepting articles with a mathematical content it has been able to maintain its appeal to the new generation of economists.

REVIEW OF ECONOMICS AND STATISTICS

This is the second Harvard quarterly journal, and publication began in 1919: it should not be confused with the British *Review of Economic Studies*. Post-war the *Review of Economics and Statistics* has covered the full range of theoretical and applied economics, though the emphasis has always been on applied economics. Economic statistics have always been a declared interest of the *Review,* though this has been less evident in recent years. There used to be many articles on statistics sources and their evaluation, but there are few now. The emphasis, now, and it is an all-pervasive one, is on econometrics and especially methodology. Agricultural economics, income, international trade, monetary theory and policy, monopoly and employment are all strong subjects, with a slight emphasis on United States, and in the 1950s, Soviet affairs. Some twentieth-century economic history is also included, but there are few articles on public finance, economic development or the history of economic thought, and an increasing number on business economics.

The contributors' institutions are not noted, but there is an impression of American university bias, with some from government and industry. An interesting difference from the other major journals is the occasional 'symposium': a group of shorter articles on the same general topic, such as economics and operational research, or recent monetary policy.

Like its sister publication *Review of Economics and Statistics* is a high-quality, sound, established journal. Rather better than *Quarterly Journal of Economics,* however, it has managed to keep abreast of the changing methodology of economics and retain the interest of the mathematical economists.

'ECONOMETRICA' AND 'REVIEW OF ECONOMIC STUDIES'

The rise in importance of **econometrics** and **mathematical economics** has been matched in some of the general journals as noted above. There are two journals, however, which are especially important in this approach to economics. *Econometrica* is the quarterly publication of the Econometric Society which, although based in the United States and that country providing most of the journal's contributions, is an international society. The subject coverage is wide, including business cycles, growth, economic behaviour, income and production theory, and, of course, methods, models and techniques. The level of reader aimed at is Ph.D., rather higher than the other major economics journals, and the standard of the contributions is extremely high. The econometrics 'schools' in Europe seems not to have the influence in *Econometrica* that one could expect. *Review of Economic Studies* has been published three times a year since 1933, the same year as *Econometrica* began. It opened as a general economics journal, which to a great extent it remains. In the 1950s and 1960s, however, under various editors, the emphasis has become more on the mathematical approach to economics, so that its rise in importance has been rapid, and it is now regarded as one of the top rank economics journals. Like *Econometrica, Review of Economic Studies* has a wide subject coverage including monetary policy, taxation, industrial economics, international trade and cycles. The contributions are very international in origin, coming from Europe and the United States, Great Britain, India and Japan. This has been termed the 'journal for the young tigers', the new generation of mathematically-minded economists.

The new (1969) *Journal of Economic Theory* from the Wharton School at Pennsylvania University shows promise of being another journal for the mathematical economist, and well worth watching in the future.

Smaller Academic Periodicals

Both Great Britain and the United States have strong schools of economics in universities outside the main centres. These schools publish the third group of economics journals which are generally of less weight academically and physically than the leading titles described above. This is not to say that they are unimportant, but only that they are of less prestige value than the leaders. All are valuable, and some have carried key articles in the development of economic thinking in the past and present.

MANCHESTER SCHOOL OF ECONOMIC AND SOCIAL STUDIES

Emanating from the Faculty of Economic and Social Studies of the University of Manchester, this journal has been published three times a year since 1930, which makes this the oldest of the British 'smaller academic' group. In this group the subject content will tend to reflect more closely the teaching and research interests of the sponsoring institution. In the *Manchester School* this gave rise to emphasis on economic policy and planning in the early 1950s, and agricultural economics and economic development in the later 1950s. But always there has been the overriding emphasis on practical, empirical applied economics, and especially industrial economics in all its aspects: pricing policy, the effects of corporate taxation, and the theory of the firm. There is little regional bias in the *Manchester School* and although articles on the cotton and engineering industries are there, the locale is less important than the industrial structure or the economic problem. This is one of the best of the smaller British journals, having always maintained a high standard, and although it has increased in size since the war, at about eighteen articles a year there is a good chance that the quality will continue.

YORKSHIRE BULLETIN OF ECONOMIC AND SOCIAL RESEARCH

The Department of Economics at Hull University began this journal in 1948, then combined with the departments at Sheffield and Leeds Universities to publish this small semi-annual periodical. There are only about ten or twelve articles a year, but of a good standard; there is much more regional emphasis in the *Yorkshire Bulletin* than in the *Manchester School:* studies of wool prices, the clothing industry, coal mining and housing. There are more articles now on national rather than local topics, and a few on foreign economic problems. This is an interesting and useful small economics journal. With the change in emphasis in economic history from the national to the local scale, this type of journal will provide the vehicle for the publication of the results of these narrower, more detailed studies which have theoretical and practical implications at the national level.

SCOTTISH JOURNAL OF POLITICAL ECONOMY

The Scottish Economic Society, revived in 1953, began publishing this journal the following year, and it now appears three times a year. It is unashamedly Scottish, aimed for the Scottish audience and concerned with Scottish problems or research being carried out in Scottish universities. The contents are, however, not exclusively concerned with Scotland, or with economics: there have been articles on the finance of education (long a favourite topic of the Scots), and business history; history of economic thought and the nature of economic study, strong subjects in Scottish economics courses, are also represented. The level of the writing is deliberately set so that the educated layman interested in the subject can appreciate the articles. Again this is a small journal, containing only about twenty articles a year, but meeting the need for a local voice, and a voice that is more widely understood than the usual academic one. This journal will flourish because of this, and because of the importance in economics of the Scottish economics schools.

JOURNAL OF ECONOMIC STUDIES

This new (1965–) journal, also originating in Scotland, deserves a mention here. Its aim is to provide a vehicle for the younger lecturer in economics who finds it almost impossible to break into the established journals, but who nevertheless has something worth saying. It is too early yet to evaluate the contents of the journal, but the aims are admirable, and there is a useful section of notes on research in progress in British universities' economics departments. The editors say they are interested in bibliographical articles: the only economics journal actively seeking such material.

BULLETIN OF THE OXFORD UNIVERSITY INSTITUTE OF ECONOMICS AND STATISTICS

The *Bulletin* began in 1939 as a mimeographed diary of current economic events, then articles were added, but it was not until 1955/56 that it settled down as a quarterly journal in its present form. The early interest in all aspects of economic conditions in the United Kingdom and abroad has continued, always with a statistical bias. Recently a few theoretical articles have appeared, and with the interests of the Institute turning to economic development and the problems of developing countries, these aspects of economics have come more to the fore.

SOUTHERN ECONOMIC JOURNAL

The Southern Economic Association launched this publication as a regional forum for economic discussion in 1933, but in 1936 it had to be financially supported by the University of North Carolina. Since then it has gained in strength as it has become less regional, drawing on the nation for its subjects and for its contributors. Now containing over thirty articles a year of rising standard, *Southern Economic Journal* like other smaller economics journals, is looking for international acceptance as a valuable economics periodical.

WESTERN ECONOMIC JOURNAL

The organ of the Western Economic Association based in California, this is a growing journal which began in 1962 and has now settled into a regular quarterly publication pattern. The full range of economics subjects is covered, with a good percentage of mathematical and statistical articles. In addition it includes abstracts of papers given at the annual conference of the Western Economic Association.

YALE ECONOMIC ESSAYS

Yale University Press began publishing this unusual journal in

1961 and there are semiannual issues. It contains all doctoral dissertations in economics accepted at Yale University in full or as an extended summary, in addition to the normal academic articles by staff and students of the University. About twelve long articles a year are published on a range of subjects with a slight emphasis on growth and development, and monetary and fiscal economics.

Other Academic Periodicals

The next group of journals is those emanating from the recently developed countries of Canada, Australia and New Zealand, South Africa and Japan.

CANADIAN JOURNAL OF ECONOMICS

This quarterly publication of the Toronto University Press for the Canadian Economics Association began in 1935 as the *Canadian Journal of Economics and Political Science* covering both economics and politics. By 1968 it had become clear that separate journals were needed, and feasible, for the two subjects and the new title was adopted for the economics section: the separation has resulted in a considerable increase in size. A full range of economics subjects is covered, in both theoretical and applied economics, with perhaps a slight emphasis on labour and industrial economics. About half of the applied economics articles refer to economic conditions in Canada, but there is an increasingly large number of articles on economic theory.

ECONOMIC RECORD

The quarterly journal of the Economic Society of Australia and New Zealand began in 1924, the year of the birth of the Society, and of Australian economics. In new and fast developing countries it is inevitable that the emphasis should be on applied economics rather than on economic theory. Between the wars most articles were studies of aspects of the Australian or New Zealand economies, especially industry, agriculture, trade and labour, with some articles on demography and some statistical studies. Postwar the emphasis has shifted towards more non-Australian subjects, and more theoretical and methodological articles have appeared, but there are still usually two articles a year surveying the Australian economic situation. From the beginning there was an insistence on book reviews, and with recent expansion this has become one of the best book review sections in an economics journal. This is one of the best 'overseas' economics journals begun in the interwar period. Almost all the contributions are from the Australian or New Zealand universities, but with the steady entrenchment of quality in the economics departments there, it is likely that the *Economic Record* will maintain and enhance its position, and become better known throughout the world.

SOUTH AFRICAN JOURNAL OF ECONOMICS

The quarterly publication of the Economic Society of South Africa is mostly in English, but has a small percentage of Afrikaans-language articles. Its subject matter is devoted to the home country to a much greater degree than the other journals in this group. This is possibly because there are very few articles on South Africa in other academic economics journals.

INTERNATIONAL ECONOMIC REVIEW

Of the Japanese journals founded since the war, one is outstanding and well worth noting here: *International Economic Review* began publication, three issues a year, in 1960, and is the product of the Kansai Economic Federation in Osaka. It was founded 'to facilitate ... the introduction of new national schools of thought (e.g. the newly developing Japanese school) to the world community of economists' and 'to foster the development of quantitative economics'. The articles are, then, mathematical studies of problems, analyses, research results, models and descriptions of methods. There is no particular Japanese bias in subject material, and the mathematical approach is being applied to trade, prices, income, investment, business capital and economic growth. About a third are by Japanese authors with the remainder from the United States, and in recent years, the United Kingdom and India. *International Economic Review* has made a remarkably swift impact on this rapidly growing area of economics, and if the 'younger new generation of editors' who were given control in 1967 can maintain the vitality which the founders had, then the *Review* has a satisfactory future before it.

Developing Countries

Some of the developing nations have backgrounds of economic study and thought of varying lengths, and have given rise to academic journals. *Pakistan Development Review* is a large quarterly publication of the Pakistan Institute of Development Economics which began in 1961. About thirty long and forty shorter articles are published each year, many by well-known and respected economists from the West and from the sub-continent. Emphasis is on development economics, both theoretical and descriptive, without any overwhelming bias towards Pakistan's development problems and programmes. This is a journal which deserves more scrutiny than it usually receives in the West. *Social and Economic Studies* from the University of the West Indies is a much slighter journal which deals almost exclusively with Caribbean problems, chiefly economic, but including social, demographic, administrative and governmental. *Indian Journal of Economics* (University of Allahabad, 1916–) is the longest established of the Indian economics periodicals, and probably the best. Most contributions are from the Indian universities and concern the problems and theory of economic development: labour, resource allocation, finance, industrialisation and the role of agriculture. A large percentage, but probably not the majority, refer to Indian conditions.

European Periodicals

Only a few of the major European titles can be briefly noted here. *Revista de Economía Política* from the Institut de Estudios Políticos in Madrid is devoted almost entirely to Spanish economic problems. *Revue d'Économie Politique* is a general economics journal which covers the full range of economics subjects and a few relating to other social sciences. *Rivista di Politica Economica* is the general Italian economics journal for all aspects of the subject; *Rivista di Politica Economica: Selected Papers* is a special annual issue containing English translations of the most important articles which appeared in the Italian edition during the year. *Swedish Journal of Economics,* previously *Ekonomisk Tidskrift,* is now entirely in English, and provides the vehicle for the Scandinavian economics schools: its 15–20 articles a year show the expected emphasis on econometrics and mathematical economics. *Zeitschrift für Nationalökonomie* is now an international journal with about half its articles in English, with strong emphasis on mathematical economics. *Weltwirtschaftliches Archiv* from the University of Kiel is also worth noting.

Non-academic Journals

Most journals reflect **current economic conditions,** in that the subjects interesting economists are these conditions, and the problems and policies associated with them. In addition there are many periodicals of which economic reports of the present state of the economy are the main content. *National Institute Economic Review* is the quarterly publication of the National Institute for Economic and Social Research and began in 1959. Its annual review of the United Kingdom economy is detailed in content and of a very high standard. Overseas countries are dealt with in less detail except in so far as they affect the British economy. In addition there are articles throughout the year on specific aspects of the UK economy: taxation, aid, imports and exports, labour supply, economic growth, and housing, for example. This journal has gained an important place in the economics field as a result of the quality of its articles and its forecasts. *The Economist* is one of the longest established of the British weekly commentaries on current affairs. Whilst still covering economic affairs in some detail, there is a tendency for political affairs to take a greater share of the content. The reporting and comments are of high quality, remarkably unbiased politically and held in good esteem by specialists and laymen alike. Political and Economic Planning publishes a series of pamphlets under the running title *Planning,* recently changed to *Broadsheet.* These are by journalists, commentators and academic experts on current economic and social problems. The tone is not unbiased politically, but the quality of most of the series is high. There are no exact equivalents of these titles for the United States. *Business Week* has a much lighter, more journalistic approach than *The Economist,* but has the same emphasis on business affairs. There are short statistical sections and commentaries on federal and international affairs. It is a very readable journal, and politically unbiased. *Dun's Review* fills a similar role, whilst *Harvard Business Review,* monthly, is aimed at a higher level of business executive and comprises mainly academic and professional articles in the business economics area.

The British joint stock **banks** are unusual in producing a series of free journals, published three or four times a year, containing very readable articles on economic problems and policies. Aimed at the intelligent layman, most are written by specialists and some provide excellent material on specific topics such as regional planning. The recent spate of bank mergers has reduced the number, but the following are, or were, especially valuable: *District Bank Review, Westminster Bank Review* (now the *National Westminster Bank Quarterly Review), Lloyds Bank Review, Three Banks Review* and *Midland Bank Review*. Each of the US Federal Reserve Banks publishes a free monthly periodical containing articles on regional and national economic and business conditions, and monetary and fiscal matters. The most widely used are those of the banks in Boston (*New England Economic Review*) and New York (*Federal Reserve Bank of New York, Monthly Review*).

Translations

There are two journals which specialise in translations into English of articles published in less well known languages: *International Economic Papers* is not concerned with international economics, but is a collection of translations of articles first published in Scandinavian, Dutch, Italian and other European languages which the editorial board of the International Economic Association feel should be more widely available. *Problems of Economics* contains English translations of articles in Russian and other East European journals which are of wider significance than purely the study of communist economies.

CHAPTER SIX

UNPUBLISHED MATERIAL

JOHN FLETCHER

In the literature of economics the volume of 'unpublished' material is large and increasing in size and importance. This chapter is concerned with this material and the sources of information about it. It is a difficult area to define, but it includes research in progress (even though no written material is available), research reports, working papers, internal memoranda and academic theses or dissertations. Occasionally this type of material is printed, but more often it is produced by duplication or lithographic process; most is not offered for sale through the normal channels, but is only available on application to the author or his academic or research institution.

Research in economics is undertaken in a wide variety of institutions, but the majority is done in university departments or research units, government departments, and a few private or sponsored research institutions. Initially there are no written results, but it is nevertheless important for a researcher to know who, if anyone, else is working on his subject. Guides to **research in progress** in the social sciences are rare. For Great Britain the Ministry of Technology's Warren Research Laboratory used to issue a *Register of Research in the Social Sciences*. Since 1967 the Department of Education and Science and British Council's joint annual publication *Scientific Research in British Universities and Colleges* has included a third volume: *Social Sciences*. Arrangement is by very broad subject ('Economics' is not subdivided) and then by the universities and colleges. Under each department there is a list of the research projects and personnel concerned. There is similar information on projects being pursued in non-academic institutions such as government departments, a few private firms, local authorities and national and industrial research institutions such as the National Institute of Economic and Social Research. There is also a personal name index and a fairly detailed subject index.

From its first issue, winter 1965, *Journal of Economic Studies* has included a section of Research Notes, which gives brief details of research work being carried out in the economics departments of British universities.

Written results of research work can take several forms: an internal research report to the sponsoring body, a working document or discussion paper made available to a select group of colleagues for critical comment, an article published in a professional journal, a paper given at a conference (whose proceedings may or may not be published) or a published monograph. Here we are concerned only with the first two categories, for to an increasing extent the first publicly available results of research in economics is the **working paper** or **discussion paper.** One eminent academic described his sequence of publication as: a first draft of a paper circulated to a small select group of colleagues upon whose discretion he could rely if the paper was bad; a second revised draft duplicated in sufficiently large quantities to send to any interested individual or organisation; and the final draft which would be submitted for publication in a learned journal. Since there would inevitably be a time lag between these steps to allow for comments from colleagues, and between submission to, and publication in, the journal, the working paper has become an ever more important type of academic 'publication'.

Unfortunately, working papers are by definition transitory, unpolished, and issued in a less-than-well-organised manner either by the author or his academic department or research institution. Because they are not published at this stage they do not appear in bibliographies or abstracting and indexing services. The following is a small selection of the more important series which are generally available.

Econometrics is a rapidly developing and constantly changing subject of economics, and one, therefore, in which it is important for the researcher to be up to date with the latest developments. A typical discussion paper series emanates from Michigan State University which has an Econometrics and Mathematical Economics Workshop at which papers are given and many are then circulated as *Econometrics Workshop Papers*, of which there are 15 to 20 each year. One of the largest series is from the Institute of Business and Economic Research of the University of California, now entitled *Working Papers in Economic Theory and Econometrics* and comprising almost 200 titles. The University of Chicago's Center for Mathematical Studies in Business and Economics is a joint venture of its Department of Economics and Graduate School of Business. Its *Report* series is large.

Three important schools of econometrics are in Europe: at Amsterdam, Louvain and Oslo. The Econometric Institute of the Netherlands School of Economics issues a series of *Reports* by researchers on the Institute staff, and by visiting academics: about twenty *Reports* are issued each year. The Catholic University of Louvain has a Centre for Operations Research and Econometrics whose *CORE Discussion Papers* are a very useful source of new econometric thought. The University of Oslo Institute of Economics is strong in econometrics and issues a large number of mimeographed *Memoranda* each year.

In **economic development** there are several important research institutes, most of which issue discussion papers. At Harvard University Center for International Affairs the Development Advisory Service and the Project for Quantitative Research in Economic Development issue a joint series of *Economic Development Reports*. There are now about 150 of these on such subjects as the use of models in development planning, Brazilian saving, the structure of Pakistan's foreign trade and the occupational and educational background and finance of industrial entrepreneurs. This is an important series, and it includes the papers given at the DAS conferences, most of which are not available in any other form. The results of the work of the Economic Department of the International Bank for Reconstruction and Development is available in mimeographed form in the *Economics Department Working Papers* and the *EC Reports* series. There is a wide range of these papers, the guide to which is the IBRD *Catalog of Studies* (*see* p. 71). Other useful series in this subject area are the *Discussion Papers* of the Center for Research on Economic Development of the University of Michigan, and the *Communications Series* of the Institute of Development Studies at the University of Sussex, which also includes conference papers. For the East European view of the subject there is the Centre for Afro–Asian Research of the Hungarian Academy of Sciences which issues a very interesting series of *Studies on Developing Countries.*

Economic growth is the subject of the *Memoranda* of the Research Center in Economic Growth at Stanford University and the *Center Discussion Papers* of the Economic Growth Center at Yale University.

The number of working paper series covering **general economics** is large and only a few can be noted here. Probably the largest is the *Institute Papers* of the Institute for Research in the Behavioral, Economic and Management Sciences of Purdue University which ranges wide over economics, psychology, sociology, marketing and business behaviour. The *Seminar Papers* of the Department of

Economics at Columbia University are worth mentioning, as is the *Discussion Paper Series* of the Harvard Institute of Economic Research. The *Cowles Foundation Discussion Papers* from the Cowles Foundation for Research in Economics at Yale University are especially valuable, but are more difficult to obtain.

In Great Britain there are discussion paper series from most universities with active departments of economics: *Discussion Papers in Economics and Econometrics* (two series with this title, from Manchester and Southampton), *Discussion Papers in Economics* (Bristol and Reading), *Discussion Papers* (Essex and Birmingham), and *Warwick Economic Research Papers* (University of Warwick) to mention a few.

From Canada there are *Carleton Economic Papers* (Carleton University) and *Discussion Papers* of the Department of Economics of the University of British Columbia; and from Japan the *Discussion Papers* of Osaka University's Institute of Social and Economic Research. Most of these series, whilst not limited to one area of economics, inevitably tend to stress those subjects with which the current staff and research are most concerned.

Research Reports of academic institutions are occasionally printed and sold in the normal way, or made available on request to the research institution. For American reports of this type the Associated University Bureaus of Business and Economic Research publishes an annual *Bibliography of (date) Publications of University Bureaus of Business and Economic Research* (the author, 1963– ; earlier volumes for 1950–56, and annually 1957 to 1962 were entitled *Index of Publications of Bureaus of Business and Economic Research*). The *Bibliography* lists the publications first by institution then by subject, and ends with an author index. The US Small Business Administration published a useful *Survey of University Business and Economic Research Reports* (USGPO, 1963) which is an annotated list of some 2300 items compiled by Texas University Bureau of Business Research.

Such research units attached to universities are less common outside the United States and comprehensive lists of their publications are not available. A few of the more prolific issue lists of their own, and some of the most useful in economics are those from international organisations. The United Nations Conference on Trade and Development (UNCTAD) makes available its working documents, including commissioned surveys and reports, and has issued a two-part list of those relating to the second UNCTAD Conference held in New Delhi in 1968: *Guide to Documentation: UNCTAD II* (TD/INF 3). Part one lists the documents by the items on the conference agenda, and part two by subject. The

Economics Department of the International Bank for Reconstruction and Development and the International Development Association issues some very useful occasional papers, reports and working papers resulting from research or survey work done on problems of economic development. The Department's quarterly *Status of Studies* catalogue listed these reports as issued, gave advance notice of future reports, research in progress and research projects under consideration. *Status of Studies* has now been replaced by *Catalog of Studies* (IBRD/IDA, 1969) which will be updated semi-annually by supplements, to form a cumulating catalogue. The same information on research and reports is given in the new publication.

Much of the research carried on in the economics departments of universities is by post-graduate students working for a master's or doctor's degree. The **theses** or **dissertations** submitted are sometimes published commercially at a later date, but most are not. With the steady increase in post-graduate activity in most universities, this volume of research literature deposited in university libraries is growing in importance. One or two *ad hoc* international lists of theses have been compiled, the most useful of which is the UNESCO: *Thèses de Sciences Sociales ... Theses in the Social Sciences: An International Analytical Catalogue of Unpublished Doctoral Theses, 1940–1950* (UNESCO, 1952) in which over three thousand entries are arranged in broad subject order, with subject, author, and geographical indexes.

There are two major current sources of information about theses in general: for Great Britain, *Index to Theses Accepted for Higher Degrees in the Universities of Great Britain and Ireland* has been published by Aslib since 1953 (the first volume covering the academic year 1950/51), and now indexes more than six thousand masters' and doctors' theses each year. Arrangement is by broad subject groups ('Economics' has twelve subdivisions, plus 'Economic Geography') within which theses are listed with author, university, title and degree. There is also an author index, and a chart showing the availability of theses from each university.

There are three general lists of American and Canadian dissertations published by University Microfilms. *Dissertation Abstracts International* (University Microfilms, 1969–) is the new title of *Dissertation Abstracts* published monthly from 1952 to 1969, which itself replaced *Microfilm Abstracts* published from 1938 to 1951. It gives long ($\frac{1}{2}$ to $\frac{3}{4}$ page) abstracts of doctoral dissertations which the company has available for sale on microfilm or as full-size Xerox copy. It therefore only includes theses from universities allowing this: now 255 institutions including

California, Yale, Princeton and Stanford, but excluding the economics dissertations of Harvard and Chicago, among others. About 20 000 dissertations in all subjects are abstracted each year, and arranged by broad subject ('Economics' has only five subdivisions, and 'Labor Relations' is subsumed to 'Sociology'). Title of the dissertation, author, degree, university, year, and in some cases supervisor, are given before the abstract which usually gives the aim, methods and brief results of the work. There are author and keyword subject indexes, both of which cumulate annually.

American Doctoral Dissertations (University Microfilms, 1957–) which replaced *Doctoral Dissertations Accepted by American Universities* (Wilson, annual, 1934 to 1956) is an annual publication which until 1965 was published as issue 13 of *Dissertation Abstracts*. It aims to be a complete listing of all doctoral dissertations accepted by American and Canadian Universities, arranged under alphabetical subject headings and then under the name of the university. Only the author and title of the dissertation is given, and there is an author index. *Masters' Abstracts: Abstracts of Selected Masters Theses on Microfilm* (University Microfilms, quarterly, 1964–) is a classified sequence of abstracts of selected masters' essays from American and Canadian Universities. The National Library of Canada, Ottawa, compiles the annual *Canadian Theses* (The Library, 1960/61–) which lists Canadian theses in a broadly classified order.

Many universities publish lists of their own theses, for example Cambridge University publishes *Titles of Dissertations Approved for the PhD, MSc and M Litt Degrees of the University of Cambridge* annually since 1925/26 (up to 1956/57 it was entitled *Abstracts of Dissertations Approved for the PhD, MSc and MLitt Degrees in the University of Cambridge*) and the Committee of Advanced Studies of Oxford University issues *Successful Candidates for the Degree of D Phil, B Litt and BSc with Titles of their Theses* (annual, 1940/49– ; previously *Abstracts of Dissertations for the Degree of Doctor of Philosophy*, annual, 1925/28 to 1940). Harvard University Graduate School of Arts and Sciences issues *Summaries of Theses Accepted in Partial Fulfilment of the Requirements for the Degree of Doctor of Philosophy* (annual, 1925–).

Probably the most useful list of American doctoral dissertations in economics is that published annually in *American Economic Review* since 1911 (the list began in 1904 as a separate publication, then was incorporated in the *Bulletin*, and finally in *American Economic Review* when the journal began in 1911). Since 1923 it has appeared in the September issue, and until 1965 included theses completed and in progress and consisted only of a title list. From 1966 there have been short abstracts of about half the titles listed and only completed theses are included. Entries are arranged in broad subject groups: the net is cast fairly wide, though some related subjects such as economic geography and industrial sociology are omitted, and the list now includes over six hundred dissertations a year.

From September 1952 each issue of *Journal of Finance* has long abstracts of up to ten PhD dissertations accepted by American Universities in the economics and business finance field. *Journal of Business* has included a list of doctoral dissertations accepted in the January issue since 1956: entries are in broad subject categories with bare details of author, university and thesis title. *Journal of Economic History* has included a small number of long abstracts of theses in recent years.

Industrial and commercial firms and government departments are undertaking an increasing amount of research work, especially in agricultural and industrial economics, management, and mathematical methods applied to business. Most reports on this research by private firms and consultants are confidential, and only a small number are available outside the sponsoring institution. These are usually only traceable through the normal bibliographical services noted on pp. 34–42, or by word of mouth. Some 'private' reports, however, are published for example in the *Kiplinger Newsletters* and *Monetary Notes* by Walter Spahr. In the United States a large amount of research work is now being sponsored by federal agencies, and reports of this work are increasingly becoming freely available. *United States Government Research and Development Reports (USGRDR)* (US National Bureau of Standards, fortnightly, April 1965–) continues the earlier *United States Government Research Reports*, and lists reports and translations with short abstracts under broad subject headings. The vast majority are, of course, scientific or technical, but the researcher in the economics fields mentioned would do well to check this listing regularly. There are no specific subject or author indexes in the fortnightly issues, but detailed subject, personal, and corporate author indexes are published annually. Most reports listed are available from the Clearinghouse for Federal Scientific and Technical Information, for American inquirers, or on microfiche from the National Lending Library for Science and Technology (obtained through the inquirer's university library) for British researchers.

The Rand Corporation is responsible for a large amount of official United States research work, and publishes the results in three series of *Reports, Papers* and *Rand Memoranda*. The Corporation issues a quarterly guide to these reports: *Selected Rand Abstracts* (Rand Corporation, 1963–) in which short abstracts are given (in code number order) with detailed subject and author indexes. Many of these reports are on subjects of interest to economists, including cost-benefit analysis, studies of economic conditions overseas, especially in communist countries, mathematical and statistical methods, manpower and industrial studies. Rand Memorandum RM2800-2 (and supplements) is an index to and abstracts of Rand Economics Department open literature published between 1948 and 1969. compiled by Harriett Porch.

British Research and Development Reports (National Lending Library for Science and Technology, 1966–) is a monthly index of unpublished research reports selected from those deposited with the library. Again, most are in the science and technology area, but the section 'Behavioural and social sciences' includes some reports of use to economists. This is the only service which includes even a few of the British discussion papers referred to above.

CHAPTER SEVEN

BRITISH GOVERNMENT PUBLICATIONS

D. C. L. HOLLAND and SUSAN EDGE

The first step towards using this material is to find a library which takes it in. The second step is to acquire sufficient understanding of the nature of government publications to be able to trace and use them efficiently. In such a short chapter it is only possible to give the briefest outline of the system of classification employed. For a fuller description the reader should consult the following:

H.M. Treasury: *Official Publications* (HMSO, 1958).
P. and G. Ford: *A Guide to Parliamentary Papers* (2nd edn, Blackwell, 1956).
J. G. Ollé: *An Introduction to British Government Publications* (Association of Assistant Librarians, 1965).
S. Horrocks: *The State as Publisher* (Library Association, 1952).

Some of the above works also contain bibliographical material: for example, Chapter 4 of *An Introduction to British Government Publications* includes lists of government publications. The author lists the government departments, covering most of the main publications of interest to the economist. *Published by HMSO: a Brief Guide to Official Publications* (HMSO, 1960) has a similar chapter, giving the departments and their chief publications.

A useful and up-to-date bibliography is to be found in *Britain: an Official Handbook*, which is published annually by the Central Office of Information (COI). On a more sophisticated plane the Interdepartmental Committee for Social and Economic Research produced a series of *Guides to Official Sources*. Those on *Census of Production Reports* (HMSO, 1961) (*see* p. 80) and on *Labour Statistics* (HMSO, 1958) are of particular relevance to the economist. Some of this series have been superseded by the set of Central Statistical Office *Studies in Official Statistics*. Bibliographies for statisticians are dealt with in a separate chapter.

75

The economic historian will find useful the *Breviates of Parliamentary Papers* by P. and G. Ford, published by Blackwell. There are three of these, for the periods 1900–16 (published in 1957), 1917–19 (1951), and 1940–45 (1961). They follow the aim and pattern of *Hansard's Catalogue and Breviate of Parliamentary Papers, 1696–1834* (reprinted in facsimile with an introduction by P. and G. Ford, Blackwell, 1953), which was first published in 1837 by James and Luke G. Hansard, whose name is more famous in connection with the report of the daily debates in Parliament. The *Breviates* are intended to give a full guide to the reports of Royal Commissions and other important committees on the assumption that these are the source of policies and hence of history. Since a Treasury economy drive of 1921 some of these reports have been published as non-Parliamentary publications, but they are nevertheless included. Some regular returns and 'information papers' are excluded. Each volume follows the same broad subject arrangement; and for every item in each *Breviate* there are the terms of reference of the committee and its date of appointment, a list of signatories of the report, the argument summarised, the conclusions and the recommendations. The Hansard *Breviate* and the Fords' twentieth century ones are linked by the *Select List of British Parliamentary Papers, 1833–1899*, also edited by P. and G. Ford (Blackwell, 1953).

Parliamentary Publications

It is not easy to make a clear distinction between Parliamentary and non-Parliamentary publications, as examples of inconsistencies can always be found. The purest form of a Parliamentary publication is one emanating from, and ordered to be printed by, one of the two Houses. Both Houses also order Public Bills to be printed, **Commons Bills** forming one of three numerical series in its sessional output of Parliamentary Papers, while Lords Bills and Papers are united in a different series. Thus, for example, what eventually became the Industrial Development Act, 1966, which introduced investment grants, was first published in May 1966 as Bill 12 of session 1966–67 in the Commons series and in July 1966 as Number 69 in the Lords series of Papers and Bills. It became an Act as Chapter 34, 1966. Public General Acts (the Statute Book) emanate from the Crown in conjunction with Parliament and therefore, although for convenience Her Majesty's Stationery Office (HMSO) classes them as Parliamentary publications, they do not rank as Parliamentary Papers, a term usually confined to Commons Bills, House of Commons Papers and Command Papers. **House of Commons Papers** are numbered in one sessional series but are of two kinds: those, such as Select Committee reports, which originate within the House, and those which are ordered to be printed in compliance with an Act, such as annual reports of statutory bodies. For instance, the annual report for 1968–69 issued under the Industrial Development Act, 1966, by the Board of Trade was House of Commons paper 329 of session 1968–69 (written as HC329 of 1968–69). Confusingly, however, following the Treasury economy measure of 1921, many statutory reports which used to be classed as Parliamentary Papers are now published as non-Parliamentary publications. **Command Papers** are also confusing because, although they form the third numerical series of Parliamentary Papers, they emanate from government departments and reach Parliament without being requested. Command Papers are numbered neither sessionally nor annually, but there have so far been five series: the first numbered 1 to 4222 ran from 1833 to 1869, and the four subsequent series are distinguished by different abbreviations of the word Command: C., Cd., Cmd., and the present series, prefixed by Cmnd., which began in 1956. As an example, the proposals which were enacted in the Industrial Development Act, 1966, were first published by the Board of Trade, the Department of Economic Affairs and the Treasury in *Investment Incentives* (Cmnd. 2874) in January 1966. In addition to various business papers, such as their respective *Journals*, both Houses publish transcripts of their debates, known as **Hansard**, which are important not only for Ministerial expositions of policy but also for statistical and other information given in answer to questions to Ministers. The indexes to Hansard, however, leave a lot to be desired.

Indexes to Parliamentary Publications

In order to trace a Parliamentary publication one should consult one of the official indexes. The main ones are as follows:

Fifty-year general indexes: there are three of these for the periods 1801–52, 1852–99 and 1900–49, the last named being entitled *General Index to Bills, Reports and Papers printed by order of the House of Commons and to the Reports and Papers presented by Command, 1900 to 1948–49* (HMSO, 1960). Like the decennial and sessional indexes mentioned below, these give volume number and page references for use with the bound sets of Papers. The 1900–49 index also has an alphabetical list of the short titles of

77

Bills. **Decennial general indexes:** the most recent one, *Parliamentary Papers (House of Commons and Command): General Alphabetical Index to the Bills, Reports and Papers printed by order of the House of Commons and to the Reports and Papers presented by Command, 1950 to 1958–59* (HC 96 of 1962–63), follows on from the last fifty-year index. As well as the alphabetical index, there is an alphabetical list of the chairmen of committees and the authors of reports included in the first part. **Sessional indexes:** one is published for each session: for example, *Parliamentary Papers (House of Commons and Command): Sessional Index for Session, 1965–66* (HC 128 of 1965-66). The contents are the same as for the decennial index, with the addition of numerical lists of Bills, House of Commons Papers and Command Papers. The sessional indexes for House of Lords Papers and some historical indexes are described in detail on page 21 of *The State as Publisher* by S. Horrocks.

Non-Parliamentary Publications

These comprise all government publications other than Parliamentary publications. They were originally called Official Publications and later Stationery Office Publications. The great majority are issued by government departments and by certain other bodies for which the government is responsible, such as the University Grants Committee. Most minutes of evidence of Royal Commissions have also been published in this form since the economy measures of 1921. The publications of the government departments of particular interest to the economist are dealt with separately below.

The only comprehensive **lists of non-Parliamentary publications** are the catalogues issued by HMSO. These, of course, also include Parliamentary Papers but in a less convenient form than in the indexes.

The *Daily List of Government Publications from Her Majesty's Stationery Office* covers for each day the publications issued by HMSO. It has sections for Statutory Instruments, Parliamentary publications, non-Parliamentary publications and publications sold but not published by HMSO. This latter category contains, for instance, the publications of international organisations. The monthly list, *Government Publications issued during ...* cumulates the *Daily Lists* and is arranged in the same way. Since 1947 the monthly list has been indexed.

The annual list, entitled *Catalogue of Government Publications*, is probably the most useful catalogue for the student. It has been published since 1918 and a consolidated index has been issued for five-year periods since 1936. It has three sections: the first shows Parliamentary Papers in numerical order; the second lists all government publications under the names of the bodies authorising publications, usually a government department; the third is a list of periodicals published by HMSO. The indexes to the annual and monthly lists are based on keywords from the titles of the publications, but personal authors and chairmen of committees are also included.

In addition there are *Sectional Lists*, each of which covers all the publications of one department, organisation or occasionally subject. There is one for each of the government departments of interest to the economist: their value is limited, however, in that they are not comprehensive and because obsolete titles are omitted at the periodic revisions.

The terms Blue Book, White Paper and Green Paper are frequently used without clarification and it may be useful to define them. The term **Blue Book** was originated in the nineteenth century for reports presented to Parliament in thick, blue covers because they were too large to have only the normal paper binding. The phrase is less common now, and to an economist it often signifies only the *National Income and Expenditure* Blue Book, although this is in fact a non-Parliamentary publication. The term **White Paper** is of more recent origin and is applied to Parliamentary publications with white covers. It refers especially to notes on policy presented in anticipation of Bills, returns printed for the House and, occasionally, to reports prepared for a debate. Most White Papers are, therefore, Command Papers. The term **Green Paper** is of most recent origin, having been used in 1967 to describe the joint Department of Economic Affairs–HM Treasury publication, *The Development Areas: a Proposal for a Regional Employment Premium* (HMSO, 1967). The intention was that these documents should not commit the government, but should be a stimulus to public discussion, the results of which would be incorporated in a White Paper leading to legislation. Thus the above paper was followed by the White Paper, *The Development Areas: Regional Employment Premium* (Cmnd. 3310, 1967). In this case legislation was not necessary, the premium being paid under the Selective Employment Payments Act, 1966 (Chapter 32).

Departmental Publications

One cannot hope to be comprehensive within such a short chapter and what follows is a mere indication of the types of publications for which the government departments and other bodies of interest to the economist are responsible. The chief difficulty of making such a classification is that responsibility for a topic can be transferred from one department to another. (*See* p. vi.)

The Board of Trade

In the course of its long history the Board has acquired many responsibilities. It was this department which initiated much of the industrial development legislation and consequently has several annual reports issued in its name. There are, for example, reports under the Control of Office and Industrial Development Act, 1965 (Chapter 33) which give numbers of Industrial Development Certificates approved during the year. Since the government reorganisation of October 1969 responsibility for industrial development has been transferred to the Ministry of Technology under whose name future annual reports will be published.

The Board of Trade is responsible for the *Census of Production* which has been taken every four or five years since the war. There was one in 1963, for which the results will all be published by 1970. A *Census* is being taken for 1968, but it is intended that this will be the last one in the present form, as annual and quarterly figures are to be collected by the new Business Statistics Office. A *Census of Distribution* is taken less frequently: the last full one was for 1961 and the next is planned for 1971, although there was a sample census for 1966. In support of its work on production the Board also publishes the *Business Monitor: Production Series*, in which many industries are covered in monthly or quarterly booklets.

Input-output tables are produced by the department, but the only complete set published since the war relates to 1954 and was published in 1961 as a joint effort of the Board of Trade and the Central Statistical Office. Preliminary tables for 1963 have appeared in the issues for August 1966 and August 1968 of the periodical *Economic Trends*, and complete figures were published in 1970.

As well as annual reports, the **Monopolies Commission** publishes a report of each of the investigations which it has been asked to make by the President of the Board of Trade. These usually appear as House of Commons Papers, although some have been Command Papers. Since 1965 the Commission has been asked to study some proposed mergers as well as potential abuses of monopoly power as defined in the earlier Acts. Its policy regarding mergers, particularly among conglomerates, is set out in an appendix to *Unilever Ltd. and Allied Breweries Ltd.: a Report on the Proposed Merger and General Observations on Mergers* (HC 297 of 1968–69). The 1969 government reorganisation envisaged the amalgamation of the Commission with the National Board for Prices and Incomes and the transference of the joint body, the Commission for Industry and Manpower, to the Department of Employment and Productivity.

The Board of Trade retains its authority acquired under the Companies Acts to make investigations of individual companies and it publishes the reports as non-Parliamentary publications.

Not surprisingly the Board is responsible for publications dealing with foreign trade: the *Overseas Trade Statistics of the United Kingdom*, known as the *Overseas Trade Accounts of the United Kingdom* before 1970, appear monthly and each month the figures are cumulated so that the December issue contains the totals for the year. The more summary *Report on Overseas Trade* is also monthly and a non-Parliamentary publication. Trade agreements are published as White Papers: so too are accounts of negotiations under international trade agreements, *The Kennedy Round of Trade Negotiations, 1964–67* (Cmnd. 3347, 1967), for instance.

The Board's periodical is the weekly *Board of Trade Journal*, which has annual articles on trade and overseas investment, recent statistics and a running index to the statistical series.

The Department of Economic Affairs (DEA)

The Department of Economic Affairs was set up in 1964. Its powers were successively reduced and in October 1969 it was finally abolished, its remaining responsibilities being transferred to the Ministry of Technology, except for supervision of the Regional Planning Councils which is now carried out by the Ministry of Local Government and Regional Planning.

The Department's first publication of note was *The National Plan* (Cmnd. 2764, 1965), but there was no follow-up until the much less ambitious Green Paper, *The Task Ahead: Economic Assessment to 1972* (HMSO, 1969) appeared. From its inception the DEA took over responsibility for regional planning and most of the regional development studies have been published under its auspices as non-Parliamentary publications: for example, *The Challenge of the Changing North* (HMSO, 1966) prepared by the Northern Economic Planning Council. Regional planning documents before 1964 were issued as Command Papers: for instance,

The North East: a Programme for Regional Development and Growth (Cmnd. 2206, 1963) which was presented by the Secretary of State for Industry, Trade and Regional Development. The Regional Employment Premium has already been mentioned in the section on Green Papers (*see* p. 79) as a joint project of the DEA and the Treasury.

Planning is closely linked to the restructuring of industry. The White Paper, *Investment Incentives* (Cmnd. 2874, 1966), was part of a long-term programme. So too is the **Industrial Reorganisation Corporation**, which was heralded by a White Paper of that title (Cmnd. 2889, 1966) and implemented by the Industrial Reorganisation Corporation Act, 1966 (Chapter 50). The IRC publishes its annual reports as House of Commons Papers, but unlike the National Board for Prices and Incomes and the Monopolies Commission it publishes no other reports of its activities.

The **prices and incomes policy** was originally supervised by the Department of Economic Affairs but was handed over to the Department of Employment and Productivity in April 1968. The first set of White Papers, which included *Prices and Incomes Policy: an Early Warning System* (Cmnd. 2808, 1965) the Prices and Incomes Act, 1966 (Chapter 33) and the early reports of the National Board for Prices and Incomes were, however, sponsored by the DEA.

The Department made one contribution to the Common Market debate, *Britain and the EEC: the Economic Background* (HMSO, 1967), which was published jointly with the Central Office of Information. The later White Paper on the same subject, *Britain and European Communities: an Economic Assessment* (Cmnd. 4289, 1970) was presented to Parliament by the Prime Minister himself.

The National Economic Development Council (NEDC)

The National Economic Development Council was set up in 1962 and has the status of a Royal Commission. As it is not a statutory body, it does not have to publish an annual report, but the National Economic Development Office does from time to time submit to the Council reports on the economic situation and these have occasionally been published under the title of *Productivity, Prices and Incomes: a General Review* (HMSO): there was one for each of the years from 1966 to 1968.

The Economic Development Committees, which consist of representatives of management, trade unions and government and which now exist for most industries, issue studies and reports dealing with their own subjects. Some of these are published by HMSO, others come direct from the Committees and are free. The National Economic Development Office is the co-ordinating organisation and has put out several works, such as *Conditions Favourable to Faster Growth* (HMSO 1963) and *Investment Appraisal* (3rd edn, HMSO, 1969).

The National Economic Development Council was preceded by the Council on Prices, Productivity and Incomes, which issued some reports now chiefly of historical interest.

The Department of Employment and Productivity (DEP)

One of the responsibilities of the Department of Employment and Productivity, which until April 1968 was known as the Ministry of Labour, is for industrial training. The present scheme was set out in *Industrial Training: Government Proposals* (Cmnd. 1892, 1962) and was enacted in the Industrial Training Act, 1964 (Chapter 16). The Central Training Council issues reports as House of Commons Papers, as do the boards for the individual industries, but unfortunately these are not of a uniform pattern and are not, therefore, comparable.

The Department published its proposals for trade union reform in the White Paper, *In Place of Strife* (Cmnd. 3888, 1969), and some of these are shortly to be enacted. They were in response to the Donovan Report, correctly called the *Report of the Royal Commission on Trade Unions and Employers' Associations* (Cmnd. 3623, 1968): the memoranda and evidence to the Commission, which contain much useful information, were published as non-Parliamentary publications. The Department of Employment and Productivity can initiate inquiries into industrial disputes and issue reports either as House of Commons Papers or as Command Papers. Alternatively, it can refer the dispute to the **Commission on Industrial Relations**, which was established as a Royal Commission in March 1969 and which publishes its own reports as Command Papers.

Manpower studies are the responsibility of the DEP. They are made by its Manpower Research Unit and published in non-Parliamentary form. Some have been issued as a series entitled Manpower Studies: No. 7, for example was *The Growth of Office Employment* (HMSO 1968).

The Department of Employment and Productivity is now solely responsible for the prices and incomes policy. It has prepared the most recent White Papers and sponsors the **National Board for Prices and Incomes** (PIB). All the reports of the Board are published as Command Papers. The annual reports give, as well as lists of the studies made, the Board's views of its effect on the economic climate. For those studying productivity bargaining the reports on *Productivity Agreements* (No. 36, Cmnd. 3311, 1967; and No. 123, Cmnd. 4136, 1969), *Payments-By-Results Systems* (No. 65 Cmnd. 3627, 1968 plus Statistical Supplement) and *Job Evaluation* (No. 83, Cmnd. 3772, 1968 plus Statistical Supplement) are valuable.

The predecessor of the National Board for Prices and Incomes was the National Incomes Commission (NIC), which was set up in 1962 and issued four reports on specific pay agreements. All were Command Papers except the last.

The DEP will be responsible for the **Commission for Industry and Manpower**, which will result from the amalgamation of the National Board for Prices and Incomes and the Monopolies Commission. The Department has also acquired responsibility for the Restrictive Practices Court and the Registrar.

Apart from the prices and incomes policy, the DEP has always been concerned with prices. The Retail Price Index, constructed in the Department, is published monthly in the *Employment and Productivity Gazette*, and the Cost of Living Advisory Committee reports to the Department from time to time on possible improvements to the Index. As a result of its most recent report (Cmnd. 3677, 1968) an index for pensioner-households has been introduced.

A section of the Department of Employment and Productivity produces annually the *Family Expenditure Survey for* ... (HMSO), although the fieldwork is actually carried out by the Government Social Survey. The survey is taken from a sample of the population and the reports are non-Parliamentary publications.

The Department publishes two periodicals: the *Employment and Productivity Gazette*, formerly the *Ministry of Labour Gazette*, and the monthly report on *Changes in Rates of Wages and Hours of Work*. A third, *Statistics on Incomes, Prices and Employment*, was discontinued in 1969 and is to be replaced by an annual volume of labour statistics.

The Treasury

As arbiter in the annual battle between departments over the allocation of public funds, the Treasury issues all documents dealing with such expenditure.

Several recommendations about the presentation of information on the subject were made in the Plowden Report on *The Control of Public Expenditure* (Cmnd. 1432, 1961). As a result of suggestions made in the report, White Papers containing 'forward looks' on public expenditure for five years ahead were published in 1963 and 1966, entitled respectively *Public Expenditure, 1963–64 and 1967–68* (Cmnd. 2235, 1963) and *Public Expenditure: Planning and Control* (Cmnd. 2915, 1966). However, the *Public Expenditure* White Papers of 1968 and 1969 (Cmnd. 3515 and Cmnd. 3936) merely detailed the effects of government policy in the immediate future. The *Public Expenditure* White Paper of December 1969 (Cmnd. 4234) was on similar lines to the papers of 1963 and 1966, but gave much more detail: it implemented some of the proposals made in the Green Paper, *Public Expenditure: a New Presentation* (Cmnd. 4017, 1969) which had already been considered in the *Report of the Select Committee on Procedure* (HC 410 of 1968–69).

In advance of the **Civil Estimates** the Vote on Account, which summarises the Civil Estimates, and the **Defence Estimates** appear as House of Commons Papers. These are followed by the individual classes of the Civil Estimates and then by a memorandum on the Estimates, which is a Command Paper and which provides a useful summary of some forms of expenditure which are spread among more than one Estimate. Later in the year come the Appropriation Accounts giving details of actual expenditure in the previous financial year. Again these are House of Commons Papers, as are the reports of the Public Accounts Committee and the Estimates Committee. These are House of Commons Committees which are able to study their subjects more closely than is possible in a debate, and they also make special investigations: there was, for instance, a report of the Public Accounts Committee on the Ferranti Affair (HC 183 of 1963–64) which led to a government inquiry and to the publication of the *First Report of the Inquiry into Pricing of Ministry of Aviation Contracts* (Cmnd. 2428, 1964).

The Financial Statement, containing the Budget proposals, is also a House of Commons Paper. Since 1969 it has incorporated a Budget report, which for the first time in 1968 included forecasts for the economy. From 1963 to 1968 the *Economic Report* on the previous year had been published as a supplement to *Economic Trends*. Before 1963 there were annual *Economic Surveys* published as White Papers.

Numerous other official accounts are issued with comments after scrutiny by the Comptroller and Auditor-General. In addition, there is an annual White Paper on *Loans from the National Loans*

Fund, which contains details of the Nationalised Industries' investment plans.

Just before each annual Budget a White Paper appears giving *Preliminary Estimates of the National Income and Balance of Payments* for the preceding year. This has replaced two separate publications and it updates the summary tables of both the *National Income and Expenditure* Blue Book and of the *United Kingdom Balance of Payments* (HMSO, annual), which come out in their final form later in the year.

The major official post-war contribution to the literature on monetary policy was the Radcliffe Report on *The Working of the Monetary System* (Cmnd. 837, 1959). Four large and useful volumes of memoranda and evidence were published at the same time as non-Parliamentary papers. As a result of recommendations in the report, the monthly periodical, *Financial Statistics*, was introduced by the Central Statistical Office in 1962.

The Bank of England issues an annual report, which contains little of value to the economist. Much more informative is the *Bank of England Quarterly Bulletin* published by the Bank itself.

International monetary policy is also the concern of the Treasury and White Papers are presented to Parliament whenever a modification of the structure is agreed. For example, there was one called *Special Drawing Rights on the International Monetary Fund* (Cmnd. 3662, 1968).

Customs and Excise

Her Majesty's Commissioners for Customs and Excise prepare an annual report, which is laid before Parliament as a Command Paper. Each issue contains data on most forms of indirect taxation collected in the United Kingdom.

Other noteworthy publications are the *Annual Statement of Trade of the United Kingdom with Commonwealth Countries and Foreign Countries* (HMSO, annual): and *HM Customs and Excise Tariff* (HMSO, irregular), which gives the rates of duty on imports.

Board of Inland Revenue

The Commissioners of Inland Revenue also issue an annual report, which covers all types of direct taxation and periodically includes the results of surveys of personal incomes and of the financial operations of industry. The report is a Command Paper but for the year 1968–69 it has been split into two parts with some of the information being relegated to a non-Parliamentary publication *Inland Revenue Statistics* which appears later in the year.

New taxes are sometimes described in White Papers amplifying the draft legislation. Such reforms are inevitably piecemeal, but entire new systems of taxation have been studied, as, for example, in the Richardson Report, the *Report of the Committee on Turnover Taxation* (Cmnd. 2300, 1964). On the other hand, *Effects of the Selective Employment Tax: First Report: The Distributive Trades* by W. B. Reddaway (HMSO, 1970) was, in fact, commissioned and published by the Treasury. The Board also produces reports of cases in tax law: and it provides useful summaries of overseas tax systems in *Income Taxes outside the United Kingdom* (HMSO, annual, 1968) of which a revised edition is expected in 1970.

The Central Statistical Office

The publications of this department are dealt with in Chapter 10.

The Nationalised Industries

The finances of these industries together have been considered in two Treasury White Papers: *The Financial and Economic Obligations of the Nationalised Industries* (Cmnd. 1337, 1961) and *Nationalised Industries: a Review of Economic and Financial Objectives* (Cmnd. 3437, 1967). Changes in the structure of the nationalised industries' sector are usually anticipated in White Papers. There was, for instance, the *Statement on Proposals for the Re-organisation of the Post Office* (Cmnd. 3233, 1967). This was followed by the Post Office Bill (Bill 1 of 1968–69), which was introduced in October 1968 and which became the Post Office Act, 1969 (Chapter 48) in July 1969.

Several of the nationalised industries came within the scope of the White Paper, *Statement on Fuel Policy* (Cmnd. 3438, 1967). The most recent publication dealing with air corporations was the Edwards Report, *British Air Transport in the Seventies: Report of the Committee of Inquiry into Civil Air Transport* (Cmnd. 4018, 1969), to which there was a government reply, *Statement on Civil Aviation Policy* (Cmnd. 4213, 1969).

The Select Committee for the Nationalised Industries makes periodic investigations of each industry and publishes the reports

87

as House of Commons Papers. It has also done more general studies, such as *Ministerial Control of the Nationalised Industries* (HC 371 of 1967–68), which runs to three volumes with evidence and appendices. Any ministerial observations on such reports are usually published in the same form.

The individual nationalised industries can and do issue their own publications independently of HMSO, but these do not come within the scope of this chapter.

Scotland, Wales and Northern Ireland

The publications of some government departments cover the whole of the United Kingdom; others deal primarily with Great Britain; yet others relate only to England and Wales. There are some publications which fill these gaps by referring to Scotland, Wales or Northern Ireland.

The **Scottish Office** produces the *Digest of Scottish Statistics* (HMSO six-monthly) and its different departments present their annual reports as Command Papers. There was a Scottish equivalent to the *National Plan: The Scottish Economy, 1965–70: a Plan for Expansion* (Cmnd. 2864, 1966); and development plans, of which a *Programme of Highland Development* (Cmnd. 7976, 1950) is an early instance, have been produced for some parts of the country.

Wales has a shorter history of administrative autonomy than Scotland and consequently fewer separate publications. The **Welsh Office** issues an annual report, *Cymru: Wales,* and there is the *Welsh Digest of Statistics* (HMSO, annual). Wales also has its regional development programme, *Wales, the Way Ahead* (Cmnd. 3334, 1967).

Northern Ireland has more autonomy than either Scotland or Wales; indeed, having its own Parliament it also has its own Parliamentary papers and other government publications, issued by the Stationery Office in Belfast. There are, for example, separate Estimates, Financial Statements and Censuses of Production for Northern Ireland. The *Ulster Yearbook* (Belfast, HMSO, annual) is the equivalent of *Britain: an Official Handbook* and there is a six-monthly *Digest of Statistics* (Belfast, HMSO).

CHAPTER EIGHT

UNITED STATES GOVERNMENT PUBLICATIONS

L. FISHMAN

There is a vast amount of economic material, statistical and historical data, and theoretical analysis to be found in United States government publications. The publications, however, are often difficult to locate because usual library rules of classification often do not apply to government documents; they tend to be a law unto themselves. In this chapter the basic rules governing United States government publications will be outlined, attention will be drawn to some major economic investigations that have played a leading role in economic literature of the United States, and we will close with a discussion of the scope and content of current materials.

The basic source for a listing of United States documents is the *Monthly Catalog of US Government Publications*. The form of the *Monthly Catalog* is that of a monthly journal, arranged alphabetically by issuing authority, and each entry numbered serially, starting anew each January. The issuing authority (Department, Bureau, Office, Agency, Commission, Committee, Subcommittee) is the key which is essential to locate a United States publication. It is also helpful to know the year and month of publication. The index in the rear of each *Monthly Catalog* lists all entries by subject, title, and author, and each December index is cumulative for the year. Publications with no specific subject or author are entered under issuing office only. All government publications issued after 12 January 1895 are entered in the *Monthly Catalog*, except those that are administrative and confidential. However, it was only in January 1963 that the *Monthly Catalog* began to index personal author entries. The appendix to the February *Monthly Catalog* is the annual *Directory of United States Government Periodicals and Subscription Publications*. The issuing office listed in the *Monthly Catalog* is always considered the publisher of Government publications, although the actual printer is usually the Government Printing Officer (an office of the United States Congress).

Since the issuing number is used by most libraries for indexing and is also used by the Superintendent of Documents to fill orders for government publications, it is familiarity with the issuing offices that brings order into government publications.

The issuing offices mirror the basic organisation of the United States government structure, with its tri-partite division into executive, legislative, and judicial branches. (For a complete description see *United States Government Organization Manual,* Office of the Federal Register, revised annually.) The President heads the executive branch, which consists of the Executive Office of the President, the twelve administrative departments (each headed by a Cabinet Officer, e.g., Secretary of Commerce), and over thirty independent offices and establishments directly responsible to the President (e.g., Board of Governors of the Federal Reserve System, Securities and Exchange Commission, and the National Labor Relations Board).

Executive Office of the President

Of the ten bodies in the Executive Office of the President, three deal directly with economic affairs: Council of Economic Advisers, Bureau of the Budget, and the Office of Economic Opportunity. The Council of Economic Advisers' annual report is published together with the *Economic Report of the President* in one document, which currently is the most important single economic publication of the United States government. The reports appraise the economic trends and current situation, analyse in detail the key economic problems confronting the nation, and make policy recommendations. The tables in the rear of the Annual Reports bring together several hundred statistical series, most of which have data from 1929 to the current year, that together provide an excellent résumé of all major aspects of the United States economy. Because of the importance of this document, its entry in the *Monthly Catalog* for 1966 is reproduced below. It is listed under the 'P' section of the March, 1966 issue of the Catalog, because the issuing office is the 'President of the United States'.

5091 Economic report of the President, transmitted to Congress

Jan. 1966, together with annual report of the Council of Economic Advisers. 1966. iv + 306 p. il.

Also issued as H. doc. 348, 89th Cong. 2d sess.

*Paper, $1·25. •Item 848

L.C. card 47–32975   Pr 36·9:966

The top left number (5091) is the journal number of the *Monthly*

Catalog, the item number (848) following the heavy circle refers to the item number sent to Depository Libraries (which in Britain include the British Museum and the British Library of Political and Economic Science). The Library of Congress card number is on the left side of the lowest line, and the key issuing number is on the right side (Pr 36·9:966). The Pr refers to the office of the President, and 966 to the year 1966. All President's Economic Reports have the same number (Pr 36·9); only the year changes. The main initials for economic material include C for all Department of Commerce publications, L for Labor, I for Interior, FS for Health, Education, and Welfare (retaining the old designation for Federal Security Agency), FR for Federal Reserve System, T for Treasury, and Y for all Congressional material.

Although the report of the Council of Economic Advisers is listed under the President, because it always has been published with the President's *Economic Report,* the publications of the Budget Bureau and the Office of Economic Opportunity are listed in the *Monthly Catalog* under their own titles. The Budget of the United States Government fiscal year 1967, is thus found in the March 1966 *Monthly Catalog* under the 'Budget Bureau, Executive Office of the President'. However, the Office of Economic Opportunity illustrates another rule to watch for: its publications are listed under 'Economic Opportunity Office, Executive Office of the President'. Presumably, it is more sensible to alphabetise on the main subject-matter word (Economic) than on the official title's first word, 'Office'. There are several other important economic series where this occurs, and these will be explained below, where they fit in the logical pattern of the US government organisation (Joint Economic Committee of Congress and the Bureau of Labor Statistics). Before leaving the office of the President, two final cautions: the *Manpower Report of the President* is issued by the Labor Department and thus is found listed in *Monthly Catalog* under 'Labor'. All three of these important messages from the President to Congress (Economic, Budget, and Manpower) are also issued as House documents and thus are also found under 'Congress', sub-section of House documents, but only the Economic Message is listed under the President. Finally, the Office of Special Representatives for Trade Negotiation in the President's Office is listed by the *Monthly Catalog* under 'Special Representative'.

Government Departments

The departments that publish most material directly pertaining to economics are Treasury, Commerce, Labor, HEW (Health, Education, and Welfare), Transportation, Housing and Urban Development, Agriculture and Defense. Few of the Treasury economic studies are published, but the *Treasury Bulletin* and the various series of *Statistics of Income* (e.g., *Corporation Income Tax Returns*) are extremely valuable statistical sources.

Department of Commerce

The Department of Commerce is one of the major United States government departments publishing economic analyses and data. The Department issues a basic catalog which covers publications issued from 1790 and also supplies a weekly list of new publications *(Business Service Checklist)*. Of the four Commerce divisions that provide most of the economic material, by far the most significant is the **Bureau of the Census**. It is responsible for the basic annual *Statistical Abstract of the United States,* which contains most of the standard series on the economy of the United States, from public and private sources *(see* p. 163). For basic reference there is the *Historical Statistics of the United States: Colonial Times to 1957* (1960 with later revisions and updating). In addition to the decennial censuses, there are special censuses, the most important of which are the *Census of Manufactures, Census of Business,* and the *Census of Governments. County Business Patterns* (annually) is especially valuable to those who need detailed information on sales and income data by geographic area. In addition, the Bureau publishes many current reports (monthly and quarterly), the most important include reports on retail sales, population, labour force, consumer intentions, foreign trade, housing, construction, and on government (federal, state, and local). Finally, there are vast storehouses of data accumulating on magnetic tapes in the Census Bureau that will never be published, but which are available for special data processing runs which can be purchased from the Bureau. The *Monthly Catalog* does not use the formal title, Bureau of the Census, but lists the publication under 'Census Bureau, Commerce Dept.'.

The **Office of Business Economics,** of the Commerce Department, publishes much of the basic economic analysis done by the Department, usually in summary form in the monthly *Survey of Current Business (see* p. 163). The office is responsible for national income and product accounts, size distribution of income, analysis of industrial production, investment, markets, and general business statistics and economic analyses that fall within the general scope of 'foreign and domestic commerce'. Major revisions of the income and product accounts are usually followed by a definitive volume reviewing the definitions and methodology and bringing them up to date: such volumes have been published in 1954 and 1958.

Business Statistics are summarised in the biennial publication of that name. Foreign investment and the international position of the United States is annually summarised in the *Survey of Current Business* (usually in the August to September issues for the preceding year), and occasional summary volumes will be published, the last of which appeared in 1960 (*US Business Investment in Foreign Countries*). The *Monthly Catalog* lists the office publications under 'Business Economics Office, Commerce Department'.

The two Commerce Department divisions already discussed (Census and Business Economics) compose the working groups under the Assistant Secretary for Economic Affairs, and are bodies designed to gather data and analyse and summarise the general business side of the United States economy. In contrast, a working administrative bureau of the Department that publishes much economic material of considerable importance in its own right is the Bureau of International Commerce. In its publications, which are designed primarily for the working exporter and businessman interested in foreign markets, the economist can trace the evolution of American overseas trade. Its *Overseas Business Reports* provide basic market and investment information on most foreign countries, and is supplemented by *Market for US Products,* which concentrates on current marketing information for most foreign countries and regions. In addition *Computerised Trade Lists* and a weekly magazine, *International Commerce,* provide up-to-the-minute information for exporters. Basic financial information on specific foreign firms and individuals is available to US firms in the form of *World Trade Directory Reports*. The *Monthly Catalog* lists the Bureau's publications under 'International Commerce Bureau, Commerce Department'.

The Department of Commerce is also responsible for the giant information service center, **Clearinghouse for Federal Scientific and Technical Information,** under which the Joint Publications Research Service operates. Its published translation service concentrates on, but is not restricted to, material from Russia, China, Eastern European countries, Cuba, North Korea, and North Vietnam. Much of this material involves industrial and economic development, and many economic journals, reports, reviews, and separate articles are available in English from the Clearinghouse. The *Monthly Catalog* lists these publications directly under the

'Joint Publications Research Service', in its own right, and provides the JPRS number, in addition to its own catalog number. It is the JPRS number that is the key when ordering a publication from the Clearinghouse, in addition to the issuing office number, if available.

Department of Labour

The Department of Labor economic material, which is most profuse among the government publications, is conveniently listed under L in the *Monthly Catalog:* under 'Labor Department', 'Labor Standards Bureau', and especially under 'Labor Statistics Bureau'. The articles, summaries, and reviews in the *Monthly Labor Review* are far ranging and remarkably comprehensive in their coverage. A considerable portion of the detailed material is also published by the **Bureau of Labor Statistics** (BLS), much of it in the form of BLS Reports and Bulletins. All BLS Bulletins have the same issuing number—L 2·3: (Bulletin number); and all BLS Reports have the same number—L 2·71 (Report number). The major material covered involves employment, earnings, labour outlook, productivity, accidents, turnover rates, labour supply, budgets, work stoppages, labour negotiations, and consumer prices. In recent decades the BLS has conducted consumer expenditure studies, in co-operation with the Department of Agriculture, to provide data for the decennial revision of the weights for the Consumer Price Index. These detailed reports provide considerable consumer information in several breakdowns, including region and income level. The BLS also pioneered in the applications of input-output analysis, in co-operation with the Commerce Department, and much of the government publication in this field is shared by these two departments.

The broad area of manpower planning and research is the responsibility of the **Manpower Administration.** Its annual *Manpower Report*, which includes the President's manpower message, does in detail for labour what the annual *Economic Report* does for the economy as a whole: its issuing number is L 1·42/2:(year). The Manpower Administration also publishes fairly regularly a complete description of the research projects which it sponsors from universities, companies, other government agencies, and institutes, and the status of these projects. The results of the research are often published in the *Manpower Research Bulletins*. Many government agencies are adopting a similar procedure: a publication regularly reporting the progress of ongoing research work, and a series to report the results of the research. Although most of the United States labour documents of interest to economists are issued by the BLS or the Manpower Administration, there are also many published by other agencies and listed by the *Monthly Catalog* in sections other than the L section, e.g., 'Women's Bureau, Labour Department', and 'Employment Security Bureau, Labor Department'.

Health, Education and Welfare

Although most of the economic material of the HEW has been published by the Social Security Administration, the recent economic emphasis on human investment has made the materials in education and health of considerable importance. The monthly *Social Security Bulletin*, and its annual statistical supplement, supplies summaries to the limited work and few materials available in this field. There has also been in recent years the Health, Education and Welfare Trends, an annual supplement to the *Health, Education, and Welfare Indicators*, and for a general review of the entire department's activities, there is always the annual report. Specifically in education, there is an extensive monthly catalogue of educational research and the National Center for Educational Statistics, with its own series. The major *Monthly Catalog* listings are under 'Social Security Administration, Education Office', and 'Public Health Service' (including pollution and environmental health series). With the spread and increased application of research and PPBS (Program, Planning, Budget System), we can expect a considerable increase in economic materials from these agencies.

Department of Transportation
Department of Housing and Urban Development

The Department of Housing and Urban Development (HUD) and the Department of Transportation are new departments, whose publications largely reflect the previous agencies' activities, e.g., Federal Housing Administration. Created because of the pressing needs of urban society, the publications from these new government departments will undoubtedly increase rapidly and provide important material for economists. For the time being, the *Monthly Catalog* is listing the documents under 'Housing and Urban Development Department' and 'Transportation Department'.

Department of Agriculture

The Department of Agriculture publications provide a direct contrast to the publications of the new departments. In Agriculture the documents are plentiful, comprehensive in coverage, and complete. Agriculture dominated the early economic and political life of the nation and the legacy of publications in this field reflect that dominance and the long time-lag before the enormous relative decrease in agriculture's role is felt in the flow of documents. For economists, probably the most important agricultural publications include the quarterly, *Agricultural Economics Research*, Marketing Research Reports, Statistical Bulletins, Agricultural Economic Reports, and Foreign Agricultural Economic Reports. The monthly *Bibliography of Agriculture* reflects the excellence achieved by the publications of this old and well funded department. The Farmers' Bulletins and Home and Garden Bulletins from the Department played an important role in the development of the economy of the United States, and provided urban consumers, as well as rural producers and consumers, with an enormous fund of useful and popular information. The two most important economic agricultural agencies listed in the *Monthly Catalog* are the 'Economic Research Service' and the 'Statistical Reporting Service'. The documents on overseas agriculture and trade are listed under the 'Foreign Agricultural Service'. For a number of years the Department issued an annual *Yearbook*, each of which highlighted a major theme or problem of agriculture and society. Several of these yearbooks achieved the position of a classic in its field and are well worth referring to in any study of the development of agriculture in the United States.

Department of the Interior

The Department of the Interior publishes material of interest to economists primarily in three fields: mining and management of natural resources, reclamation and water management, recreation and conservation, and most of the documents are in the first of these fields. The **Bureau of Mines** (listed by the *Monthly Catalog* as 'Mines Bureau') issues an annual *Minerals Yearbook* which includes a comprehensive survey of major minerals and of the mineral industry in most countries of the world and each state of the United States. The Bureau also issues Bulletins, reports of investigations, a minerals encyclopaedia, and separate publications that would be of interest to an economist working in this area.

'Independent' Agencies

The excellent supplemental work and publications of the **Resources for the Future** (RFF) should also be mentioned. RFF illustrates the growing importance of independent, usually non-profit, quasi-governmental, quasi-academic bodies that have the freedom and leisure and resources to investigate long-range problems or policies that are beyond the scope of governmental bodies. The publications of RFF do not qualify as government documents, and thus have no formal right to be included in this chapter. Yet the affinity of their research and publications to governmental policy and work makes it difficult to exclude them entirely. This tendency to use 'outside' organisations has progressed further in the Defence Department than in other agencies, but is found in many fields. Often the results of a study or a report will be published by the 'private' organisation or individual, although the funding for the project came from a government agency. Such a procedure avoids the government agency having to provide its *imprimatur* to the work, often stimulates interest and concern around a research area or problem, and develops a valuable reservoir of trained personnel. In economics, some of the more important of these independent organisations, in addition to the university institutes, are: **Brookings Institution, Twentieth Century Fund, Rand, Institute for Strategic Studies, Battelle Institute,** and Resources for the Future. Certainly in the publications of the Department of Defence, Army, Navy, and Air Force the economic documents are, to the extent that they exist, exceedingly meagre. Since the economic impact of the defence establishment is considerable, especially in the crucial fields of research and development, the economist interested in these areas must turn to Congressional material and to publications by the quasi-official research establishments like Rand, Hudson, and the Institute of Strategic Studies, university institutes, e.g., Stanford Research Institute and Denver Research Institute, and private company consultant publications.

Of the more than thirty **'independent' agencies and boards that are directly responsible to the President,** many are primarily economic in their activities. These include the Board of Governors of the Federal Research System, the Federal Trade Commission, Securities and Exchange Commission, and the US Tariff Commission. Regulatory bodies include the Atomic Energy Commission, Civil Aeronautics Board, Federal Communications Commission, Federal Maritime Commission, Federal Power Commission, and the Interstate Commerce Commission. Specialised banks and insurance bodies include the Export-Import Bank of the US, Farm

Credit Administration and the Federal Deposit Insurance Corporation. Then there are many miscellaneous bodies whose activities are economic, directly or indirectly: Tennessee Valley Authority, Tax Court of the United States, Small Business Administration, Railroad Retirement Board, National Mediation Board, National Aeronautics and Space Administration, General Services Administration, Federal Mediation and Conciliation Service, and the National Science Foundation. We will discuss in a little more detail the publications of only the first four of these bodies. For the others, the reader is referred to the current *Organization Manual*.

The monthly *Federal Reserve Bulletin* is the key publication of the Board of Governors of the **Federal Reserve System.** In addition to articles, notices, and statistics, the *Bulletin* also includes summaries of staff and research reports, copies of which are available upon request. The *Monthly Catalog* lists the Board's publications under Federal Reserve Board. The twelve regional Reserve Banks (each takes its name from the city in which it is located: Boston, New York, Philadelphia, Richmond, San Francisco, etc.), that constitute the Federal Reserve System, each publish their own Bulletins, and most carry on an active economic research programme. These publications do not qualify as federal publications, but they are important supplements to the Federal Reserve publications. In fact, the New York Bank's *Monthly Review* occupies a very special place in the banking world. The *Monthly Review* reflects the eminent position of the New York financial centre and the role of the New York Federal Reserve Bank: (1) in representing the banks that operate in the New York centre; (2) in being the agent for the Open Market Operations Committee of the Federal Reserve System; and (3) in acting as the agent for the Board in foreign currency operations. Thus, the New York Federal Reserve Bank's *Review,* when it summarises and evaluates the money market, is read with great care and occupies a position closely akin to that of a 'document'. Although publications from the other Reserve Banks may not occupy quite the same position, they are still important and each has its own emphasis and specialities. They are not listed in the *Monthly Catalog,* but can be obtained by writing to the individual Reserve Banks, whose addresses are included in each issue of the *Federal Reserve Bulletin.*

The **Federal Trade Commission** has been charged since 1915 with trying to maintain competition and to prevent unfair or deceptive acts (or 'unfair' competition). As an administrative agency with this broad charge, it is also obliged to make economic and statistical studies to remain current on the competitive situation in interstate commerce. Some of these studies, of specific industries and companies, and also for the economy as a whole, have been among the most valuable sources of information on industry in the United States. The Commission's news summaries and press releases, both listed in the *Monthly Catalog,* provide excellent summaries of the Commission's activities. The Commission, in collaboration with the Securities and Exchange Commission, also prepares a quarterly series for all manufacturing corporations, of their income statements and balance sheets, classified by both industry and asset size (FTC–SEC Quarterly Financial Series).

The **Securities and Exchange Commission** (since 1934) is a quasi-judicial body that protects the interests of investors against malpractices in the securities and financial markets. In addition to a monthly *Statistical Bulletin* and summaries of Commission actions, the SEC is the major public source of corporation financial reports and ownership data. All companies whose securities are listed upon the national exchanges must file registration applications and annual reports with the SEC, as well as all companies whose equity securities are traded over-the-counter, if such a company has $1 000 000 of assets and 500 or more shareholders. These reports are available for public inspection in the public reference room at the Commission's home office (500 N. Capitol Street NW., Washington, D.C., 20549) and reproductions of this public material may be purchased from the Commission. A Directory of companies filing annual reports with the Commission is published annually, with the companies listed alphabetically and by industry groups. The Directory is listed in the *Monthly Catalog* under the 'Securities and Exchange Commission'.

Although often viewed by historians as a political buffer organisation the **US Tariff Commission** was given a considerable new responsibility by the Trade Expansion Act of 1962. In general the Commission may investigate, hold public hearings, and issue formal reports to the President regarding an industry, firm, or group of workers who petition that they are threatened with serious economic injury because of a tariff reduction or unfair foreign competition, e.g. dumping. The published reports and public studies are listed in the *Monthly Catalog* under 'Tariff Commission'.

Congress

All Congressional bills, documents, reports, hearings and other publications are listed in the *Monthly Catalog* under 'Congress'. To locate Congressional documents in the *Monthly Catalog* the key is once again the issuing agency, most commonly a House or

Senate Committee. A bill or resolution may be introduced into either chamber, or both, or introduced as a joint resolution. These proposed laws are then assigned to a committee, the choice of which is usually, but certainly not always, determined by the subject matter of the bill. The committee to which they are assigned becomes the issuing agency for the hearings that will be held on the bill, and for the reports and studies that may be generated from the proposed law or from a resolution. The House bills (H.R.) and Senate bills (S.) and joint bills or resolutions (H.J.Res.) are their usual identification terms or symbols. By far the most important economic material published by Congress is listed under the 'Economic Joint Committee', which appears very near the beginning of the Congressional listings because it is a joint committee of both the House of Representatives and the Senate, and the joint committee materials precede the listing of material from either body.

The **Joint Economic Committee,** as a new standing committee formed after World War II, has not necessarily played a large role directly in major 'law making'. Rather it has evolved its role as the supplier to Congress Executive Departments, and the nation, of expert advice and studies on all major economic problems that face the United States economy. Its first responsibility is its annual hearing on the annual *Economic Reports* of the President and Council of Economic Advisors. Leading figures from government, business, banking, labour, and universities testify and submit comments. After the hearings, the joint committee issues its own report (usually with a minority report and individual views) and the three part exercise (original reports, hearings, committee reports) provide an unexcelled summary of the establishment view of the economy at the time. In addition, the Committee has held hearings, commissioned reports, and published studies on most major economic problems. Subcommittees of the Joint Economic Committee, each with their own hearings, studies and reports include: Fiscal Policy; Employment, Growth, and Price Levels; Economic Progress; International Exchange and Policy; Economic Statistics; Foreign Economic Policy; and Federal Procurement and Regulation. There have been several long series of major studies that have attempted to evaluate the Soviet economy, and one series on the Chinese economy. Continuing attention has been given the need for improvement in economic statistics. In recent years, considerable attention has been devoted to military procurement. In summary, the Joint Economic Committee has opened the doors wide to the study and debate of many of the most pressing economic problems of the United States. It has acted on the belief that public airing of issues, against the background of the best data and analyses available, will lead to good economic policies. The economic material in the resulting government documents has been most impressive.

In addition to the Joint Economic Committee, the House of Representatives has about twenty **standing committees,** and the Senate about fifteen. Most of these committees deal, directly or indirectly, with economic affairs. Their activities (hearings, reports, and studies) will be more directly related to specific legislative bills or resolutions, in contrast to the activities of the Joint Economic Committee. Some of the House committees that deal directly with economic matters are: Agriculture, Appropriations, Armed Services, Banking and Currency, Education and Labour, Foreign Affairs, Government Operations, Interior and Insular Affairs, Interstate and Foreign Commerce, Science and Astronautics, Ways and Means. The Senate Committees include: Agriculture and Forestry, Appropriations, Armed Services, Banking and Currency, Commerce, Finance, Foreign Relations, Interior and Insular Affairs, and Labour and Public Welfare.

In addition to the standing committees of Congress and their subcommittees, there are also special **select and investigating committees,** which have included some of the most notable producers of significant economic documents. A few of the most important of these special committees, which resemble Royal Commissions, will next be discussed in more detail. Congressional or administrative investigations are the United States counterpart of the Royal Commissions and their hearings and reports include some of the most significant US government publications for economists. A congressional investigating committee is a committee authorised by a resolution passed by the House or the Senate or both (joint) to investigate matters concerning which information is not regularly or readily obtainable. It may be a standing or a select committee, but its purpose must be inquisitorial. An administrative commission is appointed by the President, and there have also been joint administrative and congressional committees. There are few economic problems which have not been subject to inquiry by governmental committees, but the areas most often probed by significant committees are those of concentration of economic power, industrial relations, and the general field of the money and stock markets.

Although there were investigating committees from 1792, the first broad economic investigation was **The Industrial Commission** (1898). The hearings lasted more than two years and the *Final Report* (1902) consisted of nineteen volumes. Three of the volumes deal directly with *Industrial Combinations in Europe.* Seven volumes deal with various aspects of labour relations and legislation, and one volume with *Foreign Labor Legislation*. In addition, transportation and agriculture are both treated in considerable detail, as is immigration and education. The last volume is the *Final Report* of the Commission and consists of a review and recommendations. Stemming from the report was the Bureau of Corporations (the forerunner of the Federal Trade Commission), which was established in 1903. Economists wrote all of the reports which provide, with the Hearings, the most comprehensive survey of the US economy around the turn of the century.

The second and last major economic survey conducted by a commission was done by the **Temporary National Economic Committee (TNEC)**, which followed the Industrial Commission by forty years. Its terms of reference were to investigate how to revive and strengthen competition in order to achieve full employment and preserve capitalism. Thirty-seven volumes and 17 000 pages of hearings, monographs, and reports provide abundant materials on the 'concentration of economic power'. After publication of the TNEC *Final Report*, many economists expressed disappointment at the failure of the committee to question and analyse fundamental relationships, such as the impact of the distribution of income on effective demand and employment. With hindsight, however, it may have been more important to gather together, as the Committee did, an enormous set of empirical evidence on the actual pricing, production and decision-making practices of many key American industries. Stemming from the investigation was the post-war creation of the Council of Economic Advisers, the so-called 'Full Employment Act', and a re-dedication, albeit temporary, to more vigorous anti-monopoly prosecutions. The TNEC documents provide the economist with an unparalleled mine of information on American industry just prior to World War II, definitive studies of special problems, e.g. patents, and a vast literature to explore industry-government-academic relationships and attitudes in the late Great Depression period.

The investigations into the money and stock market fields were more specific in scope and usually addressed themselves directly to gathering information that would help draft new laws to meet special problems. The **Armstrong Investigation** (1905) addressed itself to abuses and practices of insurance companies. The **Monetary Commission** (1912) resulted from the panic of 1907 and investigated how a stable and secure organisation of capital and credit markets could be achieved. Although the specific plan (the 'Aldrich Plan') found in the report was not enacted, the Commission paved the way for the Federal Reserve System created in 1913. One of the most famous commissions was the **Pujo**

Committee (1913), which was concerned with the concentration of banking control and the use of 'other people's money'. Finally, the **Pecora Investigation** (1933) by the Senate Banking and Currency Committee followed on the collapse of the banking system in the United States in 1933, and led to many of the basic New Deal banking reforms, including the Securities and Exchange Act of 1934.

There have been more than 600 investigating committees; most of them included some economic material and many of them dealt directly with major economic issues. In general, the committees reflected the historical period, their leading Congressional figures, and their staff. As special or emergency committees, they tend to mirror the political and economic climate of the times, from preoccupation with early development problems through the wars and industrialisation to problems concerned with management of the world economy. Often the leading Congressional figure was appointed chairman of the committee and the popular name of the report usually reflects his name. (For a listing of such names, see *Popular Names of US Government Reports*, compiled by D. F. Wisdom and W. P. Kilroy, Library of Congress, 1966.) Although the TNEC did not adopt as its popular name that of its chairman, Senator O'Mahoney undoubtedly was the most important figure in shaping that inquiry, just as Frank Walsh was in the Industrial Relations Commission of 1912, and Senator La Follette in the famous Senate Subcommittees on Education and Labor (1937–1941). Although the chairman led and directed their investigating committees, the work of the staff was usually crucial in determining the quality of their output. Famous economic staff names that have been associated with the reports include: W. Z. Ripley with the Industrial Commission (1898); Charles E. Hughes with the Armstrong Investigation (1905); John R. Commons with the Industrial Relations Commission (1912); Untermyer and Brandeis with the Pujo Committee (1913); and Leon Henderson with the TNEC (1938).

Since World War II the economic investigating committees have tended to be under new auspices, dealing with new subjects, and far more broadly based in the economics profession. Much of the post-war economic investigation has been directed and initiated by the Joint Economic Committee. Instead of dealing with the older preoccupations of monopoly, economic power, rights and liberties of labour, the major investigations have dealt with Soviet and Chinese economic power, the effects of automation, world monetary problems, urban problems, inflation, economic growth, and military procurement. Testimony and studies in these reports

103

have tended to reflect the increased professionalisation of economists in business and government. In addition, academic economists have been widely used by post-war committees for both special and general reports. Still another quantitative change has been the growing importance of 'foundation-type' reports that often parallel congressional committee investigations (sometimes preceding and sometimes following, but almost always significant). Some of the more important foundation studies in economics, which do not carry an official 'document' status, include The Brookings Foundation, National Bureau of Economic Research, Resources for the Future, and the Twentieth Century Fund. Many of these 'quasi-documents' are as important, if not more so, than their official counterparts, and should be given careful study whenever available.

CHAPTER NINE

INTERNATIONAL ORGANISATIONS' PUBLICATIONS

E. C. BLAKE

Introduction

The term 'international organisations' is widely and rather loosely
used to describe bodies such as the United Nations, the European
Communities and the International Monetary Fund, whose
members are the representatives of a group of governments. A
more accurate description is 'intergovernmental organisations' but
this term is far less often encountered. It may be helpful to state
at the outset that all the organisations dealt with in this chapter
are basically intergovernmental in character.

International organisations tend to be regarded as twentieth
century or, more specifically, post-1918 developments but they are
of considerably earlier origin. The Organisation of American
States dates back to 1890, yet even so it was preceded by the
Universal Postal Union in 1874 and the International Telecom-
munication Union in 1865. Virtually all international organisations
share the same guiding principles which have been succinctly
defined by Inis L. Claude as 'an attempt to minimise conflict and
maximise collaboration among participating states, treating conflict
as an evil to be controlled and co-operation as a good to be pro-
moted'. ('International organisation: the process and the institutions,' in *International Encyclopedia of the Social Sciences*, vol. 8,
pp. 33–40.)

For the economist the international organisations produce three
particularly valuable types of publication, namely scholarly
monographs (often issued in series), conference proceedings, and
finally specialised periodicals including statistical journals providing international or regional comparisons of data. The League
of Nations initiated a special reporting system for the compilation
of international statistics whereby figures were collected either
from the replies to questionnaires circulated amongst member

105

nations or from officially published national statistics. Similar methods are used today by many international organisations and computer processing now enables data to be analysed in increasing detail.

General Reference Works and Catalogues

The major source of concise information on the constitutions, aims, activities and membership of currently active international bodies is the *Yearbook of International Organizations* published by the Union of International Associations and now in its twelfth (1968–69) edition. Most entries also quote a number of the more important publications, mainly periodicals and series, issued by the particular organisation. The economist requiring further details of the constitutions, objectives and declarations of international organisations in his field will find in addition to the documents produced by the bodies themselves a recent comprehensive collection of such material in *International Organisation and Integration: a Collection of the Texts of Documents Relating to the United Nations, its Related Agencies and Regional International Organisations* edited by H. F. van Panhuys and others (Deventer, Kluwer, 1968).

It must be admitted that in view of the tremendous publishing output of the international organisations the existing forms of bibliographical control are seldom fully adequate to the purpose. A survey of the position containing much useful information may be found in the article 'Current bibliographical control of international intergovernmental documents' by James B. Childs, in *Library Resources and Technical Services*, vol. 10, 1966, pp. 319–331. Catalogues or indexes of varying frequency and detail are issued by individual organisations but it is nevertheless difficult to obtain a general view of the potentially available economics literature. The problem is complicated by the fact that in addition to publications placed on sale many international bodies distribute a large amount of other material, often mimeographed, free of charge.

In Great Britain Her Majesty's Stationery Office acts as sales agent for a considerable number of international organisations. An annual catalogue entitled *International Organisations and Overseas Agencies Publications* (1955–   ) is issued and is supplemented by entries in HMSO's daily and monthly lists. Noteworthy exclusions from this catalogue are the publications of the International Labour Organisation and the World Bank.

League of Nations

The events of the war of 1914–1918 gave an urgent impetus to the movement which sought to create a framework for the peaceful discussion and solution of international problems. The Paris Peace Conference of 1919 adopted the Covenant of the League of Nations which advocated amongst other measures world wide co-operation in matters of economic and social importance. Throughout its existence the League had its headquarters at Geneva though during the Second World War part of the Economic, Financial and Transit Department operated from Princeton University.

A knowledge of the League's publications is essential for any researcher concerned with international economic developments of the period 1920–1945. The early work of the League's Economic and Financial Organisation was largely devoted to tariffs and the financial restoration of those European countries which had been severely affected by the war, but later its programme was considerably extended to cover all important aspects of the world economy.

The documentation system of the League like that of its successor, the United Nations, is complex. The most comprehensive work on the subject is the *Guide to League of Nations Publications* by Hans Aufricht (Columbia U.P., 1951) in which the publications are listed and discussed against the background of the League's structure and evolution. In addition, a chapter is devoted to the publications of the International Labour Organisation. A shorter but nevertheless valuable introduction is *Sources of Information: a Handbook on the Publications of the League of Nations* by A. C. de Breycha-Vauthier (Allen and Unwin, 1939).

The Publications Department of the League produced various general catalogues, the most important being the *Catalogue of Publications 1920–1935* (1935); five supplements supply details of further publications issued up to the end of 1945. Of particular use to the economist is the *Catalogue of Selected Publications on Economic and Financial Subjects* (1943) which, with annotations, lists documents of permanent interest with emphasis on material relevant to the formulation of economic policies after the Second World War.

Two further aids to detailed research should also be mentioned. The *Key to League of Nations Documents Placed on Public Sale 1920–1929* by Marie J. Carroll (Boston, World Peace Foundation, 1930) and its four supplements extending to 1936 provide a year-by-year listing of the publications of individual organs of the League in the order of their sales or official numbers together with a subject index. Complementary to this work is the *Subject Index to the Economic and Financial Documents of the League of Nations 1927–1930* by Eric C. Wendelin (World Peace Foundation, 1932), in which publications are listed under specific subject headings.

The League issued much monographic material on economic subjects. Its early concern with the recovery of war-stricken nations may be exemplified by the many reports on the financial reconstruction of Austria. The later widening of interests is reflected by publications such as *Remarks on the Present Phase of International Economic Relations* (1935 IIB 11) and *The Agricultural Crisis* (2 vols, 1931 IIB 12/I-II). Works of leading economists were also published by the League and included *Prosperity and Depression* by Gottfried von Haberler (1936 IIA 24), *Statistical Testing of Business Cycle Theories* by Jan Tinbergen (2 vols, 1938 IIA 23 and 1939 IIA 16) and *International Currency Experience* (Princeton, 1944 IIA 4) for which Ragnar Nurske was mainly responsible. *Commercial Policy in the Post-War World* (1945 IIA 7) demonstrates the League's work in preparation for the transition to a peace-time economy. Other diverse topics encountered in the League's output include cartels, raw materials, air transport and merchant shipping.

The League was responsible for organising a considerable number of international conferences on economic affairs. The report, proceedings and papers of the International Financial Conference, Brussels, 1920 were amongst its earliest un-numbered publications. Later meetings of special note include the International Economic Conference, Geneva, 1927, International Conference with a View to Concerted Economic Action, Geneva, 1930–31 and the Monetary and Economic Conference, London, 1933.

The basic value of the League's statistical publications and annual surveys is apparent when one considers how many of them the United Nations later took over or adapted for its own publishing programme. The *Monthly Bulletin of Statistics* (1919/20–1946) and the *Statistical Year-Book of the League of Nations* (originally *International Statistical Year-Book*, 1926–1942/44) provided world-wide data on a considerable range of economic, financial, demographic and social matters. These compilations offered a welcome short-cut to information which otherwise would have had to be culled from numerous national statistical sources. The annual *Memorandum on Trade and Balances of Payments* (1910/23–1931/32) which underwent several changes of name and format contained both analyses and statistics. It was eventually

108

divided into three separate annuals, the *Review of World Trade* (1932–1938), *International Trade Statistics* (1931–1938) and *Balances of Payments* (1931–1938). The latter was taken over by the International Monetary Fund and continued as the *Balance of Payments Yearbook*.

The *World Economic Survey* (1931/32–1942/44) gave an objective description of international economic trends; it was preceded by a single publication *The Course and Phases of the World Economic Depression* (1931 IIA 21) which covered the period 1921–1930. Other yearly reviews of interest to economists dealt with world production and prices, public finance and money and banking.

An account of the inter-relationship of League and UN material is given by Marie J. Carrol in her article 'League of Nations documents and publications comparable with or continued in United Nations publications', in *College and Research Libraries* (vol. 13, 1952, pp. 44–52. Information concerning publications of the League which are still available may be obtained from the Palais des Nations, Geneva or United Nations Publications, Room 1059, New York, N.Y. 10017.

United Nations (UN)

The UN, the largest and most familiar of present-day inter-governmental bodies, came into being in 1945 following the San Francisco Conference on International Organisation. In common with its predecessor, the League of Nations, its declared object is the peaceful settlement of international questions and the preamble to its charter announces its intention of promoting the economic and social advancement of all peoples.

The main organ dealing with economic affairs is the Economic and Social Council which acts as a policy-making and co-ordinating unit, whilst detailed work is carried out by its four Regional Economic Commissions for Africa, Asia, and the Far East, Europe and Latin America. Linked to the UN are various specialised agencies including, amongst others working in the field of economics, the International Labour Organisation, the International Bank for Reconstruction and Development and the International Monetary Fund. Information on the structure and activities of the UN and its agencies may be found in such publications as the *Yearbook of the United Nations* (1946/47–   ) and the New Zealand Department of External Affairs annual *The United Nations and Related Agencies Handbook* (1961–   ).

The best introduction to the documentation system is *A Guide to the Use of United Nations Documents including Reference to the Specialised Agencies and Special UN Bodies* by Brenda Brimmer and others (Oceana Publications, 1962). This work not only gives details of basic tools and guides but also offers much practical advice on how to organise research in UN and related material.

The majority of UN's output falls into one of three basic categories:

(a) material of wide interest issued in the sales number series,
(b) official records of the main organs,
(c) mimeographed documents.

Publications issued during the period 1946–49 may be traced in two ways. The *Checklist of United Nations Documents* provides both lists and subject indexes for the documents of the main organs and their commissions. Part 5, for instance, is devoted to the Economic and Social Council, Part 7B to the Economic Commission for Asia and the Far East. Sales publications appearing in this early period are covered by the catalogue *Ten Years of United Nations Publications 1945 to 1955* (1955 I 8). The *United Nations Documents Index* (1950–) subsequently provided a systematic approach to all types of UN publications. Up to and including Vol. 13, 1962, it included publications of the specialised agencies but from that point onwards these must be sought elsewhere. The *Index* is issued in monthly parts which are superseded by a cumulative check list and subject index. The latter also contains details of UN depository libraries throughout the world. Several catalogues of sales publications have appeared since the one mentioned above; the latest is the *Catalogue: United Nations Publications* (1967) which lists with informative annotations all currently available sales items issued between 1945 and 1966.

Two further specialised aids to research may be mentioned. *A Reference Catalogue: United Nations Official Records 1948–1962* (64 I 3) gives a consolidated chronological listing of official records including those of the Economic and Social Council. For researchers whose work may entail extended use of mimeographed documents the *List of United Nations Document Series Symbols* (65 I 6) provides a subject index to the symbols.

Statistics comprise a very considerable proportion of the UN's publishing output. A **Statistical Office** is maintained which operates on lines similar to those pioneered by the League of Nations. The Office's best known publication is its comprehensive *Statistical*

Yearbook (1948–) the information in which is supplemented by the more recent data contained in the *Monthly Bulletin of Statistics* (1947–). To obtain the fullest benefit from these sources they should be used in conjunction with the volume of notes entitled *1967 Supplement to the Statistical Yearbook and the Monthly Bulletin of Statistics: Methodology and Definitions* (E68 XVII 9). World population figures obtained from the latest censuses are conveniently summarised in the *Demographic Yearbook* (1948–). Passing from general to more specialised statistics, the *Yearbook of International Trade Statistics* (1950–) provides summary tables and detailed data for about 150 countries presented, wherever possible, in accordance with the Standard International Trade Classification. The multi-volume *World Trade Annual* (1963–) is prepared by the Statistical Office but published commercially by Walker and Company of New York. It gives detailed figures relating to the commerce of some two dozen major trading countries. Information on national product, national income, capital formation and private expenditure for about 100 countries over a ten-year period is contained in the *Yearbook of National Accounts Statistics* (1957–). Earlier figures of this nature were given in *Statistics of National Income and Expenditure* (1951–57). As another example showing the range of the Office's publications *World Energy Supplies* (No. 1, 1929/50–) may be cited; it covers the production, trade and consumption of gas, electricity and other energy sources in about 170 countries. These last two publications form parts of the series issued by the Office under the overall title *Statistical Papers*, details of which may be found in the 1967 *Catalogue*. The most extensive section of *Statistical Papers* is *Series M*. Though mainly composed of items concerning statistical organisation it also includes frequently updated bibliographies on input-output analysis and industrial and distributive trade statistics. At irregular intervals industrial statistics have been published under the title *The Growth of World Industry*. Commencing with the 1967 edition (published 1969) which covers the period 1953–1966 this will appear annually. The first of its two volumes contains national figures together with tables illustrating world and regional developments, whilst the second is devoted to data on the production of industrial commodities.

The publications of the **Department of Economic and Social Affairs** deal, generally speaking, with matters of international scope. The annual *World Economic Survey* (1945/47–) places particular emphasis on world trade, production and the balance of payments. Since 1955 each issue has contained an extended study on a topic of current interest. The *International Flow of*

111

Long-Term Capital and Official Donations (1951/59–) provides commentary and figures concerning economic assistance to the developing countries.

The four **Regional Economic Commissions** were established in order to study the economic problems of the areas concerned and to assist in their development. The Commissions for Europe (ECE) and Asia and the Far East (ECAFE) were set up in 1947 and that for Latin America (ECLA) a year later. The Commission for Africa (ECA) came into operation in 1958. To some extent their publications follow a common pattern. Each issues an annual report which appears as part of the *Official Records* of the Economic and Social Council and each issues an annual survey of economic conditions supplemented at intervals by a bulletin. ECLA and ECA produce regional statistical bulletins. Other publications follow different lines. In those of ECAFE the stress is on industrial development and natural resources as in the *Development Programming Techniques Series* and the *Mineral Resources Development Series.* An important new serial is the *Statistical Yearbook for Asia and the Far East* (1968–) which, however, does not cover mainland China, North Korea or North Viet-Nam. ECLA, which has been concerned with the movement towards a Latin American common market, has published a considerable amount on regional economic co-operation whilst series such as *Analyses and Projections of Economic Development* and *The Textile Industry in Latin America* contain studies of individual countries. ECA tends to concentrate on trade as for instance in its *Foreign Trade Statistics of Africa* (1962–). This is issued in two parts. *Series A* dealing with direction of trade and *Series B* with trade by commodity. Its *African Economic Indicators* (1968–) is a combination of charts and analytical text covering such matters as imports and exports, financial flows and gross domestic product. The publications of ECE reflect the activities and policies of a highly industrialised continent. Analytical and statistical publications are available relating to such subjects as agriculture, transport, gas, coal, steel, engineering products and electric power, many of which appear as mimeographed documents. In this category the non-serial works are often technical in nature but others such as *International Comparisons of Labour Productivity in the Iron and Steel Industry* (67 IIE Mim 9) and *Housing Costs in European Countries* (63 IIE Mim 7) are of more general relevance. A list of these documents is available from the Distribution and Sales Section in Geneva. The specialised statistics issued by ECE may be exemplified by the *Annual Bulletin of Gas Statistics for Europe* (1957–) and the *Bulletin of*

112

Statistics on World Trade in Engineering Products (1963–). A detailed account of the work carried out by ECE is given in *Fifteen Years of Activity of the Economic Commission for Europe 1947–1962* (64 IIE 6).

The UN has published relatively little either in monograph or serial form on the economic affairs of the Middle East. The review *Economic Developments in the Middle East* (1949/50–1961/63) appeared as a supplement to the *World Economic Survey* but has now been replaced by the annual *Studies on Selected Development Problems in Various Countries in the Middle East* (1967–) which concentrates on Iraq, Jordan, Kuwait, Lebanon, Saudi Arabia and Syria.

The **United Nations Industrial Development Organisation (UNIDO)** whose headquarters are in Vienna was established in 1965 with the object of promoting the industrialisation process in the developing countries. Its bulletin *Industrialisation and Productivity* (1958–), issued prior to 1966 by the Department of Economic and Social Affairs, carries long, specialised articles aimed at a readership of industrial planners and development technicians. The *Industrial Development Survey* as published in its printed form in 1969 is the first of a proposed series designed to provide comprehensive assessments of progress and significant trends in industrialisation.

The first **United Nations Conference on Trade and Development (UNCTAD)** was held at Geneva in 1964 and later that year became an organ of the General Assembly. Its basic aim is the promotion of international trade with particular attention to the economic growth of the developing countries. The Conference acts as a forum for the discussion and formulation of principles and policies. The proceedings of the first Conference were published in 1964 (64 IIB 11–18); the eight volumes cover such topics as commodity trade, trade in manufactures and trade expansion within regional groupings. The second meeting took place in New Delhi in 1968 and the five volumes of its proceedings follow a similar pattern (E68 IID 14–18). UNCTAD's annual *Commodity Survey* (1966–) replaces an earlier publication of the same title issued by the Commission on International Commodity Trade. Its scope includes recent developments and trends in commodity trade, the activities of commodity groups and the latest information concerning specific commodities.

UN Agencies

The specialised agencies are bodies created by inter-governmental

113

agreement and formally associated with the UN. The oldest of them is the **International Labour Organisation (ILO)** which stems from the Treaty of Versailles and originally operated in conjunction with the League of Nations. ILO's main concern is the improvement of working and living conditions by means of its labour conventions and recommendations. The International Labour Office acts as the Organisation's secretariat and is the originator of a large proportion of the publishing output. The *Catalogue of ILO Publications* is issued at irregular intervals; the most recent appeared in 1969 and lists all currently available English language sales publications. Other more comprehensive catalogues are found in the *Bibliographical Contributions* series and include *Catalogue of Publications in English of the ILO, 1919–1950* (1951) and *Subject Guide to Publications of the ILO, 1919–1964* (1967). Details of new publications are given in the *International Labour Review*, the announcement list *ILO Publications* and the weekly general bibliographical survey *International Labour Documentation (New Series)*. The latter includes documents as well as sales material. A two-volume *Subject Index to International Labour Documentation, 1957–64* (1967) distributed by G. K. Hall of Boston contains over 12 000 references to periodical articles listed during the period mentioned.

ILO publishes a number of periodicals including the important *Year Book of Labour Statistics* (1935/36–   ). Employment and unemployment, hours of work, wages, consumer prices and industrial disputes are amongst the topics covered and the data relates to over 170 countries and territories. Supplementary figures are supplied by the quarterly *Bulletin of Labour Statistics* (1965–   ). The series *Studies and Reports* offers a variety of subject matter such as workers' management, productivity and the minimum wage. Other publications include monographs and reports prepared for ILO committees, the International Labour Conference and numerous meetings. Many advisory reports made to governments under the Expanded Programme of Technical Assistance are also issued.

The **International Institute for Labour Studies** is an offshoot of ILO and, like the parent body, is situated in Geneva. It is active in promoting conferences and seminars for the discussion of labour and allied problems. Many of the working documents produced for these occasions are available on an exchange basis. More substantial works emanating from the Institute including collected conference papers have been commercially published in Great Britain as, for instance, *Industrial Relations and Economic Development* edited by Arthur M. Ross (Macmillan, 1966).

114

The **Food and Agriculture Organization (FAO)** was established in 1945 and operates from its permanent headquarters in Rome. Amongst its publications there are a considerable number on the economic aspects of agriculture, forestry and fisheries. The *Catalogue of FAO Publications* appears at two-year intervals; the latest covers all sales publications issued over the period 1945–68. The *Catalogue* is kept up to date by quarterly supplements whilst *FAO Documentation: Current Index* (1967–) lists all new main documents and working papers in addition to the latest sales items. One of FAO's leading publications is *The State of Food and Agriculture* (1947–) which reviews the year's developments and assesses future prospects. The *Production Yearbook* (1958–) and *Trade Yearbook* (1958–) which from 1947 to 1957 appeared as the *Yearbook of Food and Agricultural Statistics* provide a wide range of statistics including retrospective figures. More recent data may be obtained from the *Monthly Bulletin of Agricultural Economics and Statistics* (1948–) which until 1952 was entitled *Monthly Bulletin of Food and Agricultural Statistics*. The *Yearbook of Fishery Statistics* (1947–) and the *Yearbook of Forest Products Statistics* (1947–) are two valuable sources of specialised information. As well as large-scale studies such as *Agricultural Commodities: Projections for 1975 and 1985* (2 vols, 1967) and *Agricultural Development in Nigeria 1965–1980* (1966) there are various series containing items of economic interest. As examples the *FAO Agricultural Development Papers, Commodity Policy Studies* and *Commodity Reference Series* may be quoted. The latter includes compendia such as *The World Sugar Economy in Figures 1880–1959* (1961). The decennial world census of agriculture is organised by FAO and results have been published for the 1950 and 1960 censuses. The Documentation Centre is producing a series of computer-processed analytical subject indexes of FAO publications and documents issued mainly during the period 1945–1966. The twelve volumes so far issued include *Statistics* (1968), *Commodities* (1969) and *Economic Analysis* (1969).

The **United Nations Educational, Scientific and Cultural Organisation (UNESCO)** was set up in 1945 and operates from Paris. Its sales material may be traced in the *General Catalogue of Unesco Publications and Unesco Sponsored Publications, 1946–1959* (1962) and the subsequent *Supplement*. The *Current List of Unesco Publications*, the quarterly *List of Unesco Documents and Publications* and frequent brochures record new titles. A number of monographs on economic topics have been issued including *Manpower, Employment and Education in the Rural Economy of*

Tanzania (1966) and *The Role of Savings and Wealth in Southern Asia and the West* (1963). The series *The University Teaching of Social Sciences* contains a volume on *Economics* (1954) in which a general report is followed by eleven country studies describing curricula and aims and methods of teaching. This series also has volumes on *Statistics* (1957), *Demography* (1957) and *Business Management* (1966).

UNESCO has sponsored much bibliographical work. The *World List of Social Science Periodicals* (3rd edn, 1966) prepared by the International Committee for Social Science Documentation (ICSSD) includes most of the scholarly economics journals current at the time of compilation. UNESCO's most valuable contribution to the economics literature is undoubtedly the *International Bibliography of Economics* (1952–   ) which is also prepared by ICSSD. The first eight issues were actually published by UNESCO; subsequent volumes have been put out in London by Tavistock Publications. This classified bibliography is restricted to scholarly books and journal articles, duplicated reports and a certain amount of material by governments and international organisations. UNESCO's *Statistical Yearbook* (1963–   ) which contains figures on book production, paper consumption, newspapers and other mass media is potentially useful with regard to market research and trade promotion.

The **International Bank for Reconstruction and Development (IBRD)**, also known as the **World Bank**, originates from the Bretton Woods Conference of 1944 and came into operation in 1946. It was established to assist member countries in the work of post-war reconstruction, to promote the flow of capital for productive purposes and to foster the balanced growth of international trade. Its headquarters are in Washington. From time to time the Bank issues lists of its free material. For many years Johns Hopkins Press has acted as publisher or distributor for IBRD's more substantial publications, details of which are given in the Press's advertising matter. IBRD has been responsible for many economic surveys, mainly in developing countries, and the subsequent reports, for instance *The Economic Development of Morocco* (Johns Hopkins Press, 1966), form a high percentage of the Bank's output. However, it should be noted that on occasions some IBRD surveys are published by the governments for which they were conducted as was the case with *The World Bank Report on the New Zealand Economy, 1968* (Wellington, Government Printer, 1968). The series *Staff Occasional Papers* is mainly devoted to works on aspects of development planning and finance. The Bank's activities are reviewed in its annual report

(1946–) which since 1963/64 has also included the annual report of the **International Development Association (IDA).** The summary proceedings of the annual meeting of the Bank's board of governors have been issued since 1946.

The **International Finance Corporation (IFC)** is also affiliated to IBRD and assists in the promotion of private capital investment in private enterprises. An annual report and also the summary proceedings of the annual meeting of its board of governors have been issued since 1956. The inter-relationship and activities of these three bodies are described in the IBRD publication *The World Bank, IDA and IFC: Policies and Operations*, the latest edition of which appeared in 1969. The **International Centre for Settlement of Investment Disputes (ICSID)**, an associate body with the same membership as the Bank, has issued an annual report since 1966/67.

In 1955 IBRD established the **Economic Development Institute** in order to provide training courses for government administrators from developing countries. At intervals it has issued a bibliography entitled *Selected Readings and Source Materials on Economic Development*, the 1966 edition of which lists over 200 books, pamphlets and periodical articles. As with IBRD the larger works are published by Johns Hopkins Press and include *Economic Development Projects and their Appraisal: Cases and Principles from the Experience of the World Bank* by John A. King (1967) and *Development Planning: Lessons of Experience* by Albert Waterston (1965, 3rd printing 1969). The latter is particularly noteworthy on account of its extensive bibliography of national development plans and its list of names and addresses of central planning agencies.

The **International Monetary Fund (IMF)** also has the same membership as IBRD and, in common with that body, stems from the Bretton Woods Conference. Since 1945 IMF has worked to promote international monetary co-operation particularly through consultation over exchange practices. The Fund's financial resources are available to assist member countries in balance of payments difficulties. Most IMF publications from 1946 onwards are listed in the selected bibliographies which appear at intervals in *IMF Staff Papers* (1950–). This periodical carries substantial research articles on a wide variety of monetary and financial topics. The quarterly *Finance and Development* (1964–), published jointly with IBRD is in the nature of a factual record in the field of development economics and also includes announcements of new publications. The annual report of IMF's executive directors (1946–) surveys the Fund's activities in the context of world

117

economic conditions whilst the *Annual Report on Exchange Restrictions* (1950–) provides a comprehensive country by country account of foreign exchange developments. The summary proceedings of the annual meeting of the Fund's board of governors have been issued since 1946. With regard to statistics IMF's major contributions are the *Balance of Payments Yearbook* (1938/1946/47–) supplemented by the monthly *International Financial Statistics* (1948–) which in turn is supplemented by *Direction of Trade* (1958/1962–). The latter is a joint IMF/IBRD publication which superseded the United Nations annual *Direction of International Trade*. The trade values are quoted in US dollars. The *Yearbook* appears in loose-leaf form and has a coverage of nearly 100 countries. Each country's position is presented in a basic global statement and also where possible in a more detailed basic regional statement. *International Financial Statistics* presents by country data on such matters as exchange rates, international transactions, central, commercial and development banks, interest rates, cost of living and national accounts. IMF is now in the process of publishing a series of *Surveys of African Economies*. Each volume is devoted to a group of countries the economic structures of which are described with particular reference to the financial aspects.

The **General Agreement on Tariffs and Trade (GATT)** which operates from Geneva has an involved constitutional history dating back to 1947. The International Conference on Trade and Employment which met at Havana in 1947/48 discussed an International Trade Charter and the setting up of an International Trade Organisation which would administer the General Agreement. In the event, however, this body was not established and GATT is administered by a secretariat for the Interim Commission of the International Trade Organisation. GATT aims by consultation to eliminate discrimination from trade and in particular is concerned that only the customs tariff should be used to afford protection to the industries of its member countries. It has initiated numerous tariff negotiations including the 'Kennedy Round' which was concluded in 1967.

The publications of GATT and the International Trade Centre are listed in an annual catalogue. The *GATT Bibliography* (1954) and its supplements cover books, pamphlets, articles and newspaper reports relating to the General Agreement. The annual *International Trade* (1952–) surveys current world developments and includes information on the trade of the eastern European member countries of the Council for Mutual Economic Aid (COMECON). The work of the organisation is described in *The*

Activities of GATT (1959/60–) which appears at irregular intervals. The volumes of the *Basic Instruments and Selected Documents Series* together with supplements provide the text of the General Agreement and subsequent important resolutions, decisions, recommendations and reports adopted by GATT. Amongst the subjects covered by GATT's monographic publications are trade in agricultural products, cotton textiles, quantitative restrictions and the trade of less-developed countries. This last category includes a series of *Development Plans Studies* in which since 1962 there have been surveys of plans for India, Pakistan, Nigeria and Uganda.

In conjunction with the United Nations Conference on Trade and Development GATT operates the **International Trade Centre** which was established in 1964. The main object of the Centre is to assist developing countries in the promotion of their export trades and to provide information on export markets. Its publications include bibliographies, guides to export promotion techniques and numerous market surveys. Reference works such as *Compendium of Sources: International Trade Statistics* (1967) and *Compendium of Sources: Basic Commodity Statistics (1967)* have also been produced giving details of coverage and classification employed in the cited publications.

Before passing on to other international organisations it is convenient at this point to mention three development banks which work in co-operation with the UN. The **Asian Development Bank** and the **African Development Bank** were sponsored respectively by ECAFE and ECA and commenced operations in 1966. Each issues an annual report. Amongst its non-serial publications the Asian Development Bank has published the proceedings of a *Regional Seminar on Agriculture* (1969) which surveys in some detail the economic aspects of agriculture in ECAFE countries. The **Inter-American Development Bank** was founded in 1959 under the auspices of the Organisation of American States and has close links with ECLA. Its headquarters are in Washington and it is the most prolific publisher of the three. The annual report and the proceedings of the annual meeting of the board of governors have appeared since 1960. Round table discussions on a particular theme are held in conjunction with the governors' meetings and subsequently printed, as for example the *Round Table on Financial Aspects of Economic Integration in the Hemisphere* (1963). The Bank's Social Progress Trust Fund issues an annual report entitled *Socio-Economic Progress in Latin America* (1961–) which contains a regional analysis of economic trends as well as a survey of socio-economic conditions in each member state.

Bank for International Settlements (BIS)

Though at one remove from direct governmental membership the Bank for International Settlements must be mentioned as an international organisation of considerable importance. BIS was established in 1930 in order to promote co-operation between central banks and to provide facilities for international financial operations. Its headquarters are in Basle and it has a current membership of 26 central banks. Its main publication is the *Annual Report* (1930/31–), the greater part of which is given over to a review of world financial developments with reference to such topics as world trade and payments, gold reserves, foreign exchange, the Euro-currency market and the working of the European Monetary Agreement. Monographs are produced occasionally but are not widely announced or distributed. One of the Bank's most substantial works in recent years is the commercially published *Eight European Central Banks: Organization and Activities* ... (Allen and Unwin, 1963), which deals with the central banking mechanism in Belgium, West Germany, UK, France, Italy, the Netherlands, Switzerland and Sweden.

Benelux

The economic integration of Belgium, the Netherlands and Luxembourg stems from plans made in the 1940s by the governments in exile. After the war a series of co-operative measures finally resulted in the signing in 1958 of the treaty of economic union which came into force two years later. Benelux, which has its secretariat in Brussels, is not a large publisher but two serials of interest to economists may be mentioned. The Annual *Étude Comparative des Dépenses et des Recettes des Pouvoirs Publics des Pays du Benelux* analyses in text and tables the budgetary policies of the member countries. The *Bulletin Trimestriel Économique et Statistique* (1954–) superseded the *Annuaire Statistique Benelux* of which there were three issues. The *Bulletin* contains articles in French and Dutch on a wide range of topics concerning the joint economy of the group. A statistical section provides data on national product, industrial production, employment and unemployment, foreign and intra-Benelux trade, transport, prices and finance.

European Communities

The bodies comprising the European Communities are the European Economic Community (EEC), also known as the Common Market, the European Coal and Steel Community (ECSC) and the European Atomic Energy Community (EURATOM). Headquarters are in Brussels. The first in order of establishment was ECSC which started work in 1952, its aim being the creation of a common market for coal and steel. The Treaty of Rome was signed in 1957 as a further step towards a complete common market and EEC and EURATOM began to operate the following year. The member states of the Communities are Belgium, France, Western Germany, Italy, Luxembourg and the Netherlands. Greece, Turkey, Madagascar and eighteen francophone African countries are associate members of EEC.

The publications of the Communities deal with matters of common interest and in the main are closely concerned with the current activities of the parent bodies and the member states. The official languages of the Communities are German, French, Italian and Dutch but some publications are also issued in English. French and English editions of *Publications of the European Communities: Catalogue* are issued from time to time listing the sales and free material of all three Communities, their common institutions and joint services. An annual account of the work of the three organisations has been given in the *General Report on the Activities of the Community* since 1967; prior to this date each Community issued its individual *General Report*. There are also annual reports on the relations between EEC and its associate members.

The **Statistical Office** serves each of the Communities and issues a considerable number of monthly, quarterly and annual serials. The monthly *General Statistics,* formerly *General Statistical Bulletin* (1960–) relates mainly to the member countries with the type of subject coverage found in national publications of this nature. The quarterly *Energy Statistics* (1962–) together with a yearbook provide data on production, trade and consumption of coal and other solid fuels, gas, petroleum and electrical energy. *Iron and Steel* (1962–) appearing bi-monthly and supplemented by a biennial yearbook is a source of detailed information on these industries. Production figures for all major industries in member countries are given in the quarterly *Industrial Statistics* (1960–) and its auxiliary yearbook. *National Accounts* (1966–) provides retrospective figures for a ten-year period for member countries together with summary comparative figures for the UK, USA and Japan. Trade figures are produced in great quantity. The annual *Tariff Statistics* (1962–) presents import and export data arranged in accordance with the Tarif Douanier Commun (TDC) code. Details of imports and exports of coal, iron and steel may

121

be found in the annual *Commerce Extérieur: Produits CECA* (1964–). The monthly *Foreign Trade: Analytical Tables* was originally arranged by the Statistical and Tariff Classification for International Trade (CST) but from 1966 onwards the Harmonised Nomenclature for Foreign Trade Statistics of the EEC Member Countries (NIMEXE) has been used. Annual volumes for imports and exports classified according to the CST are still issued to enable comparisons to be made with previously published figures. A CST/NIMEXE correlation table is provided in the monthly series. The annual *Statistiques Sociales* (1968–) contains information on wages, cost and standard of living and employment. Another range of publications is devoted to the overseas associates of EEC and includes a general statistical bulletin and yearbook and a foreign trade yearbook.

EEC has issued studies on many topics including agricultural, economic and regional policy, competition and manpower. There are also specialised series such as *Économie et Finances, Transports* and *Développement de l'Outre-Mer*. Amongst periodicals originating from EEC the quarterly *Economic Situation in the Community* (1961–) is of particular interest. Annual reports on the activities of the **European Investment Bank** and the Monetary Committee have been published since 1958 and 1958/59 respectively.

ECSC's publications tend to be rather more technical yet provide much of economic interest. There are monographs on such subjects as economic forecasting, the steel market, wages, productivity and collective bargaining. Series include *La Conversion Industrielle en Europe, Programmes de Développement et de Conversion* and *Études Régionales d'Emploi*. Amongst periodicals there are an annual *Financial Report* (1953/55–) and a report on *Investment in the Community Coalmining and Iron and Steel Industries* (1956–).

Since 1967, however, the publishing programmes of the individual Communities have been brought under the aegis of the Commission of the European Communities. This body's name now appears as the issuing authority not only for new monographic material and series but also for series and periodicals previously issued by individual Communities.

European Free Trade Association (EFTA)

EFTA, the headquarters of which are in Geneva, was set up in 1960 in order to promote free trade particularly in industrial and agricultural products. Its members are Austria, Denmark, Norway, Portugal, Sweden, Switzerland, Iceland and UK with Finland as an associate member.

Though EFTA's publishing output is relatively small, the economist will find a number of items of interest. The monthly *EFTA Bulletin* (1960–) contains short articles on the Association's work and on topics of general economic concern to the member countries. The *Bulletin* also carries a list of currently available publications. The *Annual Report* (1960/61–) reviews the economic developments within the group and contains information on EFTA's relations with other international organisations. The agricultural side of EFTA's activities is dealt with in a separate *Annual Review of Agricultural Trade* (1964–). The annual *EFTA Trade* (1964–) analyses in text and statistical tables the trends in the trade of individual member countries generally and also the pattern of trade within the group. *Structure and Growth of the Portuguese Economy* by V. Xavier Pintado (1964), *The Effects of EFTA on the Economies of Member States* (1969) and *Regional Policy in EFTA: an Examination of the Growth Centre Idea* (1968) may be cited as perhaps the three most substantial studies produced by EFTA. The latter was commercially published by Oliver and Boyd and is the only publication mentioned here which is not available free of charge. In the UK, EFTA publications may be obtained through the EFTA Information Centre, 1 Victoria Street, London, S.W.1.

Nordic Council (Nordisk Råd)

The Nordic Council was established in 1952 and its five members (Denmark, Finland, Iceland, Norway and Sweden) pursue, amongst other aims, a policy of economic co-operation. The Council operates from regional secretariats in each of the member countries. A number of publications on economic matters have been published in the *Nordisk Udredningsserie* though with the exception of the *Yearbook of Nordic Statistics* (1962–) few of these are in English. The *Yearbook's* subject coverage is similar to that of other international compilations of this nature and its main emphasis is on population, agriculture, trade, transport and communications.

North Atlantic Treaty Organisation (NATO)

Though its concern is with international defence NATO has sponsored a number of conferences on topics such as manpower planning, queuing theory, critical path techniques and the theory of games, the proceedings of which are of potential interest mainly to mathematical economists. These conference proceedings have been issued in the UK by various commercial publishers and details may be found in the *British National Bibliography*.

Organisation Commune Africaine et Malgache (OCAM)

OCAM was founded in 1965 as the successor of the Union Africaine et Malgache de Coopération Économique (UAMCE). Its headquarters are in Yaoundé, Cameroun and its members are the Malagasy Republic and the francophone states of central and West Africa. Amongst other objects it seeks to develop the economies of the member countries and establish an African common market. Its quarterly review *Nations Nouvelles,* formerly *New Nations* (1962–   ), surveys economic, political and social developments within the organisation's member countries. The annual *Compendium des Statistiques du Commerce Extérieur* (1965–   ) provides foreign trade figures for one year. The quarterly *Bulletin Statistique de l'O.C.A.M.* (1966?–   ) does not follow a regular pattern but each issue is devoted to a particular topic with special attention to foreign trade.

Organisation for Economic Co-operation and Development (OECD)

OECD was established in 1961 with headquarters in Paris to succeed the **Organisation for European Economic Co-operation (OEEC).** At intervals of two or three years OECD issues a *Catalogue of Publications* which is kept up to date by supplements. OEEC's *General Catalogue of Books Published from 1948 to 1958* includes the publications of the **European Productivity Agency (EPA)** which was set up in 1953. Later OEEC publications are listed in supplements to its catalogue and in the earlier catalogues issued by OECD.

OEEC was formed in 1948 to deal with the problems of post-war economic reconstruction and the allocation of Marshall Plan aid. The object of the associated EPA was to further productivity through the application of advanced technical methods. Though the majority of OEEC and EPA publications are now out of print they are of great value to anyone tracing the course of western European recovery and development. OEEC's annual reports

(1948–1960/61) covered the activities of the organisation in such fields as liberalisation of trade and the restoration of financial stability. They also reviewed the economic and financial position of western Europe generally and in due course individual reports of a similiar scope were issued for each member country. The important work of the **European Payments Union** is recorded in annual reports between 1950/51 and 1958. A general statistical bulletin was published with occasional supplementary issues such as that on *Industrial Statistics, 1900–1955*. Four series of foreign trade statistics provided data on trade by areas, commodities and countries of origin and destination. Numerous studies and reports dealt with fuel and energy supplies, chemical products, machinery, textiles, agriculture and transport. Amongst subjects of economic interest EPA produced publications relating to business management, marketing and distribution, trade unions and automation.

OECD was created to promote economic growth and the standard of living amongst its member countries and the expansion of world trade on a multilateral, non-discriminatory basis. The organisation has 21 members, mainly European, but also including Canada, Japan and the United States. Yugoslavia is a special status member and is the only representative of the eastern bloc. A useful account of the Organisation's development, activities and publications is given in *OECD at Work* (1969). The publications reflect the work done by committees, working groups, conferences, international seminars and specially commissioned experts. Output is high as may be seen from the fact that the Economics and Statistics Department is currently publishing over 12 000 pages of statistical tables per year. The monthly *Main Economic Indicators* (March, 1965–) replaced both the OEEC/OECD *General Statistics* and its supplementary series of *Main Economic Indicators*. Information in the new series is in tabular and graphic form giving details of the latest changes in the economy of the member nations. There are quarterly supplements dealing with industrial production and consumer price indices. From time to time volumes of historical statistics covering a ten-year period are produced as further supplements to *Main Economic Indicators* and *Industrial Production*. *Statistics of Foreign Trade* began in 1950 and now appears in three series. *Series A: Overall Trade by Countries* is issued quarterly with monthly supplements and covers a four-year period. *Series B: Trade by Commodities: Analytical Abstracts* is also published quarterly in six parts; the classification system used is SITC (revised) and comparable figures are given for one, sometimes two previous years. *Series C: Trade by Commodities: Market Summaries* is half-yearly with import and export data in separate volumes. A half-yearly supplement provides a detailed analysis for selected SITC items. From what has already been said it will be noted that a feature of many OECD statistical publications is their retrospective coverage. *The Statistics of Energy* (1950/57–) issued annually now spans a 15-year period and occasional publications with figures usually ranging over a period of about ten years have dealt with national accounts, labour force, balance of payments and agriculture and food.

The twice-yearly *OECD Economic Outlook* (1967–) reviews developments in major countries and examines general trends within the OECD group. Following the practice of OEEC, annual *Economic Surveys* of each member country, including Yugoslavia, have been produced since 1961/62. These provide a critical assessment of the effectiveness of financial, monetary and economic policies. Latest news of OECD deliberations and activities together with articles of general interest and announcements of publications may be found in *The OECD Observer* (1962–).

Though OECD's non-serial publications are mainly concerned with the practical aspects of economic co-operation, theoretical and mathematical studies are also to be found. *Perspectives of Planning* edited by Erich Jantsch (1969) records the proceedings of a symposium on the techniques of long-range forecasting and planning whilst the *Economic Studies* series contains such items as *An Econometric Analysis of International Trade* by F. G. Adams and others (1969). OECD's **Development Centre** undertakes research into the major problems encountered by the developing countries. Its *Development Centre Studies* include such diverse works as *Supply and Demand Prospects for Fertilizers in Developing Countries* (1968) and *Reflections on Nigeria's Economic Growth* by W. Arthur Lewis (1967). The *Problems of Development* series has ranged over public finance, agricultural co-operation and economic development in particular countries, for instance Spain and Turkey. The **Manpower and Social Affairs Directorate** produces several series of relevance to economists including *Industrial Relations Aspects of Manpower Policy, Reviews of Manpower and Social Policies*, and *Labour Mobility*. The **Library** of OECD is responsible for the *Special Annotated Bibliography* series, recent examples of which are *International Monetary System* (1967), *Economic Growth* (1968) and *Capital Markets* (1969). A comprehensive listing of current serials in the field of economics is provided by the annual *Catalogue of Periodicals*, the 1969/70 edition of which contains 3020 entries arranged by subject under country or organisation of origin.

Organisation of American States (OAS)

The Organisation of American States is the name adopted in 1948 by the former Union of American Republics which was established in 1890. The Organisation has its headquarters in Washington.

An annual catalogue of currently available publications is issued by the **Pan American Union (PAU),** the General Secretariat of OAS. PAU's Statistics Department in conjunction with the Inter American Statistical Institute produces *América en Cifras* (1960-) every two years. The section entitled *Situación Económica* appears in five parts dealing with agriculture, industry, commerce and communications, finance and national accounts and finally prices, wages and consumption. Figures are given for South and Central American states, USA, Canada and some Caribbean countries. More recent information may be obtained from the monthly *Boletín Estadístico* (1965-). The **Inter-American Statistical Institute** has also produced the series *Actividades Estadísticas de las Naciones Americanas.* Though now somewhat out of date this series forms a useful guide to the statistical work of OAS member countries. English summaries and lists of major publications are provided. Various series of official records are published including those of the Inter-American Economic and Social Council. The activities of OAS are summarised in the *Annual Report of the Secretary General* (1947/48-).

The Organisation's monographic publications cover such subjects as agricultural and industrial development, trade, public finance and transportation. From time to time books of wide general interest are published for OAS by Johns Hopkins Press. Amongst these have been the *Economic Survey of Latin America, 1962* (1964), *Latin America: Problems and Perspectives of Economic Development, 1963-1964* (1966) and *The Alliance for Progress and Latin-American Development Prospects: a Five Year Review, 1961-1965* (1967). In recent years the Press has also published joint OAS/IDB fiscal surveys of Panama and Colombia and works on taxation prepared under the OAS/IDB/ECLA Joint Tax Program.

CHAPTER TEN

ECONOMIC STATISTICS

British Statistics Sources

As the quantitative approach to economics gained in importance, and as government, industry and academic economists became more concerned with controlling the speed and direction of economic change, the need for more statistical data became apparent. Some official and unofficial data had been collected from early times: statistics of Exchequer returns and foreign trade, for example, were collected in medieval times, but the great increase in published sources has come since 1945. Unlike books and journal articles, however, statistical tables are rarely indexed in any comprehensive manner, and for British sources there are no up-to-date complete subject indexes. A Joint Working Party of Librarians and Economic Statisticians set up by the Library Association and the Royal Statistical Society has drawn up a list entitled *Recommended Basic Statistical Sources for Community Use* (Library Association, 1969) which is a useful handlist of titles. A survey was conducted to discover the holdings of these 58 titles in 91 provincial centres, and the results are published in *Board of Trade Journal*, vol. 198, No. 3804, 11th February, 1970, pp. 379–383, and provide an invaluable guide to the location of key British statistical sources.

There are some partial lists and guides to sources of British statistics which are of great value to the economist. One of the most recent and valuable is Joan M. Harvey's *Sources of Statistics* (Bingley, 1969) which emphasises British sources, but also includes notes on the principal United States and international statistical publications. In her eleven chapters Miss Harvey divides the major sources by subject and includes population, education and social statistics in addition to chapters on labour, production, trade, finance, prices, transport and communications and tourism. This

128

is probably the best all-round guide to British statistics sources. The only recent official guide was compiled by the Central Statistical Office and entitled *List of Principal Statistical Series Available* (HMSO, 1965). This also groups sources by subject within the three main areas of economic, financial and regional statistics. Under each specific subject is given the government department responsible for the collection of statistics, the frequency with which they are published and the publications in which they appear. The sections are completed by short notes on the methods of collection and publication, which are invaluable in tracing the latest, or first publication of current series. Unlike Miss Harvey's book, however, the *List of Principal Statistical Series Available* does not give the sources of earlier series, but limits itself to current publication, and to official British sources.

The series of articles published in *Journal of the Royal Statistical Society* on the sources of British statistics was reprinted in *The Sources and Nature of the Statistics of the United Kingdom*, edited by Maurice G. Kendall (2 vols, Oliver and Boyd, 1952 and 1957). The articles are on specific subjects and by expert users of statistics in that area. Now somewhat dated, the volumes are still a valuable guide especially to the early post-war series.

The Interdepartmental Committee on Social and Economic Research compiled between 1948 and 1961 six Guides to Official Sources which varied considerably in quality, but aimed to give the user details of the methods of collection and publication of official statistical series, and a guide to their contents. Subjects covered include labour, census of production and agricultural and food statistics. A new edition of this last guide, entitled *Agricultural and Food Statistics: a Guide to Official Sources* (HMSO, 1969) was compiled by the Ministry of Agriculture, Fisheries and Food. Once again these guides are still useful for details of the post-war series: that on the *Census of Production* is particularly useful in listing all the publication details of the *Census* from the first in 1907 to that of 1958.

Some economic texts have been written on British economic statistical publications and are worth noting here: Ely Devons' *Introduction to British Economic Statistics* (Cambridge U.P., 1956) was a classic, and it was a great pity that Professor Devons was not able to produce a second edition. F. M. M. Lewes' *Statistics of the British Economy* (Allen and Unwin, 1967) is less comprehensive, whilst R. J. Nicholson's *Economic Statistics and Economic Problems* (McGraw-Hill, 1969) uses the sources to show how statistics demonstrate economic relationships.

Information about new statistical data, and the methods of

compilation of official series were, and to some extent still are, published irregularly in *Economic Trends*. Some of the more useful of these articles have been reprinted in the series of volumes *New Contributions to Economic Statistics*, by the Central Statistical Office. The same Office began publishing in 1968 a quarterly *Statistical News: Developments in British Official Statistics* which includes articles on the methods of compiling statistical series and short notes on new developments in the collection and publication of official statistics. There is a useful cumulating index in each issue.

The major compendium of British statistics is the *Annual Abstract of Statistics* produced by the Central Statistical Office from series collected by itself and other government departments. Most series have been published previously in other sources such as *Financial Statistics, Board of Trade Journal* and *Employment and Productivity Gazette* but a few are published for the first time in the *Annual Abstract of Statistics*. The main chapters of economic statistical series are labour, production, retail distribution, transport and communications, external trade, overseas finance, national income and expenditure, home finance, banking and prices. For each table the government department responsible for collecting the data is given, and there is a list of original sources. Since the *Annual Abstract*, as its title indicates, summarises statistics, more detailed figures are available in the original sources, which in addition are usually published more frequently than annually, and are therefore more up to date.

Many of the series included in the *Annual Abstract of Statistics* appear as monthly or quarterly series in *Monthly Digest of Statistics*, also produced by the Central Statistical Office. Again many series are reproduced from other sources, but more receive their first publication in the *Monthly Digest of Statistics* than do in the *Annual Abstract*. The *Monthly Digest of Statistics* is mentioned in the notes on sources of statistics which follow only where it contains the first publication of a series, or the useful juxtaposition of several series.

National Income and Expenditure is one of the most heavily used sources of economic statistics. Its coverage is so wide, and the series so valuable that they are dealt with in the subject sections of the remainder of this chapter. The tables are in groups: summary tables, expenditure and output at constant prices, industrial input and output, personal sector, companies, public corporations, central government, local authorities, combined public authorities, public sector, capital formation, and financial accounts. The key to the methods of compilation and description of the contents is Rita Maurice's *National Accounts Statistics: Sources and Methods* (HMSO, 1968) which supersedes the Central Statistical Office's *National Income Statistics: Sources and Methods* (HMSO, 1956). *Preliminary Estimates of National Income and Balance of Payments* is an annual white paper whose title is self-explanatory.

The following list of the major statistical serials published currently by HMSO is arranged by the government departments responsible, with notes on the frequency of publication, starting date and changes of title (past changes in departmental names or responsibility are ignored). The list is far from comprehensive, but includes all the important titles which are analysed later in this chapter. (*See* p. vi.)

Board of Trade

Bankruptcy: General Annual Report (annual, 1883–)
Board of Trade Journal (weekly, 1886–)
Business Monitor, Civil Aviation Series (monthly or quarterly, 1968–)
Business Monitor, Production Series (monthly or quarterly, 1962–)
Census of Distribution and Other Services (irregular, 1950–)
Census of Production (irregular, 1907–)
Company Assets, Income and Finance (irregular, 1957–)
Insurance Business: Statistics (annual, 1968– ; continues *Insurance Business: Summary of Statements Deposited with the Board of Trade*, annual, 1949–1967)
Overseas Trade Statistics of the United Kingdom (monthly, 1970– ; continues *Overseas Trade Accounts of the United Kingdom*, 1965–1969; which continued *Accounts Relating to the Trade and Navigation of the United Kingdom*, monthly, 1848–1964)
Report on Overseas Trade (monthly, 1950–)

Central Statistical Office

Abstract of Regional Statistics (annual, 1965–)
Annual Abstract of Statistics (annual, 1946– ; continues *Statistical Abstract of the United Kingdom*, issued by the Board of Trade, which covered 1840/53–1924/38)
Economic Trends (monthly, 1953–)

Financial Statistics (monthly, 1962–)
Monthly Digest of Statistics (monthly, 1946–)
National Income and Expenditure (annual, 1938/40–)
United Kingdom Balance of Payments (annual, 1946/57–)

Chief Registrar of Friendly Societies

Report (5 vols, annual, 1875–)

Commissioners of Inland Revenue

Inland Revenue Statistics (annual, 1970–)
Report (annual, 1857/58–)

Department of Employment and Productivity

Changes in Rates of Wages and Hours of Work (monthly, 1966–)
Employment and Productivity Gazette (monthly, 1968– ; continues *Ministry of Labour Gazette*, monthly, 1893–1968)
Family Expenditure Survey (1957/59, 1960/61, annual, 1962–)
Household Food Consumption and Expenditure (annual, 1965– ; continues *Domestic Food Consumption and Expenditure*, annual, 1950–1964)
Time Rates of Wages and Hours of Work (annual, 1946– ; continues various titles, 1893–1929)

Exchequer and Audit Department

Trading Accounts and Balance Sheets (annual, 1920–)

H.M. Customs and Excise

Annual Statement of Trade of the United Kingdom (annual, 1853–)
Protective Duties (annual, 1959–)
Report (annual, 1909/10–)

Ministry of Agriculture, Fisheries and Food

Agricultural Statistics, England and Wales (annual, 1939/44–)

Agricultural Statistics, Scotland (annual, 1939/44–)
Agricultural Statistics, United Kingdom (annual, 1939/44– ;
reports of inquiries were published irregularly from 1908)
Annual Review and Determination of Guarantees (annual,
1951–)
Farm Incomes in England and Wales (annual, 1944/48–)

Ministry of Housing and Local Government

Local Government Financial Statistics (annual, 1934/35–)
Rates and Rateable Values (annual, 1921–)

Ministry of Overseas Development

British Aid Statistics (annual, 1963/67– ; continues *British
Aid*, annual, 1961–1963)

Ministry of Power

Capital Investment in the Coal, Gas, and Electricity Industries
(1960)
Digest of Energy Statistics (annual, 1968/69– ; continues
Ministry of Fuel and Power *Statistical Digest*, annual, 1938/
43–1967)

Ministry of Public Building and Works

Monthly Bulletin of Construction Statistics (monthly, 1947– ;
published by the Ministry, not HMSO)

Ministry of Technology

Statistics of Science and Technology (annual, 1967–)

Ministry of Transport

Passenger Transport in Great Britain (annual, 1962– ; continues and extends *Public Road Passenger Transport Statistics*,
annual, 1949–1962)

Northern Ireland, Cabinet Office, Economics Section

Digest of Statistics, Northern Ireland (2 p.a., 1954–)

Scottish Development Department

Local Authority Financial Returns (annual, 1961–)
Rates and Rateable Values in Scotland (annual, 1939–)

Scottish Statistical Office

Digest of Scottish Statistics (2 p.a., 1953–)

Treasury

Civil Estimates (annual)
Consolidated Fund and National Loans Fund Accounts (annual, 1968/69–)
Financial Statement and Budget Report (annual, 1968/69–)
Finance Accounts of the United Kingdom (annual, 1880/81–1968/69)
Preliminary Estimates of National Income and Balance of Payments (annual, 1952–)
Public Expenditure (annual, 1969–)
Supplementary Estimates (irregular)

Welsh Office

Digest of Welsh Statistics (annual, 1954–)

Other important non-serial sources of statistical information are the reports of the Monopolies Commission and the National Board for Prices and Incomes. These studies of specific industries or occupations often contain valuable statistical data not available elsewhere. Another important, though unofficial, source of statistics is *National Institute Economic Review* which includes regular surveys of the economic climate and forecasts of future trends.

The remainder of this chapter is a review of some of the regular statistical series published in these titles, with the addition of a few unofficial publications which contain statistics of value to economists. Generally the sources quoted are those in which the series are first published, but it should be mentioned that many figures are released as press notices before official publication: details of these can be found in the Central Statistical Office's *List of Principal Statistical Series Available* noted above.

The aim of this chapter is to give detailed notes on the series most used by economists in a relatively small number of publications. Readers wanting information on other series and titles are advised to consult the guides mentioned at the beginning of this chapter, especially the *List of Principal Statistical Series Available* and Joan M. Harvey's *Sources of Statistics*. Miss Harvey's book is particularly useful in noting the location of earlier runs of statistical series, which are not given in this chapter. The series are described as they are published at the beginning of 1970: *Statistics on Incomes, Prices, Employment and Production*, begun in 1962 by the Ministry of Labour ceased publication at the end of 1969 and has been omitted from these notes.

Note: The indexing of statistical tables is difficult, but certain conventions have been used in the past and are followed here: the subdivision and crosslinking of subjects is noted thus: 'unemployment by sex and by standard region' and 'unemployment by sex, by standard region ...' mean there are separate figures for each sex and for each standard region, but the regional figures are not divided by sex; 'unemployment by sex by standard region' indicates that the regional statistics are given separately for each sex. 'Notes and coin' signifies separate figures for banknotes and coin, whereas 'notes/coin' means one total figure only is given. 'Adjusted' normally means series which have been adjusted to take into account known normal seasonal variations.

Economic History

Economic historians usually have to rely on estimates of economic trends based on partial contemporary statistical data. There are few British official statistical series before the late nineteenth century other than those collected together in *Statistical Abstract of the United Kingdom* produced annually by the Board of Trade from 1854 to 1938. This was the forerunner of the current *Annual Abstract of Statistics,* and included a long time series, usually fourteen years, so that the first issue contains statistics from 1840.

Many unofficial estimates of economic time series have appeared in books and journal articles, and the best of these have been brought together in B. R. Mitchell and P. Deane, *Abstract of*

British Historical Statistics (Cambridge U.P., 1962). The volume is in sections, each devoted to one economic subject, in which the different series are compared with each other and with official statistics where these exist. The subject areas covered are population and vital statistics, labour, agriculture, coal, iron and steel, tin, copper and lead, textiles, transport, building, miscellaneous production statistics, overseas trade, wages and standard of living, national income and expenditure, public finance, banking and insurance, and prices. The starting dates vary forward from the coal trade statistics for 1655, but the majority of series begin in the nineteenth century. Sources of the original estimates are quoted, and each section begins with a short review of the statistical problems involved.

Other estimates or compilations of economic statistics for historical periods are to be found in journal articles and in books: the monographs and abstracting and indexing services quoted in Chapters 11-24 are the key to these sources.

For researchers needing to start from basic statistical material the sources are very large in number, detailed in content, and specific in coverage. Histories of companies sometimes provide some statistical evidence on the growth of an industry, but most are descriptive and journalistic. Original archival material is more satisfactory, but much more difficult to trace and handle. The Business Archives Council, (Ormond House, 63, Queen Victoria St., London, E.C.4) advises firms on which records to keep, and how; the Council maintains a list of collections of business archives kept by firms, libraries, archives offices, and public records offices throughout the country. Its journal, *Business Archives,* includes short articles, a list of recent deposits of business archives, and notes on archives being sought by researchers. Occasional surveys are made to try to locate unknown caches of archival material, and the Council has a small specialist library.

The Historical Manuscripts Commission National Register of Archives published *Sources of Business History in Reports of the National Register of Archives* in 1964 and there have been annual supplements since. There are no subject or geographical indexes, and collections are listed alphabetically by the name of the company or individual. Some notable collections of business histories in British libraries are mentioned in Chapter 1.

Industry

For the statistician, and for the economist using statistics, the industrial sector of the economy is one of the most difficult to handle. First there is the problem of collecting the statistics from the thousands of industrial establishments; second, the problem of ensuring the comparability of series; third, the necessity for limiting the number of statistics collected, since this is a costly operation for many small firms, whilst still meeting the increasing needs of government, economists and the industry itself; and last, the need to retain confidentiality of the statistical information supplied by firms.

The Central Statistical Office is at present engaged on a large operation to rationalise the collection and dissemination of industrial statistics, and to reconcile these conflicting needs. The new Business Statistics Office will attempt to make the available statistical series more comparable, more quickly released, and more closely geared to the needs of users. One of the BSO's first jobs is to reconcile the different groupings and definitions of industry used by different government departments, so that statistics collected for different purposes can be compared. The first step is the creation of the 'Central Register' of establishments by which every production and accounting unit supplying statistical information to government will be allocated to an industry group. The classification used is the *Standard Industrial Classification* (3rd edn, HMSO, 1968) devised by the Central Statistical Office and closely related to the United Nations' *International Standard Industrial Classification of All Economic Activities* (rev. edn, UN, 1968). In the SIC the first division is by 'orders', then by 'minimum list headings'. The SIC has been in use for many industrial statistics since the first edition in 1948, though there are differences between the three editions.

There are many official and unofficial publications containing statistics relating to British industry, its activities and intentions. The notes which follow give details of the more important sources.

The *Census of Production,* now taken every five years, is the most comprehensive and detailed general collection of statistics about industries. Industry as a whole is divided into 128 SIC groups, each establishment being allocated to a group depending upon its principal product. For each group the *Census of Production* has a pamphlet giving the same statistical series in so far as these are applicable. The major series are: analysis by size of firm, total wage bill, employment, sales by product (for all principal products, and for subsidiary products of the larger firms), purchases of raw materials and fuel by product, transport costs, total and per capita output, stocks and capital expenditure. There are summary tables for each industry, and for the *Census of Production* industries

137

as a whole. Guides to Official Sources, No. 6 by the Interdepartmental Committee on Social and Economic Research is entitled *Census of Production Reports* (HMSO, 1961) and details the content, layout and publication of all the *Censuses* from 1907 to 1958. The results of the 1968 *Census of Production* will be the last to be published in this form. The new form has yet to be finalised, but will probably be as the result of quarterly, annual and three-yearly inquiries.

The index of **industrial production** is first published in summary form in the *Board of Trade Journal* monthly, then in more detail in *Monthly Digest of Statistics* as adjusted and unadjusted series for each of 29 SIC industry groups. Statistics of the quantity and value of the production of individual industries are scattered through many publications. The Board of Trade publishes some in its *Journal* including footwear, machine tools, man-made fibres, motor vehicles, textiles (monthly), and computers and other electronics industry products (quarterly).

Board of Trade Business Monitor, Production Series is a group of more than sixty series of leaflets, each on a specific product, published monthly or quarterly giving statistics of deliveries or sales and, for some products, orders in hand. The list of products covered is increasing, and so far includes such widely varied goods as bedding, rubber, mechanical handling equipment, stationery, gloves, salt, watches and clocks, safety razor sets and blades, soap and synthetic detergents, and internal combustion engines. The Central Statistical Office is currently engaged in detailed discussions with trade organisations in a very wide range of industries with a view to improving or beginning statistical publications relating to specific industries and products. The results of these discussions will become evident in the near future in the extension in scope and detail of industrial statistical series, especially in relation to sales figures.

Some of the Board of Trade series are reproduced in *Monthly Digest of Statistics,* which also includes production, sales or stocks data for other products including agricultural machinery, scientific instruments, synthetic dyestuffs, paint and varnish, plastics, mechanical and electrical engineering products (both industrial and domestic), shipbuilding, trucks and tractors, and hosiery. These are quarterly series and the *Digest* also contains monthly production statistics for fertilisers, sulphur and sulphuric acid, and the iron and steel, non-ferrous metals, vehicle, leather, timber, paper, rubber, and textile industries in some detail.

Production of the **fuel and power industries** is well documented in the Ministry of Power's *Digest of Energy Statistics*: for each of the major types of energy source (coal, coke, petroleum, natural gas, town gas and electricity) there are detailed tables of production, sales, prices, consumption and stocks. Productivity and employment data are given for coal, and separate production figures for anthracite and open-cast coal. The *Digest of Energy Statistics* also contains annual statistics of energy consumed by user by type, by industry by type, and by region by type. Summaries of many of these series are published and kept up to date in *Monthly Digest of Statistics,* and the Ministry of Power is examining the possibility of producing a new statistical publication at more frequent intervals.

Of all British industries the **construction industry** is probably the best served by the government with statistics. Two most useful and detailed guides to construction statistics have been issued by the Ministry of Public Building and Works: *Directory of Construction Statistics* (HMSO, 1968) and *Inventory of Construction Statistics* (3 vols, HMSO, 1968) (this is available only in certain libraries). The *Directory* contains a descriptive analysis of official statistical series, a list of publications analysed, and a subject index to the analysis. Overall this is an excellent guide, supported by the *Inventory* for those who require a more detailed description of the individual series. The Ministry also publishes *Monthly Bulletin of Construction Statistics* (with an annual supplement) which gives detailed statistical information about all aspects of construction and the industry in its ten sections: cost and production indices, value of output and new orders, employment, housing, production of materials and components, exports, industrial building, local authority design work, Northern Ireland, and value of work done and operatives employed by local authorities.

Annual estimates of total **stocks and work in progress** are published in *National Income and Expenditure*: net capital stock by sector by type of asset, gross capital stock by industry and by type of asset, by industry by two types of asset, changes in stocks/work in progress by fourteen industry groups (both book value and physical changes) and capital formation in stocks by sector. *Economic Trends* includes quarterly estimates of the changes in total, manufacturers' and distributors' stocks at current and constant prices (adjusted and unadjusted). Statistics of manufacturers' and wholesalers' stocks are published annually in the *Board of Trade Journal* based on the *Census of Production* and special inquiries. All are published as book values and at constant prices, adjusted and unadjusted series. Retailers' stocks are covered by indices of stocks at current and constant prices published monthly in the *Board of Trade Journal,* and based on the returns from a small sample of retailers. *Monthly Digest of Statistics* includes some data on commodity stocks for a few goods such as coal, coke, sulphur, and iron and steel.

Input and output statistics for industry are difficult to collect, and are only available in detail from the *Census of Production* returns. Until the 1963 *Census* there were input-output tables in the *Census* report, but for the latest tables a separate publication is planned. Broad input and output data are published in the annual *National Income and Expenditure* for gross domestic product by industry group by type of income, wages and salaries by fourteen industry groups, expenditure and output at constant prices, and an index of output at constant factor cost for eighteen industry groups. A similar index for nine industry groups appears quarterly in *Economic Trends*.

Statistics of **corporate finance** are published in several forms in different sources. *National Income and Expenditure* includes companies' appropriation account and capital account separately for industrial/commercial and financial companies. 'Trends in company finance' is a quarterly article with a few broad statistics in *Board of Trade Journal*: a summary balance sheet of about two hundred quoted companies. The most detailed official statistics are in the Board of Trade's *Company Assets, Income and Finance* an irregular publication which lists British quoted companies in descending order of size of net assets. In addition to assets there are for each company statistics of liabilities, stocks, income, reserves, and depreciation provisions. Other tables give the distribution of companies by industry, by net assets, and by average income. *The Times 500* is an annual list of British quoted companies, again in descending order of size.

Financial details of over 5000 British quoted and unquoted companies are to be found in the card services of Extel Statistical Services Ltd. and Moodies Investors Service Ltd. Both offer details of companies' financial position in a card service which is continuously kept up to date. The information on each company is standardised as far as the sources will allow and includes capital structure, dividends, summary balance sheet and any other financial information such as the value of sales, stocks, etc., which is available. The main source of the data is the annual report and accounts of the company, and up-to-date information is culled from newspaper and stock exchange reports. Dun and Bradstreet's *Guide to Key British Enterprise* and *Middle Market Directory* contain summary information about public and private companies whilst the *Stock Exchange Official Year Book* includes only public companies.

A quarterly article containing and commenting on the statistics of industry's **capital expenditure** appears in the *Board of Trade Journal* with data by industrial sector and by type of asset. *National Income and Expenditure* contains annual estimates of gross domestic fixed capital formation at constant and current prices by sector and by type of asset, by twelve industry groups, and by industry by type of asset. There are also tables of capital consumption by sector and by type of asset, and of net domestic fixed capital formation by sector and by type of asset. *Economic Trends* includes quarterly estimates of gross domestic fixed capital formation at current and constant prices by nine industry groups, by sector and by type of asset.

The *Board of Trade Journal* publishes annual and quarterly estimates of **investment** in manufacturing industry and distributive and service trades based on returns from a sample of firms. A similar sample also provides data on **investment intentions** published in the *Journal* three times a year, though there is little industrial detail available. The Ministry of Power's *Capital Investment in the Coal, Gas and Electricity Industries* includes investment plans for these industries. Housing and industrial building intentions are estimated by the Ministry of Public Building and Works semiannually, and the Board of Trade quarterly, respectively.

The annual *Report of the Commissioners of Inland Revenue* includes statistics of **profits** assessable for tax purposes by trade group, appropriation of corporate income, trading profits and incomes under different tax schedules by trade. From 1970 most statistical series previously in the annual *Report* appear in *Inland Revenue Statistics*. Tax returns also form the basis for the item in the factor incomes table of *National Income and Expenditure*: the table of trading profits by twenty-two industry groups. There are also quarterly statistics of corporate income and its allocation in *Economic Trends* in addition to a quarterly index of companies' gross trading profit.

Acquisitions and mergers of companies are analysed by the Board of Trade if the assets are more than £0·5 mill. A quarterly article in the *Board of Trade Journal* gives data on the number of acquisitions and the expenditure in cash and shares by twenty-three industry groups. For mergers or takeovers where more than £10 mill. is involved details of the transaction are given, with the names of the companies. Statistics of **bankruptcies** are published by the Board of Trade in *Bankruptcy: General Annual Report* which includes the amount of insolvency, the number of cases by County Court area and the number and amount of insolvency by type of business.

So far we have been considering chiefly statistics emanating from official sources and government departments. There is a vast amount of statistical data collected by trade associations, employers' federations, industrial research organisations and semi-official bodies such as the nationalised industries. Some of this data is available only to members of the organisation, but some is published and thus made more widely available, either in separate publications, in articles in journals or in the annual report of the organisation.

The most comprehensive guide to these sources is Gordon Wills' *Sources of UK Marketing Information* (Nelson, 1969) which was sponsored by the Market Research Society. Professor Wills includes official and unofficial sources both serial and non-serial, giving for each title notes on the population sampled and the coverage, and where relevant, sample size and method of collection. This is a very good guide, and especially useful for its detail of **unofficial sources,** only a few examples of which can be noted here.

The Society of Motor Manufacturers and Traders publishes an annual volume, *Motor Industry of Great Britain* which gives very detailed figures of car and commercial vehicle production in the UK and in selected overseas countries, registrations of vehicles, and overseas trade. The UK statistics on all these subjects are kept up to date in the Society's *Monthly Statistical Review*. A similar annual volume, *Iron and Steel: Annual Statistics for the UK* and the monthly *Iron and Steel: Monthly Statistics* are issued by the British Steel Corporation. The annual volume contains very detailed data on the industry, including raw materials, fuel, scrap, labour, production, prices, capital expenditure, uses of steel and foreign trade. There is less detail on the UK industry in the monthly publication, but it includes some production and export figures for overseas countries. The Electricity Council publishes an annual *Handbook of Electricity Supply Statistics* which includes details of plant capacities, output, lines, distribution, costs, sales, users, employment, prices and earnings in the industry.

As examples of the statistical publications of other, widely differing bodies, one can quote the Tobacco Research Council's irregular *Statistics of Smoking in the United Kingdom* (5th edn, The Council, 1969) which includes the sales of tobacco products by type of product and by sex, age group, social class, district and occupational group of consumer. *Birds' Eye Annual Review* is a general review of the frozen food market, with a few pages of useful statistics, mostly culled from other sources. The Scientific Instrument Manufacturers' Association of Great Britain has an irregular series of circulars on the production, trade and potential markets for scientific instruments, taken for the most part from official sources, but very usefully gathered together and republished. The Economic Development Committee for Electronics has been leading the field in interest in the publication of industry statistics: they produce an *Annual Statistical Survey of the Electronics Industry,* a guide to sources: *Electronics Industry Statistics and their Sources* (NEDO, 1968) and the Committee has surveyed the publication of statistics relating to the industry and made recommendations in *Statistics of the Electronics Industry* (NEDO, 1967). More work of this nature is to be encouraged, and should be forthcoming from the 'little Neddies'. A firm of hop merchants, Wigan Richardson and Co. publish an annual *Hop Report* which reviews the season's hop production and comments on trends in the industry. The report contains a small number of very detailed data of production, yield and trade.

Agriculture

As with the periodicals, abstracts and monographs, the statistics of agriculture tend to be found in most detail in separate specialised publications. There are three main sources of detailed annual statistics, *Agricultural Statistics, Annual Review and Determination of Guarantees,* and *Farm Incomes in England and Wales.* An interesting and useful volume of historical agricultural statistics is the Ministry of Agriculture, Fisheries and Food: *A Century of Agricultural Statistics: Great Britain, 1866–1966* (HMSO, 1968) which outlines the history of British agricultural statistics and surveys the available series. It provides a very clear demonstration of the increase in statistical data published since 1945. The Ministry's new edition of *Agricultural and Food Statistics: a Guide to Official Sources* (Studies in Official Statistics, No. 14, HMSO, 1969) is the most up-to-date guide to this subject, and the National Economic Development Office has issued a complementary volume: *Food Statistics: a Guide to Major Official and Unofficial United Kingdom Sources* (NEDO, 1969).

Production statistics are published in *Agricultural Statistics,* of which there are separate volumes for England/Wales and Scotland, with a third volume summarising the first two for the UK as a whole. There are detailed figures of acreages by crop, number of livestock, production of individual crops, horticultural production by crop, machinery in use, employment, and price indices for products and materials. The England/Wales and Scotland volumes give more detail including yields per acre, size of holdings by crop

143

acreage or livestock numbers, have more detailed prices sections, and many of the tables give series by counties. *Monthly Digest of Statistics* summarises many of these annual figures and gives more frequent production, stocks and sales data for many products: there are semi-annual figures of the numbers of cattle, sheep, pigs and poultry, all by type and/or age, and quarterly figures for the production of compound feedingstuffs by type. Monthly production, stocks and sales of cereals and some cereal products appear in the *Monthly Digest of Statistics* and monthly production, disposals and stocks of the main animal feedingstuffs, potatoes, sugar and jam/ marmalade. Production figures only are published for a range of agricultural products including meat, bacon/ham, canned meat, oilseeds, margarine, milk, milk products, eggs, canned fruit and vegetables, chocolate/sugar confectionery, tea, coffee, soft drinks, spirits and beer. The number of animals slaughtered by type, quantity of fish landed and home consumption of wine and beer are also given monthly.

Indices of **agricultural prices** are published monthly in *Monthly Digest of Statistics* and include indices of market and gross prices of wheat, cattle and pigs, market prices of barley, and gross prices of milk, eggs and potatoes. More detailed annual price statistics are published in *Agricultural Statistics*. The annual *Household Food Consumption and Expenditure* includes very detailed indices of prices, purchases and demand for a very wide range of food products.

Proposals for **subsidies** to agricultural producers are in the *Annual Review and Determination of Guarantees,* a white paper published by the Ministry of Agriculture, Fisheries and Food. It gives a general review of the state of the industry, and for each major product a review of the present situation and future prospects, including subsidy proposals. For each product there is also the estimated costs of exchequer support by price guarantees or production grants.

The **income** of the industry depends very largely on the price structure and the extent to which the government is willing to support this. *Farm Incomes in England and Wales* is published annually and gives a great amount of detailed data on farm income by type of farm, by crop, and by region. Estimates of the **stocks** of certain individual products and agricultural inputs are given in *Monthly Digest of Statistics*.

Agriculture is treated as an industry in the *Standard Industrial Classification* so that many statistics relating to industry also include agriculture as an industrial division. Thus statistics of agricultural employment, unemployment, earnings and wage rates are to be found in *Employment and Productivity Gazette* where this data is published with an industrial breakdown.

Labour

The first pamphlet in the series *Guides to Official Sources* issued by the Interdepartmental Committee on Social and Economic Research is on *Labour Statistics* (rev. edn, HMSO, 1958). This is a useful, but now somewhat dated guide to British sources. Most British official statistics on labour matters are first published in *Employment and Productivity Gazette,* and many are later reproduced in *Monthly Digest of Statistics.* Quarterly, semi-annual and annual statistics are first published with a commentary as an article in the *Gazette.* These often contain more detailed statistics than are repeated in the regular monthly statistical section. The series described below are in the *Gazette* except where indicated. The Department of Employment and Productivity is about to produce a *Yearbook of Labour Statistics,* the first volume relating to 1969, which will summarise the full range of employment, prices, wage rates and earnings statistical series for the year. The last similar volume, *Abstract of Labour Statistics* was published in 1936, and the Department intends to publish a preliminary historical volume of the *Yearbook of Labour Statistics* to fill the gap between 1936 and 1969.

Total working population is given quarterly as both adjusted and unadjusted figures by different sectors of civilian and service employment. Statistics of **employees in employment** are quarterly by standard regions, and monthly by eighteen industry groups. Monthly estimates are made of employees by sex by *Standard Industrial Classification* minimum list heading groups. The *Census of Production* contains statistics of total employment and employment by size of firm for the specific industries covered by the *Census* enquiry. Employment in the construction industry is given in *Monthly Bulletin of Construction Statistics.* A basic volume of labour statistics for agriculture was produced by the Ministry of Agriculture, Fisheries and Food: *The Changing Structure of the Agricultural Labour Force in England and Wales: Number of Workers, Hours and Earnings, 1945–1965* (The Ministry, 1967), which brings together new analyses of the results of many inquiries by government departments in this period.

Unemployment is an important economic indicator, and the statistics are suitably detailed. Three types of unemployment are recognised: temporarily stopped, wholly unemployed and

145

registered unemployed. For the first two there are monthly statistics by sex and by standard region (separating school-leavers who obviously affect the data at certain times of the year), and by sex by SIC minimum list heading industries. Statistics of wholly unemployed are given monthly for men, women and young persons separately by duration of unemployment, and by sex by standard region by duration. Quarterly statistics of wholly unemployed by occupation by sex by region, and monthly statistics of the wholly unemployed excluding school-leavers by eight industry groups in both adjusted and unadjusted series are published. Unemployed workers registered at employment exchanges are much easier to count, and the statistics of this group are more detailed: monthly figures of men, women and young persons separately, the percentage rates in development areas and local areas (i.e. selected large towns), and semi-annually the number by sex by twelve age groups by duration of unemployment, and by sex by three age groups by duration by standard region.

The number of **unfilled vacancies** registered at employment exchanges is also a useful indicator of the industrial climate, and statistics are published monthly for men and women (adjusted and unadjusted series) and young persons. *Employment and Productivity Gazette* also contains quarterly figures of notified vacancies by sex by occupation (by region annually). There are also monthly figures of vacancies for men, women, boys and girls by twenty-seven industry groups and by standard region. Similar details are published of the number of **placings** made by employment exchanges.

Statistics of **overtime and short-time** working ('short-time' separates stood off for the whole week from working part of the week) are published monthly in the *Gazette*: the number of operatives involved, hours worked (or lost) by thirteen industry groups and up to eighteen selected SIC minimum list heading industries.

The *Gazette* includes monthly indices of total and average **hours of work** by operatives in six industry groups. More detailed statistics of actual average hours worked by manual workers in twenty-two industry groups are available twice a year. *Time Rates of Wages and Hours of Work* and *Changes in Rates of Wages and Hours of Work* give details of the collective national and local agreements on hours of work for specific industries and occupations.

Strikes were always a statistical problem for the labour economist, but the published figures have improved in recent years. The *Gazette* now includes monthly data on the number of workers involved in **stoppages,** the number of working days lost by twenty-seven industry groups cumulating from January each year, with comparative statistics for the previous year. Statistics of stoppages by cause, showing the number, and the number of workers involved, are published monthly.

There are few official statistics on the membership of **trade unions.** Part 4 of the annual *Report of the Chief Registrar of Friendly Societies* includes data on the total membership of registered unions by sex, and of the membership of individual unions with more than 100 000 members. Registered unions are then grouped into twenty-eight industry groups and for each total membership, income, and expenditure, including political fund transactions is given. Similar figures are given for employers' associations, but with no industrial breakdown. The *Report* of the annual *Trades Union Congress* contains a list of unions affiliated to the TUC with the membership of each given separately for men and women. Since many of the white-collar unions are not affiliated to the TUC the statistics for these are difficult to obtain.

Prices and Incomes

The main source of the first publication of statistics of prices and incomes is the monthly *Employment and Productivity Gazette* issued by the Department of Employment and Productivity.

There is a monthly index of **earnings** of all employees by twenty-four industry groups, but more detailed statistics are available less frequently. These annual and semi-annual statistics are first published in an article in the *Gazette* which often gives more detail than is reproduced later in the regular monthly statistical section. Semi-annual statistics published in this way include manual workers' average weekly earnings and average hourly earnings by sex by twenty-two SIC industry groups as a value figure. For adult males in manufacturing there are semi-annual indices of average weekly earnings including overtime, and average hourly earnings excluding overtime, both by occupation in four industry groups. Administrative, technical and clerical employees are taken together in an annual table of average weekly earnings by twenty industry groups, each by sex. Separate tables for clerical employees and 'salaried' employees give average weekly earnings as value and index figures annually. Some of these tables of earnings are summarised in *Monthly Digest of Statistics*. A new survey of earnings, using different methods and breakdown of results was published in *Employment and Productivity Gazette* during 1969. The new survey is now being evaluated, and the recommendations of the expert group on its future use may entail the replacement of some of the earlier series noted above.

Employment and Productivity Gazette includes for manual workers only, monthly indices of basic weekly and hourly **wage rates** separately for men, women and juveniles, and by eighteen industry groups. The most detailed figures of wage rates are published in the annual *Time Rates of Wages and Hours of Work* and kept up to date monthly by *Changes in Rates of Wages and Hours of Work*. These publications give summaries of all collective agreements between workers and employers at both the national and local level on wage rates and the normal working week. The information is very detailed and there is no industrial approach since these agreements are based on trades and occupations, rather than across-the-board agreements for whole industries.

The problem of **wage drift,** the relationship between wage rates and earnings, is illustrated by a series of semi-annual statistics in *Employment and Productivity Gazette*. These consist of the percentage change over the corresponding month of the previous year of average weekly-wage earnings, average hourly-wage earnings (including and excluding overtime) and average hourly wage rates.

The annual *Report of the Commissioners of Inland Revenue* is an excellent source of statistical data on incomes from various sources, and of personal incomes linked to other economic variables: family circumstances by income, incomes by region: giving income distribution by source, e.g. pensions, rents, salaries, professional earnings and wives' incomes. From 1970 these series appear in *Inland Revenue Statistics*.

National income statistics also include some aggregates for the personal sector: figures for the income and expenditure account and capital account, categories of personal income, and the distribution of personal income before and after tax by numbers and by value. These are all included as estimates annually in *National Income and Expenditure*; in rather less detail, *Economic Trends* includes quarterly estimates of personal income, expenditure and saving.

The general index of **retail prices** is first published as a single index number in the *Board of Trade Journal*. The detailed indices are published in *Employment and Productivity Gazette* where there are separate indices for foodstuffs with and without seasonal variations, home-produced and imported food, and eleven other commodity groups. These, and the indices for all groups and subgroups are published monthly. There are deficiencies in the national retail price index in that it glosses over regional differences in prices, and the differences in purchases made by households with different compositions and incomes. A *Report of the Cost of Living Advisory Committee* (Cmnd. 3677) (HMSO, 1967) advised that there should be separate 'pensioner-household' and regional price indices. The first of these relating to one-person and two-person pensioner-households was first published in *Employment and Productivity Gazette* for June 1969, and quarterly figures are to follow.

Indices of **wholesale prices** are published in an annual article in the *Board of Trade Journal* which gives details of the changes in the prices of the products and materials used in twelve industry groups, including indices of the prices of many specific industrial products. The monthly indices of wholesale prices in the *Journal* give considerably less detail, but there is a wide range of unpublished wholesale price indices available from the Board of Trade: details are given in *Board of Trade Journal,* vol. 196, No. 3753, 21st February, 1969, p. 555.

Other **price indices** are to be found in *Monthly Bulletin of Construction Statistics* for the cost of new construction (quarterly), the average price of new houses (quarterly), and the prices of more than thirty construction materials (monthly). The *Monthly Digest of Statistics* reproduces many of the price indices noted above, and also contains monthly index numbers of the market and/or gross prices of some agricultural products, and two monthly indices of merchant shipping freight rates.

National Income and Expenditure contains a most useful collection of statistics of **consumers' expenditure** by product groups, and quarterly estimates appear in *Monthly Digest of Statistics* at current and constant prices (adjusted and unadjusted series) under the following headings: food, alcoholic drink, tobacco, housing, fuel/lighting, clothing, durable goods, other goods, other services. There are subdivisions of many of these headings which give estimates for individual goods. *Family Expenditure Survey* is now published annually, and the results are used to define the 'basket of goods' used to calcuate the index of retail prices. The *Survey* is the result of returns by about 11 000 households of expenditure on a wide range of goods and services, and comprises 46 tables including household income and expenditure by quarterly periods, by income of household, by income by composition of household, by income by broad area, by income by broad occupational group, characteristics of households, and distributions of weekly earnings. It also includes a series of regional analyses of households included in the sample. Preliminary results of the *Survey* are published in *Employment and Productivity Gazette.*

Expenditure on food is a large factor in consumers' expenditure, and there is more detailed data published than is described above:

Monthly Digest of Statistics includes quarterly estimates of expenditure on and consumption of each major food item, with an analysis by income and by composition of household. By far the most detailed statistics of food consumption by quantity are contained in the annual report of the National Food Survey Committee, issued by the Ministry of Agriculture, Fisheries and Food, and entitled *Household Food Consumption and Expenditure.* Statistics are given of geographical, social class, household composition, and family composition, differences in food consumption and expenditure, with considerable detail by specific foods. Quarterly results of the survey, in less detail, a*e published in the *Board of Trade Journal* which also includes an annual estimate of food consumption.

It is only in recent years that **productivity** statistics as such have been published regularly with an industrial breakdown. *Employment and Productivity Gazette* now includes annual and adjusted quarterly indices of output, employment, and output per person employed by nine industry groups, and annual indices of wages/salaries and labour cost per unit of output by eight industry groups. These industrial groupings are fairly broad, and for more detail of per capita output the statistics published in the *Census of Production* will provide the raw material from which the researcher must calculate his own figures.

Money and Banking

There are two major statistical sources for the economist working on the British money and banking sector: *Bank of England Quarterly Bulletin, and Financial Statistics.* The latter is a compilation of statistical series from several official, and a few unofficial, sources, and since it is published monthly includes most of the series which appear in the *Bank of England Quarterly Bulletin* though occasionally in less detail.

Banking sector assets and liabilities appear quarterly in *Bank of England Quarterly Bulletin* and in *Financial Statistics*: quarterly data for the liabilities and (in more detail) assets are given for deposit banks, accepting houses, the discount market, and, since 1968, National Giro. Current and deposit accounts and advances of these four banking groups are also analysed by broad sector: government, local authorities, public corporations, financial institutions, companies, and other. Dealings with overseas residents are shown separately. The financial accounts tables of *National Income and Expenditure* include net acquisition of financial assets by sector, and transactions in financial assets by sector by type of asset. **Bank of England assets and liabilities** are published weekly in *London Gazette* and a monthly set of statistics appears in *Financial Statistics* for the Issue Department: notes in circulation and in the Banking Department, and government securities; and for the Banking Department: deposits under four headings, securities under three, and notes/coin.

London clearing banks' balance sheets are supplied by the Committee of London Clearing Bankers monthly and published in *Financial Statistics.* Deposits and major assets are broken down into their components: gross deposits (current, deposit, and other accounts), net deposits (adjusted and unadjusted), liquid assets, special deposits with the Bank of England, investments, advances to customers, coin/notes/balances with the Bank of England (main assets being shown as totals and as percentages of total deposits), money at call/short notice, bills discounted (by type) and investments (British government securities and other investments).

Similar data, for the same dates, are available for the **Scottish banks** as for the London clearing banks and are also published monthly in *Financial Statistics*. Statistics of the **Northern Ireland Banks** are also published in *Financial Statistics,* but are less detailed and refer to different 'make-up' dates.

Accepting houses, overseas banks in the United Kingdom, British overseas and Commonwealth banks, American banks (in Britain), and foreign banks and their affiliates (in Britain): for each of these groups of financial institution quarterly figures relating to the assets and liabilities are published in *Financial Statistics.* Main headings are current/deposit accounts, coin/notes/balances with the Bank of England, balances with other UK banks, money at call/short notice, loans to UK local authorities, sterling bills discounted, British government securities, advances, other assets and acceptances.

The London **Discount Market** Association provides quarterly statistics which appear in *Financial Statistics,* giving details of assets by type, and borrowed funds by source.

Other financial institutions: this term covers a wide range of non-banking institutions concerned in the money and credit markets. Statistics of the sources and use of their funds are published in *Financial Statistics* quarterly except where indicated. **Trustee savings banks** and National Savings Bank: investment by type; **building societies:** liabilities and assets by type, mortgage advances (separating advances on new housing, other housing, and other advances), and monthly figures of shares/deposits, mortgages and net investments, in unadjusted series and some have adjusted series also; **hire purchase companies:** assets and liabilities by type, new credit extended and repayments, and monthly statistics of credit outstanding separately for durable goods shops/department stores and finance houses, indices of new hire purchase business and new credit extended; **unit trusts:** investments by type, with separate figures for UK quoted/unquoted companies and overseas companies' loan capital, preference and ordinary shares, and monthly data on the number of unit holdings, total funds and gross and net sales of units; **insurance companies:** investments by type (note that the Board of Trade's annual *Insurance Business: Statistics* gives greater detail of the insurance companies' account); **superannuation funds:** investments by type.

Bank advances are given in more detail in a quarterly analysis of outstanding amounts of advances by London clearing banks, the Scottish banks, and other banks in *Financial Statistics*. For each group of institution totals are broken down by twelve industry groups, financial (hire purchase companies, property companies, UK banks, and other), services (six groups), personal (separating advances for house purchase from other needs), and advances to overseas residents. A similar analysis of Northern Ireland banks' advances is also published in *Financial Statistics*, though in less detail.

Money supply and bank clearings are key indicators for the monetary economist: *Financial Statistics* includes quarterly statistics of money supply, credit expansion and bank clearings, and monthly currency circulation data.

The **capital market** is also an important monetary sector of the economy, and is fairly well provided with statistics. *Financial Statistics* includes monthly figures for the value of turnover and the number of transactions on the London and Scottish stock exchanges separately. These are divided into separate figures for British government and local authorities' securities, preference and ordinary shares, and (for the London stock exchange only) overseas government securities.

Capital issues and redemptions appear in *Financial Statistics* in some detail: monthly data of gross issues and gross redemptions, and of issues less redemptions in more detail: loan capital, preference and ordinary shares (separating UK public quoted companies and financial companies), and for public quoted companies other than financial there is an analysis by ten industry groups, public utilities, distribution, property companies and others.

Financial Statistics contains several statistical series on **security prices and yields**, though more frequent publication of many of these series can be found in the financial section of many newspapers, especially the *Financial Times* and weekly general economics or financial journals such as *Economist* and *Investors' Chronicle*. For **gilt-edged securities** end-of-the-month figures are published in *Financial Statistics* of net price, gross yield and grossed-up net yield for ten British government securities, net price and gross flat yield for 2½% Consols and 3½% War Loan stocks, and gross yield for the three groups short-, medium-, and long-dated stocks. Price indices for **company securities** are calculated by the *Financial Times* staff, by the *Economist*/Exchange Telegraph team, and by the financial department of *The Times*. *Financial Statistics* reproduces the *Financial Times* actuaries share indices monthly for financial, industrial, preference and debenture stock, and all classes, in addition to the yield figure for each group. The FT index (1962=100) of industrial ordinary shares, and yield is given monthly for capital, durable and non-durable consumer goods industries, and the FT index (1935=100) of ordinary industrial shares and yield. *The Times* indices of industrial share prices for large and smaller companies and capital and consumer goods industries are also published monthly in *Financial Statistics*.

End-of-the-month **rates of interest** are published in *Financial Statistics* for different short-term money: commercial and Treasury bills, deposits with local authorities and hire purchase companies, National Savings Bank, interbank lending, and London clearing banks' deposit accounts and call money. The changes in the Bank Rate, building society deposit, share and mortgage rates, and local authority loans rates (for money borrowed from the Public Works Loan Board) and the dates on which they changed are also given. There are also the end-of-the-month rates of interest on local authority long-term loans, and semi-annual rates of interest paid on deposits in trustee savings banks.

Public Finance

The Treasury controls a large and increasing proportion of the national income, and the government's actions and policies have a deep and wide effect on the whole of the British economy. The statistics of proposed and actual government income and expenditure are therefore of vital importance to the economist.

Detailed data on the **income of government** is published annually in the *Report of the Commissioners of Inland Revenue* and the *Report of HM Customs and Excise*. The former includes detailed figures of receipts from income tax, surtax, profits taxes, corporate taxation, capital gains taxes, and death, estate, and stamp, duties.

153

In addition to the statistics of taxes collected the Inland Revenue *Report* contains a great deal of information on the income, profits and wealth which is taxable: personal income, profits, investment income, and detailed estimates of the number and value of estates by type. The new *Inland Revenue Statistics* includes most of the series previously published in the annual *Report*. Monthly statistics of net receipts by type of tax are published in *Financial Statistics*. The Customs and Excise annual report contains similar detail of the receipts of import and excise duties by groups of product or by types of duty. *Protective Duties* gives detailed statistics of the value of goods imported (and the duty paid on them) under Commonwealth preference, EFTA and full rates, for all items dutiable. These annual figures are supplemented by totals published quarterly in *Financial Statistics*.

Government expenditure is approved by Parliament in the form of estimates: requests by the Treasury for approval of the use of income. The *Civil Estimates* are published annually, and give in immense detail the proposed expenditure on specific projects under the different departmental headings: government and finance, Commonwealth and foreign, home and justice, communications, trade and industry, agriculture, local government, housing and social services, education and science, museums, galleries and the arts, public buildings and common governmental services, other public departments and miscellaneous. *Civil Estimates* also includes notes on many of the proposals. *Supplementary Estimates* are approved by Parliament for additions to original grants where these become necessary during the financial year. From 1969 there is an annual white paper issued by the Treasury giving forecasts of future public expenditure. The first issue, *Public Expenditure 1968–69 to 1973–74* (Cmnd. 4234) includes statistics of public expenditure by programme, and by authority, and in more detail for some of the programmes such as overseas aid, housing, agriculture, transport, social security, education, nationalised industries' capital expenditure and law and order. There are also forecasts of receipts.

In much less detail, summaries of the current and capital accounts of the central government are published in *National Income and Expenditure*. Quarterly estimates of the current and capital accounts appear in *Financial Statistics* and are summarised in *Economic Trends*. *Finance Accounts of the United Kingdom* was an annual synopsis of the Exchequer cash transactions and assets and liabilities for the previous financial year. *Consolidated Fund and National Loans Fund Accounts, 1968–69* is the first of the new series of accounts replacing the earlier *Public Income and Expendi-*

ture Account and the *Consolidated Fund Abstract Account.* Together with its *Supplementary Statements* volume the new publication replaces and includes the information previously published in *Finance Accounts of the United Kingdom* and the *National Debt Return.* Assets and liabilities of each of the funds are given. The *Financial Statement and Budget Report* also contains valuable statistical tables in addition to a review of the economic background to the budget.

Local authorities' finance stems from local rates and from grants from the central government earmarked for specific purposes. *National Income and Expenditure* contains detailed current and capital accounts annually, and quarterly estimates are published in *Financial Statistics* with a summary of the current account in *Economic Trends.*

The most useful sources of statistics of local government finance are *Local Government Financial Statistics: England and Wales* and *Local Authority Financial Returns, Scotland.* These are annual publications giving income and expenditure by source for each rate fund service and trading service, and detailed accounts of special funds, rate fund income, salaries and wages. There are less detailed statistics by class of local authority: County Boroughs, Urban Districts, etc. *Rates and Rateable Values in England and Wales* and *Rates and Rateable Values in Scotland* give, for each authority, the poundage rate, product of a penny rate, total rateable value and the number and value by size and/or type of property. There is rather less detail in the Scottish statistics.

Combined public authorities' finance is the term used for the joint accounts of central and local government. *National Income and Expenditure* contains current and capital accounts, an analysis of current expenditure on goods and services, housing subsidies (separating central and local government subsidies), taxes on expenditure, subsidies, taxes on income and on capital. Quarterly estimates of the combined capital account are published in *Economic Trends.*

Statistics of **public corporations** are found in most detail in the annual reports and accounts of the nationalised bodies themselves, but *National Income and Expenditure* combines and summarises these in a series of tables on operations, appropriation and capital accounts (both analysed by five industry groups). Quarterly appropriation and capital accounts without industrial analysis are published in *Financial Statistics.*

Some trading or commercial services are conducted by government departments, for example, the Forestry Commission, aerodromes, the Royal Mint, Her Majesty's Stationery Office, and the

Export Credit Guarantee Department of the Board of Trade. Accounts and balance sheets for these government activities appear in *Trading Accounts and Balance Sheets* published annually as a House of Commons paper.

International Economics

The statistical needs of the economist concerned with international trade and finance are usually well satisfied. It is relatively easy to check goods passing through international frontiers, and visible trade statistics are some of the earliest and most detailed. This section contains details of the main British sources of data on foreign trade, both visible and invisible, and financial statistics of overseas dealings. International publications giving less detail about these subjects, but on a comparative basis for a large number of countries are described on pp. 171–172.

Just as industries are classified into groups by the *Standard Industrial Classification*, so products in international trade were classified according to the *Statistical Classification for Imported Goods and for Re-exported Goods* (the 'import list') and the *Export List*. These are the British lists of products in a classified scheme related closely to the United Nations' *Standard International Trade Classification* (rev. edn, UN, 1961), which in turn is based on the 'Brussels nomenclature'. Gradually more countries are adopting SITC or a close equivalent for international trade statistics, so that different countries' trade figures are becoming more easily comparable. From January 1970 the British import and export lists have been replaced by *HM Customs and Excise Tariff and Overseas Trade Classification* which combines the trade and tariff classifications of goods into one scheme. HM Customs and Excise *Guide to the Classification for Overseas Trade Statistics, 1970* (HMSO, 1969) correlates the new tariff/trade code numbers with SITC and the earlier import and export list numbers.

The most detailed British statistics of **visible foreign trade** are published in the *Annual Statement of Trade of the United Kingdom*, now in five volumes. All statistics in this publication are by both quantity and value, with the exception of trade in gold and coin, which are by value only. The *Annual Statement of Trade* is published within about twelve months of the year referred to. Volume I is the summary volume of imports and exports by product only. Volume II gives a more detailed breakdown of imports by product, and under each product the principal sources from which it comes. These countries are in geographic-economic groups

156

and there are always subtotals for the Commonwealth/Ireland. Volume II also includes, separately, statistics of re-exports and imports of gold and coin. Volume III deals with exports in the same manner as Volume II, but here the geographic-economic breakdown is for the principal countries of destination. Volume IV gives data on both imports and exports of the UK by country of origin and destination by product. Here there are subtotals under each section heading. Volume V, now published every year, is a summary of imports, re-exports and exports by port (or frontier post) by product, with rather less detail in the product divisions.

The monthly *Overseas Trade Accounts of the United Kingdom* keeps the statistics in *Annual Statement of Trade* up to date, though in a summary form. It contains quantity and value statistics for the month, and cumulating from January each year imports, re-exports and exports, and imports and exports of gold and coin. From January 1970 re-exports are not shown separately from exports. All statistics are by product by country, but with considerably less detail of both than in the *Annual Statement of Trade*. In separate tables there is a total value given for imports, re-exports and exports for each country. The new (1970–) title of *Overseas Trade Accounts of the United Kingdom* is *Overseas Trade Statistics of the United Kingdom*: more detail is now given in the product and geographical breakdown of trade.

These figures are abstracted and summarised yet again in the monthly *Report on Overseas Trade* which gives value only statistics for broad product groups and the trade with broad geographic areas. Index numbers of the volume of trade are given for even broader product groups. Some summary data is also published monthly and annually in *Board of Trade Journal*, which also includes a quarterly article on the overseas trade figures. *Economic Trends* reproduces the broad outline of the foreign trade position, and contains a quarterly commentary on it.

Detailed statistics on Britain's **invisible trade** are difficult to find. Total figures are included in most balance of payments tables, but only those in *United Kingdom Balance of Payments* give a great deal of detail. A newly-instituted series of articles in *Board of Trade Journal* entitled 'Trends in invisible transactions' gives some detail of credit and debit in the invisible trade part of the balance of payments, and there are now tables in the quarterly article on balance of payments in *Economic Trends*. **Tourism** is one item of invisible trade, and an annual article in *Board of Trade Journal* gives some details of the number of overseas tourists coming to Great Britain, and British subjects travelling abroad, with estimates of the expenditure of each group, and the British

157

Travel Association publishes *Digest of Tourist Statistics*, though this is more concerned with numbers than expenditure.

Statistics of the **balance of payments**, that vital indicator of the state of Britain's economic health, are, by their nature, liable to retrospective amendment in the light of later statistical returns. The most detailed, and reliable, data are contained in the annual *United Kingdom Balance of Payments* published about six months after the end of the calendar year referred to. Fifty-eight tables analyse the balance of payments in great detail: the general balance (summary tables), visible trade by area and by commodity, invisibles by area, government, shipping, aviation, travel, interest and investment, loans and liabilities. The *Preliminary Estimates of National Income and Balance of Payments* white paper publishes the first summary estimates about three months after the end of the calendar year.

A quarterly broad survey of the balance of payments appears in the *Board of Trade Journal* and more detailed statistics, with an article commenting upon them and their significance is published in *Economic Trends*. This includes statistics of current and capital accounts, monetary movements, balance of payments with sterling and non-sterling areas, government transactions, interest, investments, liabilities and claims in sterling, gold and currency reserves, and the UK account with the International Monetary Fund. *Financial Statistics* also contains some quarterly summary balance of payments statistics of current account, long-term capital account and monetary movements. More detailed data are included of UK external liabilities and claims by type and by region or group of countries, and monthly gold/currency reserve holdings and the IMF account. *National Income and Expenditure's* table of international transactions summarises overseas credits and debits in broad groups.

Gold and currency reserves have been mentioned above, and a bare statement of the total at the end of each month is published in the *Board of Trade Journal*.

The increasing interest in **foreign aid** has led to more detailed statistics being published. *Financial Statistics* contains quarterly statistics of multilateral and bilateral aid, separating aid to Commonwealth and to foreign countries. More detail appears in *United Kingdom Balance of Payments* in its annual statistics of aid and private investment in developing countries. The most detailed data of British aid to overseas countries are in the annual publication of the Ministry of Overseas Development, *British Aid Statistics*, where details are given of both financial and technical assistance by type by country.

The most up to date **rates of exchange** both spot and forward are to be found in the daily newspapers, especially *The Times* and *Financial Times*, for a small number of foreign currencies, and *Financial Statistics* includes the average monthly and end-of-the-month spot and forward rates for about two years for thirteen major world currencies. *Pick's Currency Yearbook* is an invaluable reference tool for detailed information on world currencies and exchange rates.

Transport

There are several official and unofficial sources of data on British transport. The most comprehensive annual statistical publication on passenger transport is compiled by the Ministry of Transport from its own sources and from those of other government departments, notably the Board of Trade: *Passenger Transport in Great Britain*. This contains very detailed statistics of passenger transport by rail and by public service road vehicles including the number of vehicles, rolling stock, seating capacity, passenger miles, vehicle miles, etc. The sections on private road transport and domestic air services are in much less detail. The 1968 volume also contains the results of the 1965 National Travel Survey. Summary monthly and quarterly statistics of inland transport are included in *Monthly Digest of Statistics*. The annual reports of the British Railways Board and London Transport Board contain details of the undertakings, capital formation, stocks and operations.

Highway Statistics, an annual statistical report by the Ministry of Transport, includes figures of vehicle registrations, estimates of road mileage and traffic, road expenditure and details of car ownership and the number and use of commercial vehicles. *Basic Road Statistics* published annually by the British Road Federation includes figures of motor vehicle registrations, road traffic and accidents, the road transport industry, roads, and motor taxation; whilst *British Shipping Statistics*, an annual publication of the Chamber of Shipping of the United Kingdom contains data on shipping by tonnage, by type, by size, shipbuilding, shipping movements, laid-up shipping, shipping as an invisible export and the cost of shipping. *Monthly Digest of Statistics* has some tables on merchant shipping compiled by the Board of Trade and the Ministry of Transport, including the size of the fleet, entrances and clearances, and passenger movement by air and by sea.

The annual reports of the state airlines contain a number of valuable statistical tables, but the most promising series of statistical publications in this field is the *Board of Trade Business Monitor, Civil Aviation Series* which so far covers air passengers, air freight and mail, airport activity and airlines' operating statistics in monthly reports.

Advertising

Industry's expenditure on advertising is an important facet of marketing which is now well handled statistically in *Advertising Statistical Review*. After many changes of style and title, it now comprises statistics of expenditure on TV and press advertising separately for a very large number of individual branded products. There are summaries by product group, by type of advertising, and for press advertising by type of publication.

Distribution

Because of the large number of reporting establishments the distributive trades are always poorly represented in the statistical sources: *Monthly Digest of Statistics*, for example, includes only index numbers of retail trade and stocks, and these are estimates based on returns from a small sample of large outlets. The only comprehensive detailed statistics available are in the irregular *Census of Distribution* which is primarily a census by region by type of retail outlet. Part 1 comprises establishment tables: the number of establishments, turnover and employment, by product sold. Parts 2 to 13 are area tables giving similar information to that in Part 1 for each borough and urban district, and for the region as a whole. Part 14 contains the organisation tables: owners and firms, rather than establishments, by form of organisation (multiples, large independents, co-operatives) by broader product group, and giving turnover, stocks, and gross profit margins. The Business Statistics Office is to publish the final results of the 1966 sample *Census of Distribution* in two volumes: volume 1 dealing with establishments and organisations, turnover, employment, margins, stocks, capital expenditure, wages and salaries; and volume 2 giving the results of supplementary inquiries on transport costs, mail order, self-service and other methods of trading. Since 1950 the *Census* has excluded wholesaling, which is dealt with by special inquiries published in the *Board of Trade Journal*.

Regional Statistics

Regional studies are becoming more important with the development of regional economic policies, and the publication of statistics for standardised regions has improved in recent years. The annual *Abstract of Regional Statistics* attempts to gather together the most useful economic and social statistics available on a regional basis. It has become a more valuable publication as the New Standard Regions are more widely accepted, making comparisons between economic series more feasible. Almost all of the sixty-four tables included now refer to these new regions, except those relating to the Coal, Electricity and Gas Board regions. The main economic groups of tables are population (including interregional migration), employment and unemployment, fuel and power, production (steel and *Census* data only), construction, investment, distribution (*Census* data only), transport (both internal and foreign are especially useful), income and expenditure. Definitions of terms are the same as for the *Monthly Digest of Statistics*. The Central Statistical Office's *List of Principal Statistical Series Available* is the only guide to the regional sources published officially.

The *Digest of Scottish Statistics* and *Digest of Welsh Statistics* are publications very similar to the *Abstract of Regional Statistics* in that they bring together and summarise the economic statistical series for their respective countries. The subject groups are also similar: population and vital statistics, industrial activity, transport and communications, finance and trade. Almost all series in both publications are annual.

Science and Technology

The part played by technological change and research and development in the growth of the British economy are important in the economist's view. A new publication, *Statistics of Science and Technology*, attempts to help economists in their need for more statistical data about this aspect of industrial development. It includes statistics of government expenditure on research and development, the supply of newly qualified manpower, stock and deployment of qualified manpower, staff and students in scientific and technical education, and examination successes. The 1968 edition includes the results of the 1966 survey of professional engineers. The emphasis so far has been on the manpower aspects of scientific development, but there are signs that more information on the financial aspects of research and development work will be made available.

United States Statistics Sources

(*See also* Chapter 8: United States Government Publications.)

The United States Government Printing Office is the largest publishing office in the world, and the United States government one of the most prolific collectors and publishers of statistical information. In the United States as in the United Kingdom, the collection and dissemination of statistics is not centralised but is in the hands of many government departments and agencies, each collecting information for its own purposes. In Great Britain the Central Statistical Office is taking a firmer hand in organising the collection and publication of statistical data, and ensuring consistency of terminology: in the United States the Office of Statistical Policy of the Bureau of the Budget fulfils a similar function, but apparently with less success. Viewing the statistical publications of the US government, one is astonished at the number of publications and the amount of duplication of statistical series.

This section is a very brief review of some of the most commonly available and useful publications of statistical data about the American economy. Most are official publications and, except where noted, are issued by the United States Government Printing Office. The best guide to these publications is *Statistical Services of the United States Government* prepared by the Office of Statistical Standards (rev. edn, 1968). This small book introduces the reader to the organisation of the collection and publication of official statistics, describes the major statistical programmes, and lists the main statistical responsibilities and publications of each government department. It lacks an index, however, and this deficiency is made up by Paul Wasserman's *Statistics Sources* (Gale Research, 2nd edn, 1965) which is an alphabetical subject index in considerable detail, to official and some unofficial sources.

For economists and businessmen one of the most useful **compendia** is *Economic Almanac* (Macmillan, 1940–), a biennial publication of the National Industrial Conference Board. The latest volume contains 580 tables of 'useful facts about business, labor and government in the United States, Canada and other world areas'. Its contents are chiefly on the American economy and include long runs of annual figures on labour, national income, agriculture, mining, construction, manufacturing, transport, trade, consumption and saving, banking and finance, foreign trade and international finance. The official compendium is *Statistical Abstract of the United States* published annually by the Department of Commerce since 1878. Its 1300 tables give it a much wider coverage than *Economic Almanac*, but much non-economic data such as climate, area, education, immigration and government are included. Otherwise the coverage is similar, often in more detail, but for a shorter period in the *Statistical Abstract*. Each subject section begins with short notes on regular sources of statistics and on terminology, and each table has notes on the publications which regularly cover that subject.

For **current economic statistics** the Office of Business Economics issues the monthly *Survey of Current Business* which with its many supplements contains most of the broad statistical series needed by the economist: general business indicators such as production figures in detail, sales, stocks, national income, balance of payments and business income, prices, construction, domestic and foreign trade, labour, employment and earnings, banking, finance and credit, transport, and food and raw materials. In addition to these monthly series there are regular articles on the national income and product tables, balance of payments (quarterly), and personal income (quarterly). There is a good index in each issue. The *Survey of Current Business* also has a large number of regular supplements which are invaluable source-books of longer runs of statistical data. The July issue of the *Survey* is the national income issue, being devoted entirely to the estimates, a long commentary on them, and details of their construction. *National Income and Product Statistics of the United States, 1929–1965* published in 1966 as a supplement to the *Survey of Current Business* provides the historical series. There is a biennial supplement entitled *Business Statistics* which gives the longer historical series of annual figures for most of the statistics noted above; *Balance of Payments Statistics of the United States* is a similar supplement covering international finance, and there have been other irregular supplements on *US Income and Output*, *Personal Income by States*, and *Foreign Business Investments in the US*. The weekly sheet *Business Statistics* gives a few weekly and monthly statistics of business indicators.

The Council of Economic Advisors compiles *Economic Indicators*: monthly statistics of output, income, spending, employment, unemployment, prices and finance displayed as charts and tables. The annual supplement gives the historical run and a descriptive commentary. *Business Conditions Digest*, the new (1968–) title of *Business Cycle Developments* is the monthly compilation of the Bureau of the Census. Its six sections of charts and tables give national income data, cyclical indicators, anticipations and intentions (of orders, prices and investments), other key indicators, analytical measures (such as sales) and some international comparisons of prices and production with about six other developed economies. There is a good index and source list.

Labour statistics are found in most of the compilations noted above, but the primary source books are the Bureau of Labor Statistics' annual *Employment and Earnings Statistics for the United States* and *Employment and Earnings Statistics for States and Areas*. These cover all aspects of employment, unemployment, hours, earnings, hiring, quitting, labour turnover, overtime and short-time, and unemployment insurance. The same department keeps these series up to date in *Employment and Earnings and Monthly Report on the Labor Force. Handbook of Labor Statistics, 1969* is a very useful compendium by the Bureau of Labor Statistics of the historical annual series from the earliest reliable figures to 1968, in some detail, and including family budgets, employee training, trade unions and stoppages. The Bureau also issues *Monthly Labor Review*, which is now chiefly statistical and has descriptive articles on labour matters, and includes a short Current Labor Statistics section of about thirty tables: less detail than in *Employment and Earnings and Monthly Report on the Labor Force*, but between them these two publications provide most of the key labour data monthly. The Department of Labor presents an annual *Manpower Report of the President and a Report on Manpower Requirements, Utilization and Training*, a large report with a small but useful statistical supplement containing projections of population and labour force by states.

Personal income and expenditure in detail are found in the Internal Revenue Service's *Statistics of Income: Individual Income Tax Returns*, one of a series of four annual reports of income statistics. Current Population Reports, series P60 of the Bureau of the Census entitled *Consumer Income* is published annually giving detailed tables of the distribution of income. **Consumer expenditure** statistics appear in the national accounts statistics sources noted above. **Prices** are given as an index in several publications, the best guide being Paul Wasserman's *Sources of Commodity Prices* (Special Libraries Association, 1960), which is now somewhat dated. Current price indices of consumer goods are published monthly in the Bureau of Labor Statistics' *Consumer Price Index*, which covers both goods and services.

Statistics on **industrial production** are detailed and, for some series, frequent. The Bureau of Defense Services Administration publishes an annual *US Industrial Outlook* which reviews the present situation and future expectations of specific industries in short statistical articles. Wholesale and retail trades and a few services such as hotels and advertising are included. The Bureau of the Census is responsible for the large-scale inquiries resulting in the quinquennial *Census of Manufactures* finally published in three volumes: summary statistics consisting of twelve reports on number of establishments, employment, stocks, investment, etc.; industry statistics, about eighty reports on specific industries with details of employment, size of establishment, sales by product, materials and fuel used, and capital investment; and area statistics, fifty-one reports on states, counties, and towns. The Bureau's *Census of Business* is also quinquennial and gives general and detailed data by area of retail, wholesale and service trades. The *Census of Mineral Industries* is carried out at the same time, and published in a similar manner to the *Census of Manufactures.* *Minerals Yearbook* is a four-volume survey of production, consumption and stocks, prices and investment by specific minerals, volume 4 including international statistics. To keep these series up to date there are the *Annual Survey of Manufactures* (Bureau of the Census) and monthly or quarterly *Current Industrial Reports* on individual, very narrowly defined industries, and *Mineral Industry Surveys*. Current industrial production statistics are published in *Federal Reserve Bulletin*, and this is widely accepted as the best monthly source of this information on a broad national basis.

The Department of Agriculture produces most of the statistical series on **agricultural production**, income and prices. One major exception is the Bureau of the Census' quinquennial *Census of Agriculture* now in five volumes covering areas, general report, irrigation, drainage, and special reports (on horticulture, etc.). The Department of Agriculture's main annual statistical publication is *Agricultural Statistics* on yield, acreage, production, and prices of agricultural products, whilst the Economic Research Service has statistical publications with such self-explanatory titles as *Situation and Outlook Reports* (irregular), *Changes in Farm Production and Efficiency* (annual), *Farm Costs and Returns* (annual), *The Hired Farm Working Force* (annual), *Agricultural Finance Review* (annual), and *Farm Income Situation* (quarterly). The Department also conducts irregular censuses on subjects such as irrigation, which are a valuable source of data.

The Board of Governors of the Federal Reserve System are responsible for the statistics on **money and banking**, including consumer credit and saving, and rather surprisingly indices of industrial production and flow-of-funds tables of national accounts: these were pioneered in the *Federal Reserve Bulletin*, a special issue (August 1959) being devoted to the launching. The monthly *Bulletin* also includes articles on current financial problems and conditions and on new or revised statistical series published in the large financial and business statistics section. Main subjects covered are banking, money supply, interest rates, stock market, federal finance, business finance and credit, and a small section of international statistics of balance of payments, gold, exchange rates and capital transactions of the United States. This is one of the key sources of US statistics covering a wide area and carrying a great deal of weight. A useful historical volume is the Board's *All-Bank Statistics, 1896–1955* (The Board, 1959). *The Federal Reserve Monthly Chart Book* graphs a range of banking, finance, national accounts, labour force, price and production data over the short run, and the *Historical Chart Book* is an annual which covers the same field for a longer period.

The Securities and Exchange Commission with its greater control over **capital transactions** than has the Board of Trade in Great Britain, provides good statistical series on security trading and prices in its monthly *Statistical Bulletin*, on corporate capital in the quarterly *Working Capital of US Corporations*, and from a sample of companies' returns *Quarterly Financial Report for Manufacturing Corporations* (jointly with the Federal Trade Commission). The Federal Home Loan Bank Board produces *Savings and Home Financing Source Book*, an annual of statistics on **mortgage** finance. All three main departments, the Federal Reserve System, SEC and FHLBB publish irregular special studies of financial and banking subjects.

Public finance statistics are issued by the Treasury in the monthly *Treasury Bulletin* and *Monthly Statement of Receipts and Expenditures of the United States Government*. The Bureau of the Budget produces the *Budget of the United States Government* which includes considerable statistical data in addition to the tax proposals. *Annual Report of the Secretary of the Treasury on the State of the Finances* gives current and historical data on federal finance. Income tax statistics are published in the Internal Revenue Service's annual *Statistics of Income* in four parts: *Business Tax Returns, Corporation Income Tax Returns, Individual Income Tax Returns* and *Fiduciary, Gift and Estate Tax Returns*. The same department also issues other data on other sources of government tax income, and some irregular special reports.

The Bureau of the Census now takes a quinquennial *Census of Transportation* which covers both goods and passenger **transport**

166

internally, and the Interstate Commerce Commission produces the annual *Transport Statistics in the United States,* and monthly *Transport Economics. Highway Statistics* is an annual publication of the Bureau of Public Roads on motor vehicles, fuel, taxation, and road construction and finance. The biennial publication entitled *Handbook of Airline Statistics* is produced by the Civil Aeronautics Board.

Foreign trade statistics for the United States are published in a great many series, both summary and detailed, and the Bureau of the Census publishes an excellent annual *Guide to Foreign Trade Statistics.* The most important summary reports are FT 900-I *Total Import Trade,* and FT 900-E *Total Export Trade,* which give monthly and cumulating value figures by nine product groups. FT 985 *US Waterborne Foreign Trade* gives volume by trade area, port and type of service, but less detail is given in FT 986 *US Airborne Foreign Trade. Highlights of US Export and Import Trade* is FT 990 and gives summary tables of trade by product by customs regions and by trade area, by method of transport, all monthly cumulative figures. The detailed monthly cumulating reports are FT 135 *US Imports ... Commodity and Country* and FT 410 *US Exports ... Commodity and Country.*

In addition there are seven series of annual reports: FT 150 and FT 450 imports and exports by commodity by country respectively; FT 155 and FT 455 imports and exports by country by commodity respectively; FT 210 imports and FT 610 exports by Standard Industrial Classification groups; and FT 246 imports by Tariff Schedule groups. Most of the detailed reports, both monthly and annual, give statistics by value and quantity This publication pattern changed in 1967, but one of the earliest annuals is *Foreign Commerce and Navigation of the United States* (Bureau of the Census, 1821–).

Balance of payments data in detail appear in the *Balance of Payments Statistical Supplement to Survey of Current Business* and are kept up to date by tables in the *Survey* itself.

Finally, the United States has an official compendium of **historical statistics**: *Historical Statistics of the United States, Colonial Times to 1957* (Bureau of the Census, 1960) with two supplements which bring the data up to 1962. These are large compilations of over six thousand very detailed series with notes on definitions and sources. The note on sources at the beginning of each of the twenty-four subject sections are an excellent guide to United States official statistics. There is a good detailed index to the series at the end of the volume.

International Statistics Sources

(See also Chapter 9: International Organisations' Publications.)

One of the greatest problems facing the economic statistician is the need to compare economic conditions in different countries. The statistical series considered so far in this chapter are concerned with one nation only, and there are obviously many nations producing similar series. Until the end of the First World War, there were few international organisations in the economics field, but with the foundation of the League of Nations and the International Labour Organisation in 1919 work began on producing international statistical series. These aimed to bring together the series produced by each country and to standardise the definitions of terms, and the methods of presenting statistics, to facilitate comparison between countries.

Although work began between the wars, it was not until the middle 1950s that one can say that the international statistical series became reliable, and useful. There remains a lot of work to be done to make the series uniform, and to persuade national governments to accept standard definitions of industries, classifications of products and occupations, and abandon the myriad other variations in terminology. The United Nations and its various agencies have done a great deal to standardise statistical publications, and some of the more important ones are noted here.

The *Standard International Trade Classification (SITC)* was first published in 1950 and the latest edition in 1961. This groups products into ten sections, which are further subdivided into divisions, groups, subgroups, and finally items. This gives a unique *SITC* number to specific products, and a coding by which all foreign trade statistics could be made comparable. Many developed nations had their own classification for trade statistics, but most are now adapting this to conform more closely with *SITC*.

There is a similar classification of industries, the *International Standard Industrial Classification of All Economic Activities (ISIC)*, the latest edition of which was published by the United Nations in 1968. This too is being increasingly adopted by national statistical services. Both *SITC* and *ISIC* are published as numerical classification schemes with alphabetical indexes. A great deal of work is done by the Statistical Office of the United Nations in making recommendations for the standardisation of other statistical series: most are published in Series M of the Statistical Office's publications and include *International Recommendation on the 1963 World Programme of Basic Industrial Statistics* (Series M,

168

No. 17, 1960), *Retail Price Comparisons for International Salary Determination* (Series M, No. 14, 1952–62), and *Report of the Seminar on Sampling Methods, Tokyo, 1965* (Series M, No. 42, 1966). Series M also includes several useful economics bibliographies, such as *Bibliography of Industrial and Distributive Trade Statistics* (Series M, No. 36, 1967), and *Input-output Bibliography, 1963–1966* (Series M, No. 39, 1967).

There are several major international or supranational organisations with economic interests, and the following notes describe some of the more important statistical publications of these bodies. As above, details are given for the latest issues of the publications available at the beginning of 1970. Dates of the first publication are given for some of the most important titles.

General compendia of economic statistics are published by several international organisations. The United Nations' *Statistical Yearbook* (League of Nations, 1926 to 1929) and *Statistical Year-* 1948 and continued the League of Nations' *International Statistical Yearbook* (League of Nations, 1926 to 1929) *and Statistical Yearbook of the League of Nations* (League of Nations, 1930/31 to 1942/44). The latest of the United Nations' *Statistical Yearbook* has sections on population, manpower, agriculture, forestry, fishing, industrial production, mining and quarrying, manufacturing, construction, energy, internal and external trade, transport, communications, consumption, balance of payments, wages and prices, national accounts, private and public finance, international capital flows, health, housing, and education. Statistics for more than 150 countries are included, though some data are not available for all countries. Generally a series of up to ten years' statistics is given.

The United Nations' *Monthly Bulletin of Statistics* keeps many of the series up to date, though there is always less detail by country, and frequently less by subject. Most series are given monthly, and a few quarterly.

The Organisation for Economic Co-operation and Development (OECD) now calls its general statistical serial *Main Economic Indicators* underlining the change in emphasis from the previously entitled *General Statistics*. The Organisation now includes twenty-one full members, with Yugoslavia as an associate member for many purposes. It is worth mentioning here that the United States, Canada, and, since 1964, Japan, are full members of OECD and their statistics appear in all the OECD series. *Main Economic Indicators* has three sections of statistical series: by subject (national accounts, industrial production, retail sales, unemployment and vacancies, wages, consumer prices, exchange rates and international liquidity, each with specific subdivisions) by country,

169

which for most series includes Yugoslavia, and foreign trade indicators. Most series are published monthly. There are supplements to the monthly issue covering historical statistics, consumer prices, and industrial production.

The Statistical Office of the European Communities publishes a *General Statistical Bulletin* which gives statistics for the six EEC countries on industrial production, building, transport, internal trade, employment and unemployment, wages, prices, foreign trade, public finance, and money and credit.

UNESCO has also published a *Statistical Yearbook* which is useful to the economist in its detailed coverage of education, and communications media such as books, newspapers, and broadcasting.

The Comparative Data Unit in the Economics Department of the International Bank for Reconstruction and Development has produced an invaluable loose-leaf volume of *World Tables*. These are eight series of tables covering annual average growth rates, population, labour force, education, selected economic relationships (such as saving as a percentage of GNP, capital-output ratio), resources, product, income, investment, saving, government revenue and expenditure, foreign trade, external debt and reserves, balance of payments and foreign exchange. Statistics are given for a wide range of countries on a comparable basis, being estimated by the Unit or amended as necessary, for 1950/59, 1960/65, and annually from 1965 (in some tables figures are for 1950, 1955, 1960, 1965–). There is inevitably a number of gaps in the tables where data are not available, but the volume is an invaluable aid to comparative studies in economics. New edition in 1971.

National accounts statistics have been available for many countries for only a few years, but their importance in economic planning and policy is paramount. The United Nations' *Yearbook of National Accounts Statistics* (UN, 1958–) now covers the accounts of 98 countries, in a uniform and fairly detailed set of tables. International aggregate tables, in less detail, include estimates for another 28 countries. The sources are quoted, but these are often only the reply of a national government to the United Nations' questionnaire, and fuller accounts are not published elsewhere. *National Accounts Statistics, 1956–1965* is the title of an Organisation for Economic Co-operation and Development publication of 1967, a date which indicates the delay common in the publication of international statistics. This gives the accounts of the twenty-one OECD countries, and there is an annual *National Accounts* volume issued by the Statistical Office of the European Communities.

Foreign trade statistics are more readily available, and as noted above are becoming more easily comparable. The United Nations' compendium *Yearbook of International Trade Statistics* (UN, 1951–) now covers 143 countries. The data are by country, with a summary table, and more details of imports and exports by *SITC* for four years. In addition there is an historical series of about 30 years with a total value figure and index numbers for imports and exports. United Nations' *Commodity Trade Statistics* is a quarterly publication in about twenty-five parts each relating to up to five countries: value and quantity of trade is given for each *SITC* item. The UN *World Trade Annual* (New York, Walker, 1964–) is a four-volume compilation of these returns rearranged under product by country for a selection of the major trading nations.

Direction of Trade is a monthly supplement to *International Financial Statistics* and published by the International Monetary Fund and the International Bank for Reconstruction and Development. It gives the statistics of value (in US dollars) of trade by country by country of source or destination. Its special value lies in its grouping of certain countries to give subtotals for, for example, industrial countries, less-developed areas, oil exporting countries, industrial Western Europe, and Latin America.

The *Statistics of Foreign Trade* published by OECD are remarkably detailed and fairly rapidly published. There are three series: series A, issued quarterly with a less detailed monthly supplement, is subtitled *Overall Trade by Countries*: total value (in US dollars) figures are given for imports and exports for each country and group of countries by source or destination of trade. Series B, *Trade by Commodities: Analytical Abstracts*, is published as six booklets each quarter, each covering about four countries or groups of countries: for each the value of trade in US dollars is given for each five-digit *SITC* group. Series C, *Trade by Commodities: Market Summaries*, is issued in two volumes (imports and exports) quarterly, each quarter cumulating from the beginning of the year. The degree of detail in the *SITC* divisions varies, but for the ten sections, the sixty-one divisions, some groups and subgroups there are volume and value figures by country by source or destination of trade. Single-line totals are given for other groups and subgroups.

Statistics of the foreign trade of the members of the European Economic Community are contained in the monthly *Foreign Trade: Monthly Statistics*, the quarterly *Foreign Trade: Analytical Tables* and the monthly *Overseas Associates: Foreign Trade Statistics*. The Food and Agriculture Organisation of the United Nations publishes an annual *Trade Yearbook* (FAO, 1958–) which with the *Production Yearbook* replaced the earlier *Yearbook of Food and Agricultural Statistics* (FAO, 1947 to 1957). The *Trade Yearbook* gives detailed statistics of trade in specific major agricultural commodities by volume and value for a seven- or eight-year period. Total value data are given for trade by countries. Foreign trade statistics are often included in general volumes of data in narrower subject areas: the Society of Motor Manufacturers and Traders' annual *Motor Industry of Great Britain* includes a very useful section on the international trade in motor vehicles from and to most countries. Similarly, many of the regular surveys of industries in OECD countries noted below contain trade figures.

The most useful compilation of **labour statistics** is the International Labour Office's *Yearbook of Labour Statistics* (ILO, 1935/36–) which now covers more than 170 countries with up to ten series of figures. Main headings include total and economically active population, employment, unemployment, hours of work, labour productivity, wages, consumer prices, industrial accidents and disputes, and there are actual figures and indices given for many of the series, the latter using a uniform base year of 1963 to facilitate comparison. The ILO's quarterly *Bulletin of Labour Statistics* (ILO, 1965–) replaces the statistical supplement to *International Labour Review* and keeps up to date a selection of the series which appear in the *Yearbook*.

Labour Force Statistics, 1956–1967 (OECD, 1969) is the latest OECD compilation: earlier volumes were entitled *Manpower Statistics* and covered the period from 1950. Series include population, total labour force, armed forces, civilian labour force, unemployment, civilian employment, and employment by branches of economic activity (*ISIC* divisions) for each of the twenty-one OECD countries. The Statistical Office of the European Communities publishes an annual review of *Wages* in its Social Statistics series, which also includes several irregular reports on real incomes, social security, accidents, employment, and labour costs in either the EEC or the European Coal and Steel Community.

The International Labour Office has published a volume of *Household Income and Expenditure Statistics, 1950–1964* (ILO, 1967) which is the compilation of the results of a large number of national and international surveys of household income and expenditure. These include sources of income, distribution of household expenditure and consumption expenditure, distribution of expenditure on food, drink, and other items, and quantities consumed of food and other items. Each section is divided into surveys by overall or geographic areas, by social or occupational groups, by economic level (i.e. income or expenditure groups), and by household size groups.

International comparisons of **production statistics** are especially difficult, and economists are indebted to the international organisations and other bodies which compile such data in standardised formats. The Food and Agriculture Organisation publishes many series of statistics on **agricultural production**, the widest ranging being its *Production Yearbook* (FAO, 1958–) which succeeds the *Yearbook of Food and Agricultural Statistics* (FAO, 1947 to 1957). There are short sections on land, population, food supply, prices and wages, and more detailed series on specific crops, livestock and livestock products, and fertilisers and machinery, all by country with up to eight years' figures in each series. The Organisation's monthly *Agricultural Economics and Statistics* keeps some of these series up to date. The FAO also produces some indices of agricultural production. *The State of Food and Agriculture* has been an annual FAO publication since 1947, and is a general review of the world agricultural situation and prospects. The commentary is well supported by statistics and each volume contains special features on important topics for that year.

The *FAO Commodity Review* (FAO, 1961–) comprises a series of statistical reviews of the general agricultural situation and outlook, of prices, of international trade, and of agricultural commodities and raw materials. There are also articles on current topics, such as the 'Kennedy Round' of tariff negotiations, of interest to agricultural economists and planners. A very useful compilation of statistics is the FAO's *World Crop Statistics: Area, Production and Yield, 1948–64* (FAO, 1966), a computer-produced series of tables of products by country. The FAO also publishes the annual *World Grain Trade Statistics* (FAO, 1954/55–) which continued *Grain Exports by Source and Destination* (FAO, 1949 to 1954/55) and *Fertilizers: an Annual Review of World Production, Consumption and Trade* (FAO, 1951– (titles varied)). The *Commodity Bulletin Series* begun in 1947 is a collection of monograph reviews of different agricultural products such as *Sugar* (No. 22, 1952), *The World Rice Economy* (No. 36, 2 vols, 1962/63) and *The World Meat Economy* (No. 40, 1965). Rice is also dealt with in the annual *FAO Rice Report* (FAO, 1963–) which replaced *Rice* (FAO, 1950 to 1962). *Yearbook of Fishery Statistics* (FAO, 1947–) is now published annually in two volumes: *Catches and Landings* and *Fishery Commodities* (disposal of catches and international trade); the *Yearbook of Forest Products Statistics* which began publication in 1947 has two useful cumulations: *World Forest Products Statistics, 1946–*

173

1955 (FAO, 1958) and *World Forest Products Statistics, 1954–1963* (FAO, 1965).

Other organisations publishing international agricultural statistics are worth noting: the Commonwealth Economic Committee publishes irregular surveys of production and trade in wool, and on fertilisers, hides and skins, tobacco, canned foods, agricultural machinery and many other products. Its monthly or quarterly series of Intelligence Services on wool, dairy produce and meat, fruit, tobacco, grain, tropical products, and hides and skins, and the annual *Commodity Series* on fruit, grain crops, meat, and dairy produce, are particularly useful in giving statistics and a commentary and review of the situation of each product. The International Wheat Council publishes an annual *World Wheat Statistics* giving area, production, yield, flour production, foreign trade, stocks, and monthly prices by country and region. The Pan-American Coffee Bureau publishes *Annual Coffee Statistics* (1954– , previously *Coffee Statistics*, annually from 1941 to 1953) which includes in addition to detailed production and consumption statistics, reports on the working of the International Coffee Agreement, and world prices of coffee. A similar publication is the *Sugar Year Book* issued by the International Sugar Organisation which keeps the statistical information up to date in the monthly *Statistical Bulletin*. *Agricultural Statistics* published by the Statistical Office of the European Communities eight times a year should also be mentioned.

Compared with agricultural products, **industrial products** are not well supplied with regular statistical publications. The Organisation for Economic Co-operation and Development published the useful volume of 'historical statistics', *Industrial Production, 1955–1964* (OECD, 1966) but does not issue a general industrial production serial. Instead there are annual surveys of specific industries: *The Chemical Industry, The Iron and Steel Industry, The Non-ferrous Metals Industry, The Engineering Industries in North America, Europe, Japan, The Pulp and Paper Industry, Textile Industry in OECD Countries*, and *The Cement Industry*. Each gives a commentary on production and trade, with statistical tables, and often trends are projected for the next year, and all cover the industries in the European member countries, the United States, Canada and Japan. The regular *Economic Surveys* of OECD countries and the new OECD *Economic Outlook* can be of use in providing some industrial statistics, though they are usually not very detailed.

Industrial Statistics is the title of the quarterly serial and yearbook covering this subject published by the Statistical Office of the

European Communities. The industrial statistics issued by the United Nations Economic Commission for Europe are, not surprisingly, more detailed than those published by other UN Economic Commissions. They include the *Annual* and the *Quarterly Bulletin of Coal Statistics for Europe* (UN, 1952–), *Quarterly Bulletin of Steel Statistics for Europe* (UN, 1950–), *Annual* and *Quarterly Bulletin of Electric Energy Statistics for Europe* (UN, 1960–) and the *Annual Bulletin of Gas Statistics for Europe* (UN, 1950–). All give detailed statistics of production, consumption, and trade for each of the European countries, and some include data for the United States. Other similar serials cover housing and building, and timber. The Economic Commissions for Asia and the Far East, for Latin America, and for Africa have issued some special reports on specific industries in these areas. All the Commissions issue their equivalent of the *Economic Survey of Europe* (annual), and some an equivalent of the supplementary semi-annual *Economic Bulletin for Europe*, which are surveys of the economic situation in the region, and include a few statistics on industries.

Other statistical publications worth noting are *Metal Statistics*, an annual issued by Metallgesellschaft Aktiengesellschaft of Frankfurt-am-Main which provides very useful detailed statistics for ten years of the production of each major non-ferrous metal by country, and *Metal Statistics* (American Metal Mart, annual, 1908–) which gives production and prices on a world-wide basis. The Mineral Resources Division of the Institute of Geological Sciences compiles the *Statistical Summary of the Mineral Industry: World Production, Exports and Imports* published by HMSO, which includes six years' figures of production and trade by country by each specific mineral product.

There are very few sources of international comparative statistics of **finance** other than the few in the *Yearbook of National Accounts Statistics*, but the International Monetary Fund publishes *International Financial Statistics* (IMF, 1948–), monthly with an annual supplement, which now covers more than one hundred countries. For each there are detailed tables including liquidity, central and commercial bank statistics, monetary survey, development banking, interest and prices, international transactions, foreign trade value and prices, balance of payments, and national accounts. Most series are quarterly and a few monthly, and the supplement gives annual data for a period of up to 18 years. Standardisation in the data shown for each country has been achieved to a reasonable and increasing degree. The IMF also publishes a *Balance of Payments Yearbook* (IMF, 1949–), originally in one bound volume each year, but now issued in monthly parts cumulating into an annual loose-leaf volume. The detail given varies between countries, but these are often the most readily available balance of payments statistics for most under-developed countries.

CHAPTER ELEVEN

GENERAL ECONOMICS

JOHN FLETCHER

So far in this book we have reviewed libraries and the way in which they are organised, and looked at the literature of economics in its divisions by type or source: reference tools, periodicals, unpublished literature, government publications, international organisations' publications and economic statistics. In the remaining chapters specialists in different fields of economics review the literature of their subjects, with reference to periodicals, monographs and series.

Most economists would agree that the day of the general economist is past (though there are a few outstanding exceptions to prove the rule), and that specialists are becoming even more specialised. Students of economics now find that they finish with general textbooks early in their courses, and thereafter use specialist texts and, increasingly, journal articles in their specific subject courses. For this reason, this introductory chapter will leave aside general textbooks and concentrate on three main areas of the literature which cover the whole conspectus of economics: abstracting and indexing services, the key to the mass of journal articles; series of monograph publications; and the series of conference proceedings now becoming more common and more important in economics.

Conference Proceedings

Conferences and symposia have in the past played a smaller role in the social sciences than in the natural sciences and technology. The traditional picture is now changing so far as economics is concerned, and national and international meetings of economists discussing a wide variety of specialist topics are becoming more common.

Papers given at conferences are often pre-printed and distributed to those attending the meeting, and some are also more widely available in the 'working papers' series described in Chapter 6. Other conferences do not publish their proceedings as collected volumes of papers, but contributions are later published as articles in professional journals, or as supplements to them: e.g. most papers given at conferences of the Econometric Society if published at all, appear in *Econometrica* or other econometrics journals, whilst the proceedings of the annual meeting of the American Economic Association are published as the special May issue of *American Economic Review*. Here we are concerned only with conference proceedings published as separate volumes.

Three organisations are outstandingly important in organising and publishing economics conferences. The **International Economic Association** was formed in 1949, and now has a membership representing thirty-nine national associations of economists. Conferences of IEA are held at least annually, and are of a very high standard. Earlier conferences have been on *Inflation* (1962) (dates quoted are of the publication, not the conference), *Monopoly and Competition and their Regulation* (1954), and *Theory of Capital* (1961). More recent subjects have included *Public Economics* (1969), *Risk and Uncertainty* (1968), *Backward Areas in Advanced Countries* (1969), and *Activity Analysis in the Theory of Growth and Planning* (1967). All are published by Macmillan in London.

Conference on Research in Income and Wealth is a section of the American National Bureau of Economic Research which organises conferences and NBER publishes the proceedings in the series entitled *Studies in Income and Wealth*. Some are very specific in subject matter, e.g. *Analysis of Wisconsin Income* (No. 9, 1948), but more recent conferences have been on wider subjects and provided excellent research and teaching material: *Input-output Analysis: an Appraisal* (No. 18, 1955), *Models of Income Distribution* (No. 28, 1964), and *Theory and Empirical Analysis of Production* (No. 31, 1967). The most recent conference proceedings have been published by Princeton U.P. for NBER, which previously published them itself.

Also in the same subject area is the **International Association for Research in Income and Wealth** formed in 1947, and with personal members from forty-three countries. It holds approximately annual conferences, since 1949, and publishes the proceedings in the *Income and Wealth* series. Early conferences were without titles, but later ones are devoted to specific topics, such as *Studies in Social and Financial Accounting* (Bowes and Bowes,

1961) and *Middle Eastern Studies in Income and Wealth* (Bowes and Bowes, 1965).

The **Universities-National Bureau Committee for Economic Research** is a joint committee of NBER and university representatives set up to organise conferences, and NBER publishes the proceedings in its *Special Conference Series.* The subjects covered are less narrowly defined than in the *Studies in Income and Wealth* series, and include *Aspects of Labor Economics* (No. 14, 1962), *Demographic and Economic Change in Developed Countries* (No. 11, 1960), *Issues in Defense Economics* (No. 20, 1967) and *National Economic Planning* (No. 19, 1967).

Many **other organisations** sponsor conferences of interest to economists, and publish their proceedings. Some are noted in other chapters in this book, and here it is necessary to mention only a few of the more prolific. The **United Nations,** and especially its regional Economic Commissions, publishes many conference proceedings in addition to the standing United Nations Conference on Trade and Development (UNCTAD). Many are on problems of economic development, and specific in subject matter, such as *Regional Economic Co-operation in Asia and the Far East* (UNECAFE, 1966) and *Seminar on Changes in the Structure of the Building Industry Necessary to Improve its Output* (UN, 1965). The **Conference of European Statisticians** is a permanent body set up by UNECE and the UN Statistical Office to consider improvements in statistical methods at its annual sessions. The Conference also issues recommendations in its series *Statistical Standards and Studies:* No. 19, is a very useful list of *National Statistical Publications issued in 1966* (UN, 1969), promised as the first of an annual series.

Organisation for Economic Co-operation and Development holds numerous conferences of interest to the economist: one series is published under the title *International Seminars,* but most are issued separately, such as *Employment Forecasting* (OECD, 1967) and *The Financing of Industrial Development* (OECD, 1968).

The **International Labour Organisation** holds the International Labour Conference annually, and the invaluable working documents of the various trade committees preparatory to the Conference are available from the International Labour Office in Geneva. The ILO also sponsors other conferences including the International Conference of Labour Statisticians (the eleventh was held in 1966), Regional Conferences (usually on labour problems in developing countries) and special Technical Meetings.

Most conferences organised by the **North Atlantic Treaty**

Organisation are on science or technology, but a few are on economics topics, e.g. *Manpower Research* (Elsevier, 1968) and *Mathematical Models for the Management of Manpower Systems* (English Universities Press, 1970).

Monograph Series

There is an increasing tendency for publishers to issue books in series: monographs by separate authors on allied subjects are grouped together under one series title. Inclusion of a title in a series is no guarantee that its quality is comparable to the remainder of the series, but it may approach its subject in a similar manner.

University Series

With so many universities now having their own publishers it is difficult, and fruitless, to distinguish the universities' series from those of the university presses. Two of the longest-established series in economics are *Cambridge Economic Handbooks* (published jointly by Nisbet and Cambridge U.P.) which includes such classics as U. K. Hicks, *Public Finance* (3rd edn, 1968) and R. F. Harrod, *International Economics* (rev. edn, 1963); and *Harvard Economic Studies,* from Harvard U.P., which includes B. Ohlin, *Interregional and International Trade* (No. 39, 1933), A. Fishlow, *American Railroads and the Transformation of the Ante-bellum Economy* (No. 127, 1965) and *An Econometric Model of Canada under the Fluctuating Exchange Rate,* by L. H. Officer (No. 130, 1968).

Cambridge U.P. also publishes two important series for the Department of Applied Economics at Cambridge University: *Monographs* (No. 6 is *Productivity and Technical Change,* by W. E. G. Salter, 2nd edn, 1966) and *Occasional Papers,* which are slighter works, but none the less important, such as No. 9, G. Clack, *Industrial Relations in a British Car Factory* (1967) and the interim and final reports on the *Effects of UK Direct Investment Overseas,* by W. B. Reddaway (Nos. 12 and 15, 1967 and 1968). A third series from Cambridge University's DAE is *Programme for Growth,* published by Chapman and Hall, which is devoted to the continuing results of work on the Cambridge Growth Project. Glasgow University's *Social and Economic Studies: New Series* are published by Allen and Unwin, whilst its *Social and Economic Studies:*

Occasional Papers and Research Papers come from Oliver and Boyd. All three series now emphasise regional studies to a large degree.

The Cowles Foundation for Research in Economics at Yale University has a series of *Monographs* published by Wiley which includes K. J. Arrow's *Social Choice and Individual Values* (2nd edn, 1963) and some conferences sponsored by the Foundation. Princeton University's International Finance Section publishes several series of pamphlets of a high quality including *Princeton Studies in International Finance, Essays in International Finance,* and *Special Papers in International Economics.* The Industrial Relations Section of the same university publishes a *Research Report Series,* and there are many others in this subject noted in Chapter 18. The Center of Planning and Economic Research in Athens is an off-shoot of the University of California, and publishes several series: *Research Monographs* and *Training Seminars* are the most valuable. The *Publications* series of Yale University Economic Growth Center is important, and published by Irwin, whilst the *Yale Studies in Economics* is published by Yale U.P., and has a less narrow subject field.

Publishers' Series

Most commercial publishers important in this field now issue at least one series in economics: several have been noted above, and only a few more of the major ones can be mentioned here. McGraw-Hill has an *Economic Handbook Series,* a *Series in International Development,* and a *Labor Management Series,* and Prentice-Hall has its *Foundations of Modern Economics Series,* and a series on *Modern Economic Issues.* The same company also issues a *Ford Foundation Doctoral Dissertation Series* in co-operation with the Foundation: most are in industrial and business economics. *Irwin Series in Economics* is that publisher's major series, but it also issues the *AEA Series of Republished Articles in Economics* for the American Economic Association.

Macmillan is an important economics publisher which is exceptional: only the IEA conference series noted above form a series; *Macmillan Series in Economics* comes from the New York publishing house of the same name. The *Praeger Special Studies in International Economics and Development* series is worth noting, as is *Reprints of Economics Classics* by Kelley, New York.

Of the European publishers North-Holland Publishing Co. of Amsterdam is outstanding in economics: its two series, *Contribu-*

tions to Economic Analysis and *Studies in Mathematical and Managerial Economics* are of a very high standard indeed. A much smaller series, *Swedish Economic Studies,* comes from Almqvist and Wiksell of Stockholm.

'Independent' Organisations' Series

There are many semi-independent research organisations in economics in both Great Britain and the United States, and some of the largest, and most influential, issue important publications directly or through a commercial publisher. Some of their series of publications are well worth noting.

National Bureau of Economic Research was mentioned above; in addition to conference proceedings it also publishes a wide range of reports and studies in series including *Publications, General Series, Occasional Papers, Technical Papers,* and the especially valuable number of series entitled *Studies in* ... covering such subjects as business cycles, capital formation and financing, consumer instalment financing, and international economic relations. **Brookings Institution,** another powerful research body in politics and economics has two series of particular interest to economists: *Studies in Government Finance,* and the *Transport Research Program.* Most of its publications, however, are not in series. The **Twentieth Century Fund** *Studies* are also worth noting.

The British **National Institute of Economic and Social Research** has several important series published by Cambridge U.P.: *Economic and Social Studies* includes J. C. R. Dow's *The Management of the British Economy, 1945–60* (No. 22, 1964) and A. Maizels' *Exports and Economic Growth of Developing Countries* (No. 25, 1968) in addition to the classic *The Structure of British Industry* by D. Burn (2 vols, No. 15, 1958); whilst the *Occasional Papers* series of smaller works includes R. R. Nield's *Pricing and Employment in the Trade Cycle: a Study of British Manufacturing Industry, 1945–61* (No. 21. 1963).

The **Institute of Economic Affairs** (another IEA, and not to be confused with the International Economic Association), publishes several series of pamphlet monographs which economists find valuable: *Hobart Papers, Eaton Papers, Occasional Papers,* and a new series *Research Monographs.* **Political and Economic Planning** published a pamphlet series entitled *Planning,* which has now been re-titled *Broadsheet.* In recent years this series has been of monographs by named authors, but some libraries still treat the series as a periodical. PEP recently began to co-operate with the

Royal Institute of International Affairs in the production of a *European Series* of pamphlets on European affairs. The **Economist** publishes a small series of *Economist Briefs*, short résumés of current economic problems which are useful introductions, and the **Economist Intelligence Unit** issues *Quarterly Economic Review Special Reports*, a similar pamphlet series linked to its *Quarterly Economic Reviews* of conditions in a large number of countries.

Official Series

Government departments, research bodies and supranational organisations all issue publications in series, many of which are noted elsewhere in this book. Especially important are the several lettered *Series* of publications of the Statistical Office of the United Nations, the *Reports* and *Bulletins* of the US Bureau of Labor Statistics, *Studies and Reports, New Series* of the International Labour Office, and many series from the Organisation for Economic Co-operation and Development and the European Economic Community too numerous to list here.

Abstracting and Indexing Services

The ever-increasing flood of economics literature is nowhere more apparent than in the journals. It has long been difficult for any researcher to keep up to date with the flow of new publications in even the narrow subject specialisations now current. Until 1969, there was no adequate current-awareness service in economics: a list of new journal articles and books by subject. With the change in content as well as title, *Journal of Economic Literature* (previously *Journal of Economic Abstracts*) now fills this role adequately for English-language material.

Journal of Economic Literature is published quarterly by the American Economic Association and comprises three or four review articles, the large book review and new books sections previously in *American Economic Review,* a list of the contents pages of new issues of journals, and a subject index to articles published in recent issues of over a hundred economics journals, a selection of which also appear with abstracts. This is a vast improvement on *Journal of Economic Abstracts* (AEA, 1963–1968) which by abstracting articles reduced the number included, and delayed the publication of the abstract. In economics a rapid, comprehensive current-awareness listing was desirable.

183

For literature searching, however, the lists in *Journal of Economic Literature* are only needed to bring up to date a bibliography produced from more cumulative sources. The sources discussed below are large in number, and some in physical size also, and all would only be used if the search was to be comprehensive. The more general sources, however, are essential for some topics on the borders of economics and other social science subjects such as politics or sociology.

Before describing these sources, a note on definition is required: both abstracting and indexing services list articles by subject, giving author, article title, journal title, and other bibliographical details, and will usually include an alphabetical author index. This is the extent of the information provided by an indexing service, whereas an abstracting service will add a short abstract, or résumé, of the main aims, content, and results of the work described in the article. Generally speaking, as noted above, the preparation of the abstract delays the publication of the article's listing, but this may be offset by more frequent publication of the service. Books and pamphlets are not abstracted (except in book reviews), though both *Economic Journal* and *Journal of Economic Literature* sometimes add notes to the titles of new publications listed.

General Indexing Services

The most comprehensive indexing service is *Internationale Bibliographie der Zeitschriftenliteratur (IBZ)* which indexes over 300 000 articles a year from about 7700 journals in all subjects. Coverage is international, with a preponderence of European titles. Entry is made under alphabetically-arranged subject headings (in German, with references from the English terms), and the journal title is indicated by a code number. *IBZ* is issued in fortnightly parts which cumulate to form one annual volume, each year's output of articles being indexed during the following year. Before 1965 there were two series: series A for German-language material, and series B for other languages: now all are in one sequence.

The *Bulletin of the Public Affairs Information Service* (*see* p. 42) is a weekly indexing service, which cumulates frequently, and covers books, pamphlets and a few government publications in addition to articles in about one thousand journals. 'Public affairs' is defined broadly with emphasis on factual and statistical material; most is in English with a bias towards American publications; arrangement is by alphabetical subject headings.

The H. W. Wilson Company of New York publishes several

indexes to books and journal articles including *Cumulative Book Index* (*see* p. 37), and *Readers' Guide to Periodical Literature.* This a general alphabetically-arranged subject index to the contents of about 160 periodicals in English. Like most Wilson indexes there is a bias towards American material. About 170 periodicals in a narrower field are analysed in *Business Periodicals Index* which is arranged in the same fashion: these indexes are easy to use, provided note is taken of the cross-references to other subject headings, and their limitations are appreciated.

The British counterpart is *British Humanities Index* (quarterly) which restricts itself to the contents of about 300 British journals in the social sciences and history: all the major British economics journals are covered. Again entry is made under alphabetically-arranged subject headings, which are very detailed. For some economics subjects it may be useful to scan some of the indexing or abstracting services covering technical subjects: *The Engineering Index* (an abstracting service in spite of its title) gives excellent international coverage of journals on all aspects of engineering industries.

Economics Services

The most valuable service for purely economics articles in English is *Index of Economic Journals* (9 vols, Irwin, for American Economic Association, 1962–) which arranges index entries for articles in more than a hundred 'major professional economic journals' from 1886. Only English-language articles are included, however, and some journals are only selectively analysed. The subject arrangement is by a specially-designed classification scheme, and a detailed author index is provided in each volume. From 1964 articles appearing in collective volumes including Festschriften, conference papers, readings volumes, hearings and studies for Congressional committees, English translations of foreign articles and some lecture series are also included: volume 7Λ covers such material for 1964–65, and volume 8 combines the analysis of collective volumes with the established index of journal articles for 1966.

International Bibliography of Economics began with UNESCO support and is now published annually, like the other parts of the *International Bibliography of the Social Sciences,* by the International Committee for Social Sciences Documentation. Books and pamphlets are included as well as articles in about 2000 periodicals, with very international coverage: Asian, Russian and

East European material is especially well represented. This is a particularly good service for items on, and from, underdeveloped countries, and for non-English-language publications. Entries are arranged in subject order by a special classification scheme, and an author index is provided. There is about a two year time lag between publication of the original and the appearance of its index entry in the *International Bibliography.*

The Library of the Economics Information Service of the Netherlands Ministry of Economic Affairs abstracts articles from about 450 American and European economics journals and publishes them in the fortnightly *Economic Abstracts* (1953–). Abstracts are short, in the language of the original if French, English or German, otherwise in English, and arranged by the UDC classification scheme. Author and subject indexes are published frequently. This is the best abstracting service for European economic publications, though not as easy to use as the other services.

Other Services

There are more than eighty abstracting or indexing services covering some aspect of economics. The researcher wishing to use more specialised sources should consult the entries in *Index Bibliographicus,* vol. 2 (4th edn, Fédération Internationale de Documentation, 1964) which lists services current at that time by subject. It should be noted, however, that many of the 'services' listed are little more than lists of new publications received by the editorial staff of economics journals. With the exception of agricultural economics *(see* Chapter 20) and possibly public finance *(see* Chapter 22) most economics subjects are adequately covered by the services described above.

CHAPTER TWELVE

HISTORY OF ECONOMIC THOUGHT

R. D. COLLISON BLACK

The student of the history of economic thought must acquire a somewhat different set of techniques from those used by his colleagues in most branches of contemporary economics. The additional skills he must seek to master are those of the historian and the bibliographer. Up to recently at least, he has been none too plentifully served with specialised reference tools, and must often learn to adapt other people's tools to his particular purposes.

Like any other historian, the historian of economic thought normally starts from the basic classification of his material into primary and secondary sources, and sub-divides his primary sources into manuscript and printed material. Unlike other historians, those who deal with economic ideas are only comparatively recent converts to the view that original documents and manuscripts are important. Hence, while no research worker today would undertake a study in the history of economic ideas without checking on the extent and location of relevant manuscript material, he still has no specific finding lists or catalogues of such material to help him in his task.

Great Britain was the cradle of modern economics two hundred years ago and has furnished most of the leading names in the history of the discipline. In view of that undisputed fact it is astonishing that even the whereabouts of the papers of leading British economists are often unknown, and no concerted attempt has been made to catalogue and preserve them. A committee of economists is at present seeking to undertake this task, and a Register of Archives for British Economics should be in existence in a few years' time. The committee consists of Professor A. W. Coats (Nottingham University), Professor B. A. Corry (Queen Mary College, London), Professor D. N. Winch (Sussex University) and the present writer, with Lord Robbins and Mr. H. S. Ellis (of the Historical Manuscripts Commission) as honorary consultants.

In the meantime, the student who wishes to verify the possible existence of manuscript sources should not neglect to check the National Register of Archives and the British Museum Catalogue of Additional Manuscripts. If his topic lies within the area of relations between economic thought and policy in the United Kingdom or its dependencies, he must be prepared to search the lists and catalogues of the Public Record Office using the *Guide to the Contents of the Public Record Office* (2 vols, HMSO, 1963) as an introduction; if his interest is in the work of a particular individual, a search of the records at Somerset House may enable him to identify descendants and executors, who can be approached for details of personal papers surviving.

In printed primary sources the researcher is confronted by a less difficult problem, but is still not over-supplied with **bibliographies** specifically related to the history of economics. Henry Higgs's *Bibliography of Economics, 1751–1775* (Cambridge U.P., 1935) was prepared for the British Academy as the first instalment of a 'comprehensive, chronologically arranged, catalogue of literature of economic interest'. It was intended to be continued 'backward and forward', but Higgs had not completed the volume for 1701–1750 when he died in 1940. Towards the end of World War II, his materials were taken over by L. W. Hanson, of the Bodleian Library. Working from this foundation Hanson produced his *Contemporary Printed Sources for British and Irish Economic History, 1701–1750* (Cambridge U.P., 1964). In both these works the material is chronologically arranged, but with the entries for each year classified under a series of subject heads. Each of the two works has an Introduction which is a valuable bibliographical essay in itself.

An earlier and more limited bibliography of eighteenth century works is Henry R. Wagner's *Irish Economics, 1700–1783* (London, J. Davy & Sons, 1907). This lists only 369 items examined by the compiler in the British Museum, the Library of Trinity College, Dublin, and the Haliday Collection of the Royal Irish Academy, but most of the entries are fairly fully annotated.

Partially overlapping the work of Higgs and Wagner but differently organised, is Judith Blow Williams: *A Guide to the Printed Materials for English Social and Economic History* 1750–1850 (2 vols, Columbia U.P., 1926). Part I, 'Works of General Reference', has a useful section on Bibliographies and Catalogues and Part II 'Works regarding Special Subjects' contains a special section devoted to Economic Theory.

For the nineteenth century itself bibliographies in the proper sense of the term are as sparse as the material is voluminous. The modern neglect of the bibliography of earlier economic thought can be sharply highlighted by stating the simple fact that one of the best bibliographies for the classical period is still J. R. McCulloch's *The Literature of Political Economy,* originally published in 1845. McCulloch's work has the sub-title 'A Classified Catalogue of Select Publications in the different departments of the Science, with Historical, Critical and Biographical Notices' and while its extensive annotations reflect the compiler's own strongly held views they are none the less frequently enlightening and useful. McCulloch was perhaps the first professional economist, and also a notable bibliophile; considerable interest therefore also attaches to the catalogue of his own library which he published as *A Catalogue of Books, the Property of a Political Economist* (1862).

The absence of general bibliographies of printed sources for this period is to some extent compensated for by the existence of special bibliographies relating to particular subjects or authors. An example of the former is the bibliography appended to D. G. Barnes: *History of the English Corn Laws,* and of the latter the *Bibliography of the Published Writings of John Stuart Mill,* by N. MacMinn, J. R. Hainds and J. McCrimmon (Northwestern University, 1945). The Bibliographical Appendix to *Robert Torrens and the Evolution of Classical Economics* by L. C. Robbins (Macmillan, 1958) deserves mention as a model of detailed but clear annotation.

For the neo-classical period there is H. E. Batson's *Select Bibliography of Modern Economic Theory 1870–1929* (Geo. Routledge & Sons, 1930) which gives a good coverage of continental European, as well as British and American, works. In addition to a subject bibliography it has an 'author bibliography' in which the works of each writer are listed chronologically. Useful bibliographies relating to particular topics for the classical and neo-classical periods can be found in Palgrave's *Dictionary of Political Economy* (3 vols, Macmillan, 1908–10) as well as in the *Encyclopaedia of the Social Sciences,* edited by E. R. A. Seligman (New York, Macmillan 1930–35) and the *New Encyclopaedia of the Social Sciences* edited by David R. Sills (Crowell Collier and Macmillan, Inc., 1968). The latter does not entirely supersede the former since the coverage is by no means identical.

Outside the field of bibliographies proper much useful information is obtained from the printed **catalogues** of the great repositories of economic literature. Among these two are outstanding: the *London Bibliography of the Social Sciences* for the United Kingdom and the *Catalogues of the Kress Library of Business and Economics* for the United States. The first now runs to twenty volumes. The first four volumes cover the holdings up to 1931 of the British Library of Political and Economic Science, the Goldsmith's Library of Economic Literature and such special collections as the pamphlets of the Reform Club, the Hume, Ricardo and other economic collections of University College, London, as well as other London libraries. Volumes 6 to 14 cover additions to most of these collections from 1931 to 1962. There are author indexes in Volumes 4 (covering vols. 1 to 3), 5, and 6 but not in later volumes; the basic classification is by subject.

Both the Goldsmith's Library and the Kress Library owe their origins to the unique enthusiasm and flair for book collection of H. S. Foxwell (1847–1936). (The fascinating story of how Foxwell accumulated these two unique collections of economic literature is told in *The Kress Library of Business and Economics* by J. M. Keynes, A. P. Usher and A. H. Cole (mentioned also in Chapter 1 of this book) (Kress Library Publication Series, No. 1)). The Kress Catalogue, which now runs to three main volumes and supplements and runs from the fifteenth century up to 1848, covers a vast range of economic literature: its arrangement is strictly chronological, but supplemented by very complete author and title indexes.

Of similar construction, but with a different scope, is the present author's *Catalogue of Pamphlets on Economic Subjects published between 1750 and 1900 and now housed in Irish Libraries.* (Belfast, Queen's University; New York, A. M. Kelley, 1969). This is in fact a union catalogue of the economic pamphlets held by seventeen major Irish libraries: not being confined to items of Irish interest it can, however, be used as a guide to the extensive pamphlet literature of the period.

For the student of the history of economic thought the availability of rarer items can often be a problem, so it is important to know the **location of major collections.** In the United Kingdom, outside of the great repositories such as the British Museum and the Bodleian, the leading special collections are those to which reference has already been made: the Goldsmith's Collection and the British Library of Political and Economic Science.

Outside London the most valuable specialised source for the history of economic ideas is surely the Marshall Library at Cambridge. Manchester has much of value both in its City Library and John Rylands Library, as well as the University to which much of the fine collection of books made by W. S. Jevons was donated. Many of J. R. McCulloch's books have found their way to Reading University and Edinburgh University has the valuable collection made by W. B. Hodgson.

In the United States the leading collection is that of the Kress Library at Harvard; less well-known, but almost as important, is the Seligman Collection at Columbia University. The collection of Henry R. Wagner is now in the Beinecke Library at Yale. Chicago holds valuable resources for the historiographer of economics, both in the University of Chicago Library and the Newberry Library, and the University of Kansas has built up considerable holdings in this field.

Of recent years, the activities of **reprint** publishers have done much to help the student who is not within easy reach of any major collection of material; but the reprinting of earlier materials has long been a useful practice in political economy:

'The Italians provided the startling example. Beginning in 1803 and continuing through 1816, they produced an amazing fifty volumes that they entitled *Scrittori classici italiani di economi politica* as Professor Arthur H. Cole has pointed out in his valuable monograph on *The Historical Development of Economic and Business Literature* (Kress Library Publication No. 12, (1957), p. 29). This was followed in the mid-nineteenth century by the first series of thirteen volumes of the *Biblioteca dell 'economista*, edited by Francesco Ferrara and consisting mainly of translations into Italian of works by English and other authors. Four other series of the *Biblioteca* followed this: Series II, edited by Ferrara (13 vols, Turin 1859–77); Series III, edited by Gerolamo Boccardo (15 vols, Turin 1876–92); Series IV, mainly edited by Salvatore Cognetti de Martiis (10 vols, Turin 1896–1904); and Series V, edited by Pasquale Jannacone (20 vols, Turin 1905–22).

The years between 1840 and 1848 saw the appearance of a *Collection des Principaux Économistes* in France. Edited by Eugene Daire, this ultimately comprised fifteen volumes mainly the works of French economists, such as Quesnay and Turgot, but also including a few *étrangers* such as David Hume. At this same period in Great Britain J. R. McCulloch was producing his series of reprints of *Early English Tracts on Commerce, Scarce and Valuable Tracts on Money* and other economic subjects: some half-dozen volumes in all.

Between 1933 and 1938 a new and revised *Collection des Principaux Économistes* appeared under the editorship of Gaetan Pirou and François Simiand (Paris, Librairie Felix Alcan). In 1945, when the Institut National d'Études Démographiques was established, a project to reprint 'the great classics of demography' was sponsored by it, and under this editions with commentaries of the works of Cantillon and Quesnay have appeared.

In Britain the practice of reprinting 'Scarce Tracts in Economic and Political Science' was revived by the London School of Economics in the inter-war years with a first series comprising twenty volumes; a second series now includes some twenty further items. The Royal Economic Society has done invaluable service by its editions of the *Works and Correspondence of David Ricardo,* edited by Piero Sraffa and M. H. Dobb (10 vols, Cambridge U.P., 1951–55), and the *Correspondence and Related Papers of Léon Walras* (3 vols, North Holland, 1965). Similar editions of the Overstone Papers and Jevons Papers are in preparation under its auspices. The Scottish Economic Society is also producing a series of Scottish Economic Classics, which already covers James Mill and Sir James Steuart, with J. R. McCulloch soon to be added. A special edition of the Works and Correspondence of Adam Smith, to commemorate the bicentenary of the *Wealth of Nations,* is being prepared by the University of Glasgow and will be published by the Clarendon Press.

Although specialist economic **journals** began to appear as early as 1842 in France and in 1862 in Germany, none of the journals in English which economists nowadays regard as 'standard' date back farther than 1886, but this does not mean that earlier British economists published no articles as such. One possible outlet for their shorter writings was in the *Journals* or *Transactions* of the Statistical Societies of London, Manchester and elsewhere, or of the Literary and Philosophical Societies which flourished in the early and mid-nineteenth centuries. (The Manchester Statistical Society, founded in 1833, preceded the London (later Royal) Statistical Society, which was formed in March, 1834. *See* T. S. Ashton: *Economic and Social Investigations in Manchester* 1833–1933 (P. S. King, 1934); *Annals of the Royal Statistical Society 1834–1934.* (London, 1934)). The Cambridge Philosophical Society and Manchester Literary and Philosophical Society *Transactions* are sources not to be overlooked: at a somewhat later date the early volumes of *Nature* and *Mind* contained a number of contributions by economists.

In the high classical period, the literary quarterlies, pre-eminently the *Edinburgh, Westminster* and *Quarterly Reviews,* provided the main forum for the discussion of questions of political economy. All of these contributions were, by tradition, unsigned: Professor F. W. Fetter has performed an invaluable service by identifying most of those written by economists in a series of articles which form an indispensable tool for the historian of ideas:

'The Authorship of Economic Articles in the *Edinburgh Review,*

1802–47', *Journal of Political Economy*, vol. 61, No. 3, June, 1953, pp. 232–259.

'The Economic Articles in the *Quarterly Review* and their Authors, 1809–52', *Journal of Political Economy*, vol. 66, Nos. 1 and 2, February and April, 1958, pp. 47–64 and 154–170.

'The Economic Articles in *Blackwood's Edinburgh Magazine*, and their Authors, 1817–1853', *Scottish Journal of Political Economy*, vol. 7, June 1960, pp. 85–107.

'Economic Articles in the Westminster Review and their Authors, 1824–51', *Journal of Political Economy*, vol. 70, No. 6, December 1962, pp. 570–596.

Professor Fetter's pioneering work was necessarily limited in scope, and there are many other nineteenth-century periodicals which contain work of interest to the historian of economic ideas. A number of these are, or soon will be, covered by the *Wellesley Index to Victorian Periodicals 1824–1900*. Planned to include ultimately author, subject and book review indexes for a wide range of Victorian monthlies and quarterlies, the first volume of the work (University of Toronto Press, 1966) provides an author index to *Blackwoods, the Contemporary, Cornhill, Edinburgh Review* (including the period 1802–1823), *Home and Foreign Review, Macmillan's Magazine*, and the *North British* and *Quarterly Reviews*. The second volume will add another thirty periodicals to this list.

Clearly the line of distinction between primary printed and secondary sources is not a sharp one in this particular subject, and each student must draw his own line according to his topic. **Secondary sources** may range from monumental surveys such as *History of Economic Analysis* by J. A. Schumpeter (Allen and Unwin, 1954) to detailed monographs and journal articles.

A good list of standard histories of economic thought and monographs on particular schools and periods is given in *The Literature of the Social Sciences* by P. R. Lewis (Library Association, 1960) but bibliographies of this material are generally found as sub-divisions of larger bibliographies, such as the *International Bibliography of the Social Sciences: Economics*, published by UNESCO (London, Tavistock Publications; Chicago, Aldine Company) in which the History of Economic Thought is classified under D.O.–D.82 in the volumes for 1960–67: in the earlier volumes simply entitled *International Bibliography of Economics* (Paris, UNESCO) and covering the years 1952–59, the relevant material is classified under 03–039·3. A similar section is included in *Bibliographie der Sozialwissenschaften* (Gottingen, Vandenhoeck and Ruprecht) as a sub-division of Section I 'Wirtschaftstheorie'. *Biblio-*

graphie d'Économie Politique 1945–1960 by R. Mossé (Receuil Sirey, 1963) contains a useful section for French writings on economic thought during its period. A work which covers both primary and secondary sources is *Handbuch zur Geschichte der Volkswirtschaftlehre* von Walter Braeuer (Frankfurt-a-M., V. Klostermann, 1952). It covers works by and about the leading members of all schools in economic thought from the ancient Greeks to Keynes; no leading thinker is omitted from the 250 names covered, but not unnaturally the minor figures listed are mainly German. Similar in character but more specialised are Burt Franklin and G. Legman: *David Ricardo and Ricardian theory, a Bibliographical Checklist* (New York, B. Franklin, 1949); Burt Franklin and F. Cordasco: *Adam Smith, a Bibliographical Checklist* (New York, B. Franklin, 1950).

The task of searching for articles on the history of thought has been immensely simplified by the *Index of Economic Journals* published by the American Economic Association; the section (4·0–4·8) on this topic is sub-divided according to both schools and individual writers. Since 1963 abstracts of a growing volume of relevant articles have been provided by the *Journal of Economic Abstracts* which with Volume 7, No. 1 (March 1969) became the *Journal of Economic Literature* and now has a classified listing of articles in 175 current journals, as well as a selection of abstracts. In the classified listing History of Economic Thought has the number 031.

These listings now cover all the major journals publishing articles on this topic. Up to recently, there have been no specialised journals in the history of economic thought but the *History of Economic Thought Newsletter* began publication in Great Britain in November 1968. The first three issues were edited by A. W. Coats of Nottingham University, but the editorship is now being taken over by D. A. Collard of Bristol University, to whom inquiries should be addressed. The *Newsletter* is intended to keep workers in the field in touch with one another and with developments in research. Similar in scope, but more ambitious in form, is *History of Political Economy,* a journal published by Duke University Press: vol. 1, No. 1, appeared in Spring 1969.

Aside from these, there are some other periodicals outside the area of economic journals proper which occasionally contain material of value to the historian of economic thought, notably the *Journal of the History of Ideas* and *Victorian Studies.* A list of relevant articles in the former journal, prepared by A. W. Coats, appeared in No. 2 of the *History of Economic Thought Newsletter,* which intends to include a number of such bibliographical lists in future issues.

From what has already been said, it should be clear that the historian of economic ideas must always be prepared to look outside the strict confines of his own discipline, and this is particularly true when he is looking for useful **reference tools.** There are some records which relate strictly to the subject such as Volume 6 of the *Proceedings of the Political Economy Club* (Macmillan, 1921) which contains a list of the questions discussed at this famous club from its foundation in 1821, Minutes of Proceedings 1899–1920, a Roll of Members and valuable extracts from some of their letters and diaries. Often, however, the most useful reference sources do not appear to be economic at all. For the searcher after biographical information, familiarity with the *Dictionary of National Biography* may be taken for granted, but for lesser known names Boase's *Modern English Biography* (3 vols, and supplements, privately printed, 1892; reprinted by Frank Cass, 1965) and *Who was Who* can often be more useful for the later nineteenth and early twentieth centuries. For earlier periods the obituaries in the *Gentleman's Magazine* often repay a search. For simply tying up chronology, the first resource is *A Handbook of British Chronology* by F. M. Powicke (Royal Historical Society, 1939); but for contemporary details or checking the holders of offices, the *Annual Register* (first published by Dodsley in 1758) and the *British Almanac and Companion* (produced under varying titles by the Society for the Diffusion of Useful Knowledge from 1827 to 1913) are frequently useful.

Identification of anonymous or pseudonymous work is a problem frequently encountered and for this it pays to be familiar with such reference books as Block and Stonehill: *Anonyma and Pseudonyma* (London, Stonehill, 1926), *Anonyms* and *Initials and Pseudonyms* by William Cushing (Cambridge, Mass., Cushing, 1889), and *A Dictionary of Anonymous and Pseudonymous English Literature* by S. Halkett and J. Laing (9 vols, Oliver and Boyd, 1926–62).

Since many economists have given evidence to, or sat upon, Royal Commissions and Select Committees, the student may often find himself turning to British Parliamentary Papers. If so, he should begin by reading *A Guide to Parliamentary Papers*, by P. and G. Ford (Blackwell, 1955). Finally, the economist who wants a guide to the principles and techniques of historical research can profitably read *The Modern Researcher* by Jacques Barzun and Henry F. Graaf (Harcourt, Brace and World, 1957).

CHAPTER THIRTEEN

ECONOMIC HISTORY

G. N. VON TUNZELMAN

Definitionally, for the purposes of this chapter, economic history studies economic phenomena occurring in historical time by applying a consistent explanatory framework. This framework is received economic theory. When the assumptions are satisfied, the logicality of the economic theory is unaffected by geographical or temporal context. If correctly applied, therefore, it provides a comparatively powerful tool to interrelate cause and effect. It is, of course, essential to recognise that economic forces alone are rarely complete explanations in themselves of particular historical events. Causation is strengthened or modified by the surrounding social, political, and other pressures. Subject to these considerations and the nature of the topic, there will generally be scope for the economic influence to be provisionally accepted, if the data so warrant. Thus economic history proper requires first an appropriate model drawn from economic theory. Having erected the hypothesis, its second aspect is a body of data to substantiate or vitiate the thesis. The appropriateness of the model depends upon the theory being satisfied in all its assumptions (or if it is not, what difference this will make to the results), and being rigorous in its application. Testing the hypothesis against the available data involves attention to the relevant statistical theory.

The demarcation of the more theoretical economic history from applied economics may not be so obvious as one might think. Even the time span is not inevitably a reliable guide. It is true that economists are generally more interested in bringing their observation period up to the present day, but this contrast too occasionally fails, and in both directions. It is also true that economists tend to be more interested in prediction, whilst economic historians 'forecast', if at all, usually for periods either within or previous to their observations.

A methodological debate over the use of theory and quantification in economic history has waxed strongly, sometimes rather heatedly, particularly in the USA in the 1960s. Some of the arguments and clarifications can be found in the *American Economic Review (Papers and Proceedings)* for 1964 and 1965. Other important methodological sources include *Studies in Econometric History* by A. H. Conrad and J. R. Meyer (the English edition and title, Chapman & Hall, 1965), and many issues of the major journals of economic history, mentioned below.

Journals

The re-unification of economic history with economic theory, such as has been claimed for the 'New Economic History', has meant that many articles in economic history have appeared in the economics journals surveyed elsewhere in this book (Chaper 5). In the USA, articles in this genre have been published in the *American Economic Review*, the *Journal of Political Economy*, the *Quarterly Journal of Economics*, and the *Review of Economics and Statistics*, to name only some of the more important. Historical articles of regional interest are published in the *Southern Economic Journal* and *Western Economic Journal* (e.g. on slavery).

The comparatively weak sway of economics over British economic history is reflected in a lower volume of publication in the 'national' economic periodicals, such as the *Economic Journal*, except by non-Britons. Regional influences, on the other hand, are comparatively strong, and find outlets in such as the *Scottish Journal of Political Economy*, the *Manchester School*, and the *Yorkshire Bulletin*. Almost every economics periodical in every country, however, has contained historical articles at one time or another. Even the *Review of Economic Studies* has not been immune.

The most important journals devoted primarily to economic history are the *Journal of Economic History* (USA) and the *Economic History Review* (UK). Though naturally specialising in works relating to the two associated countries, each does publish articles of sufficient merit and interest portraying the economic history of any other country. The *Journal of Economic History* began life as the *Journal of Economic and Business History* (1928–32) and recommenced with its present title in 1941. Proceedings of the Annual Conference of the American Economic History Association have been issued since 1942 as a separate volume of this journal, bearing the distinguishing sub-title *Tasks of Economic History*. A notable feature of this issue has been its summaries of selected American doctoral theses. The *Economic History Review* (1st Series, 1927–48; 2nd Series, 1948–) has been noteworthy not only for its articles but for its annual summaries of periodical literature relating to particular countries, and for its long-running series of review articles, entitled 'Essays in Bibliography and Criticism'. Four novella-like supplements of important articles too long for inclusion in the main body of the *Review* have been published since 1953. In addition, the *Economic Journal* created a regular supplement for its historical articles under the simple title of *Economic History* (1934–40). A further journal publishing significant articles in both US and British history is *Explorations in Entrepreneurial History* (1st Series, 1949–58; 2nd Series, 1964–69). The implied emphasis on entrepreneurial history has become less dominant, and indeed the journal has now been retitled *Explorations in Economic History* accordingly.

The role of the entrepreneur is nevertheless still stressed in writings on business history. The leading periodicals are the *Business History Review* (USA, 1942– ; before 1942 known as the *Bulletin of the Business History Society*) and *Business History* (UK, 1958–). For agricultural history the titles run conversely: *Agricultural History* (USA, 1927–) and *Agricultural History Review* (UK, 1953–).

In Great Britain especially, the boundaries between economic and social history have never been very sharply defined, and much of the literature combines the two. Prominent journals at the more academic end of the social history spectrum with considerable bearing upon economic history include *Past and Present* (1952–), *Victorian Studies* (1957–), and the *International Review of Social History* (1956–). The French *Annales: Économies, Sociétés, Civilisations* (operating under various titles since 1929) and the Italian *Economia e Storia* (1954–) are still weightier equivalents.

Smaller areas impinging upon both economic and social history are served by specialist journals. The history of organised and unorganised labour is treated in *Labor History* (USA, 1960–) and the *Bulletin* of the Society for the Study of Labour History (UK, 1960–). The related field of population and demography has concerned economic historians more than economists practically since Malthus: journals such as *Population Studies* (1947–) have published historical articles written by authors with medical or other expertise. The International Association for Research in Income and Wealth published *Papers* on its research topics 1951–65 and the *Review of Income and Wealth* since 1966. But by far the most notable amassing of data on the growth of output, wide-ranging in time and place, is to be found in *Economic Develop-*

ment and Cultural Change (1951–), principally in the issues given over to the work of S. Kuznets, entitled 'Quantitative Aspects of the Economic Growth of Nations', in ten parts, 1956–67.

Historical statistics collated with varying degrees of economic sophistication are available in statistical periodicals, especially the *Journal of the Royal Statistical Society*. Industrial archaeology, a burgeoning popular interest in Great Britain at least, has ramifications in economic history, sometimes satisfied in its publications, such as the *Journal of Transport History* (1953–). Of more sustained academic respectability are journals devoted to the social causes and consequences of invention, especially *Technology and Culture* (1960–).

A large proportion of academic journals in 'pure' history contain articles of economic relevance. There is room here to single out only a very few of the major historical journals, but they would include *History*, the *English Historical Review* and *Transactions of the Royal Historical Society* for Great Britain; and the *American Historical Review*, the *Journal of American History* (formerly the *Mississippi Valley Historical Review*), and *William and Mary Quarterly* (colonial period) for the USA. Regional historical periodicals such as are published for many US states may also be of value. The publications of local antiquarian and record societies abounding in both countries are, however, not likely to include more than a tiny proportion of material usable for the economist. In parallel fashion, geographical journals may contain articles of historical reference, if not always historical understanding.

Literature published in other countries can be dealt with in less detail. The German economics periodicals, e.g. *Kyklos* and *Zeitschrift für die Gesamte Staatswissenschaft*, frequently contain economic history, a fair proportion of it written in English. Scandinavian countries produce two English-language journals, the *Scandinavian Economic History Review* (1953–) and *Economy and History* (1958–), the former being of more general interest. Important productions of Commonwealth countries include the *Indian Economic and Social Historical Review* (1963–) and the *Australian Economic History Review* (known as *Business Archives and History*, 1962–67). These and the major journals apart, the economic history of particular Commonwealth countries appears with some regularity in the appropriate economics periodicals, including the *Canadian Journal of Economics*, the *South African Journal of Economics, Social and Economic Studies* (West Indies), *Indian Economic Journal, Economic Record* (Australia and New Zealand), *Australian Economic Papers*, and *New Zealand Economic Papers*.

Bibliographies

Much of the recent literature, especially that with a more theoretical slant, is indexed along with applied economics in relevant sections of economics bibliographies and abstracts. The *Journal of Economic Literature* (formerly the *Journal of Economic Abstracts*), for example, abstracts many of the articles from the *Journal of Economic History*, the *Economic History Review*, etc., as well as historical articles in the economic periodicals. The American Economic Association's *Index of Economic Journals* (for 1886 onwards) and the *International Bibliography of Economics* (1952–) have historical sub-sections scattered through each of their volumes. Such bibliographies are dealt with elsewhere in this book (Chapter 11).

The present concern is to approach economic history bibliographically from the historical side. Many of the bibliographies of such a kind may be arranged only by chronology or by author, and for that reason (but depending on the problem at hand) might be hard going for the economist or economic historian. A highly recommended point at which to attack a historical problem in this sphere is the American Historical Association's *Guide to Historical Literature* (New York, Macmillan, 1961). By its selection, the *Guide* contains a wide range of suggestions for following subject matter up to individual fields of interest. Its inevitable generality means that it must be eked out by specific bibliographies. The *Harvard Guide to Historical Literature* (Belknap, 1954) by O. Handlin *et al.*, is essential for research in depth. The *International Bibliography of Historical Sciences* (1926–) fulfils the same function as the International Bibliographies of the Social Sciences. It is currently published in German. *Historical Abstracts* (1955–) in its quarterly issues provides abstracts of some length for articles relating to recent history (defined as 1775 onwards), under an elaborately coded classificatory system which helps to make its five-year indexes so good. The *Annual Bulletin of Historical Literature* (1911–) gives a selection of the literature appearing in that year as rated by the contributing historian; the classifications and often the selections are not usually directly useful for the economic historian. More in the spirit of the AHA Guide, *A Bibliography of Modern History*, compiled by John Roach (Cambridge UP, 1968), is keyed to the *New Cambridge Modern History*, and its choice of topics of special interest mirrors that fact.

It is more difficult to obtain up to date historical bibliographies of greater depth for many individual countries. The series issued under the auspices of the Royal Historical Society called *Writings*

on *British History* now extends to books published between 1901
and 1945. For more recent works, the series must be supplemented by the *Bibliography of Historical Works Issued in the
United Kingdom* compiled by Joan C. Lancaster for 1946–56 and
by William Kellaway for 1957–60 and 1961–65. Another series
under the direction of the Royal Historical Society, in association
with the AHA, comprises the Clarendon Press volumes; referring
to 1485–1603, edited by Conyers Read (2nd edn, 1959), 1603–
1714 by G. Davies (1928), and 1714–1789 by S. Pargellis and D. J.
Medley (1951). The traditional chronological breakdown of British
history frequently cuts across the interests of economic historians,
but these volumes compensate by being well edited and with
generally useful critical annotations. Subsequent work is listed in
the Bibliographical Handbooks newly initiated by the Conference
on British Studies: *Anglo-Norman England, 1066–1154,* by M.
Altschul (Cambridge UP, 1969), and *Tudor England, 1485–1603,*
by M. Levine (Cambridge UP, 1968), have already appeared.

Specifically economic history of Great Britain is less well served.
The standard source is Judith B. Williams, *A Guide to the Printed
Materials for English Social and Economic History, 1750–1850*
(Columbia UP, 1926). It is quite obsolete for non-contemporary
references. Fortunately this deficiency has now been largely
remedied by K. Borchardt's bibliography of the early Industrial
Revolution in *Vierteljahrschrift für Sozial–und Wirtschaftsges-
chichte,* vol. 55, part 1, July 1968. For other periods, one must
rely a great deal on the historical bibliographies, or on publication
lists provided in the periodicals. Much the most extensive of
these is the List of Publications on the Economic History of Great
Britain and Ireland, published annually in the *Economic History
Review* since its inception.

The same is true of American economic history. *Writings in
American History* is published annually as Volume II of the
Annual Report of the AHA (1906–   ). Part of its undoubted value
is lost through being many years in arrears. Thus, very few of the
important recent books in particular topics of American economic
history referred to below yet appear in this bibliographical series.
The more primitive classification methods used for the lists in
journals such as the *Journal of American History* and the *American Historical Review* have to suffice to bring the record up to the
present. To be fair, the bibliographies for associated fields are
better for the USA than for Great Britain. Further, a work such
as the *Guide to Business History* (Harvard Studies in Business
History, vol. 12), by Henrietta M. Larson (Harvard U.P., 1948)

includes annotations of a large number of works in general economic history.

For Europe, note *A Select List of Works on Europe and Europe Overseas*, by J. S. Bromley and A. Goodwin (Oxford U.P., 1956), and A. Bullock and A. J. P. Taylor, *A Select List of Books on European History, 1815–1914* (Oxford U.P., 1957). Both these collections are highly selective, but conveniently arranged by subject matter.

Alternative to an approach by country is one via branch of study. The US Department of Agriculture has issued several series of bibliographical works on agricultural history. The University of Illinois has Bibliographical Contributions devoted to Labour history. Serial bibliographies of this kind include *Population Index* and *Bibliography on Income and Wealth*.

Amongst library catalogues of contemporary printed books, that of the Kress Library of Business and Economics, Harvard University, is outstanding (to 1848; three volumes plus supplements, 1940–64). Early agricultural history is especially well documented, with, *inter alia, Catalogue of the Printed Books on Agriculture, 1471–1840*, compiled by Mary S. Aslin (Rothamsted, 1926), and F. A. Buttress, *Agricultural Periodicals of the British Isles, 1681–1900* (Cambridge, 1950). Transport history is also well covered, e.g. *A Bibliography of British Railway History*, by G. Ottley (British Museum, 1965), and *Naval and Maritime History: An Annotated Bibliography*, by R. G. Albion (3rd edn, Munson Institute, Conn., 1963). The best chronological compilations are the consecutive *Contemporary Printed Sources for British and Irish Economic History, 1701–1750*, by L. W. Hanson (Cambridge U.P., 1963) and *Bibliography of Economics, 1751–1775*, by Henry Higgs (Cambridge U.P., 1935).

Printed Books and Texts

A weighty general introduction to economic history might begin with the multi-volume *Cambridge Economic History of Europe*, or appropriate sections of the *New Cambridge Modern History* or the *Cambridge History of the British Empire*. D. Landes' extended essay in volume 6 of the former exemplifies the traditional approach to economic history at its most relevant. It has recently been further extended into a book, *The Unbound Prometheus* (Cambridge U.P., 1969). But for the most part this section can afford to survey only the most up-to-date texts and monographs.

British economic history before the Industrial Revolution has been deficient in applying the explanatory models if not some of the concepts inspired by theory. Even the particularisation of economic variables has largely been confined to a few striking phenomena such as the 'Price Revolution'. More profound analyses of economic developments begin chronologically with B. E. Supple's *Commercial Crisis and Change in England, 1600–42* (Cambridge U.P., 1959). *England's Apprenticeship, 1603–1763* (Longmans, 1965), by Charles Wilson, is perhaps the finest study (or sequence of profiles) of the economic life of pre-industrial England. M. W. Flinn's slim *Origins of the Industrial Revolution* (Longmans, 1966) examines the latter part of the same period from the hindsight of the Industrial Revolution. Building on the statistical compilation of B. R. Mitchell and P. Deane (*Abstract of British Historical Statistics*, Cambridge U.P., 1962; *see* Chapter 10), P. Deane and W. A. Cole have established series of strategic economic variables : population growth and movement, output, labour force, capital, and the like, in *British Economic Growth, 1688–1959* (2nd edn, Cambridge U.P., 1967). Reservations have been made about the validity of some of their statistical manipulations (see the important reviews by J. Wright in the *Economic History Review*, August 1965, and by J. R. T. Hughes in the *Journal of Economic History*, March 1964). The newest textbook covering the Industrial Revolution and after is *The First Industrial Nation*, by P. Mathias (Methuen, 1969). Mathias fairly evaluates each side of the argument over the now most controversial issues. Of the older works, T. S. Ashton's *An Economic History of England: the 18th Century* (Methuen, 1955) contains valuable yet hitherto neglected flashes of intuition or perhaps revelation. Several studies of the nineteenth century confine themselves to much briefer time spans. F. Crouzet's monumental *L'Économie Britannique et le Blocus Continental* (Paris, Presses Universitaires de France, 1958) gives a balanced, analytical view of the British economy, 1806–13. The following period is dominated, historiographically, by R. C. O. Matthews' *A Study in Trade-Cycle History* (Cambridge U.P., 1954). Matthews is admirable in drawing general propositions about the character of British economic growth from its short-run behaviour (1833–42). J. R. T. Hughes's *Fluctuations in Trade, Industry and Finance* (Clarendon Press, 1960) studies the cycle from 1850 to 1860. H. J. Habakkuk's *American and British Technology in the Nineteenth Century* (Cambridge U.P., 1962) is a controversial study now greatly in need of empirical testing. For the late nineteenth century, W. Ashworth, *An Economic History of England, 1870–1939*, is solid; C. P. Kindleberger presents fresh if somewhat idiosyncratic views in *Economic Growth in France and Britain, 1851–1950*;

while a symposium on the 'Great Depression' edited by J. Saville in a special issue of the *Yorkshire Bulletin*, 1965, has achieved near-text status. S. Pollard's *The Development of the British Economy* has recently been brought up to 1967 in a new edition (Arnold, 1969). The economic history of Great Britain over the last century or more has been swayed by international considerations. Especially recommended are A. K. Cairncross, *Home and Foreign Investment* (Cambridge U.P., 1953); I. Svennilson, *Growth and Stagnation in the European Economy* (UN ECE, 1954); and A. Maddison, *Economic Growth in the West* (Allen & Unwin, 1964).

Economic histories of the United States have generally been able to draw upon a much more comprehensive and accurate range of statistical material. The National Bureau of Economic Research has been especially active in compiling and processing data: particularly in volumes 24 and 30 of its Studies in Income and Wealth. A number of highly important specific studies bear the NBER imprint, including the famous *A Monetary History of the United States, 1867–1960* (Princeton U.P., 1963), by M. Friedman and A. J. Schwartz. *Historical Statistics of the United States: Colonial Times to 1957* (US Bureau of the Census, 1960) collects many of the leading series. General texts providing valuable historical background include C. W. Wright, *Economic History of the United States* (McGraw-Hill, 1941), and C. H. Hession and H. Sardy, *Ascent to Affluence* (Allyn & Bacon, 1969). The economic angle is better specified in L. Davis, J. R. T. Hughes, and D. McDougall, *American Economic History* (3rd edn, Irwin, 1969). A standard via media is Ross M. Robertson's *History of the American Economy* (2nd edn, Harcourt, Brace, 1964). External aspects of development are stressed in J. G. Williamson, *American Growth and the Balance of Payments, 1820–1913* (North Carolina U.P., 1964), and in D. C. North, *The Economic Growth of the United States, 1790–1860* (Prentice-Hall, 1961).

For the economist, much of the most interesting feature of American economic historiography is the recent accent upon economic theory and statistics in probing controversial historical questions. The role of the railroads in American growth has been assessed in R. W. Fogel's provocative *Railroads and American Economic Growth* (Johns Hopkins U.P., 1964), and by Λ. Fishlow, *American Railroads and the Transformation of the Ante-Bellum Economy* (Harvard U.P., 1965), *inter alia*. Industrial studies in similar mould include P. Temin, *Iron and Steel in Nineteenth Century America* (MIT Press, 1964) and P. F. McGouldrick, *New England Textiles in the Nineteenth Century* (Harvard U.P., 1968).

Essays have been published in H. Rosovsky (ed.), *Industrialization in Two Systems* (Wiley, 1966), A. H. Conrad and J. R. Meyer, *The Economics of Slavery* (Aldine, 1964), and A. W. Coats and R. M. Robertson, *Essays in American Economic History* (Arnold, 1969). R. W. Fogel and S. L. Engerman are editing and introducing a large number of such essays in their collection, *The Reinterpretation of American Economic History*, to be published by Harper and Row.

CHAPTER FOURTEEN

MATHEMATICAL ECONOMICS

F. G. PYATT

Mathematical economics has come a long way since Marshall wrote in the Preface to his celebrated *Principles of Economics*: 'The Chief use of pure mathematics in economic questions seems to be in helping a person to write down quickly, shortly and exactly, some of his thoughts for his own use: and to make sure that he has enough, and only enough, premises for his conclusions (i.e. that his equations are neither more nor less in number than his unknowns) ... it seems doubtful whether any one spends his time well in reading lengthy translations of economic doctrines into mathematics, that have not been made by himself.' Yet Marshall goes on to conclude his preface as follows: 'A few specimens of those applications of mathematical language which have proved most useful for my own purpose have, however, been added in an Appendix.' The contemporary reader of these specimens will find treatment of problems which are now in the first-year textbooks.

There are numerous examples that can be quoted of how mathematics illuminates and distils economic doctrine. Let it suffice to quote two: Passinetti's article 'A Mathematical Formulation of the Ricardian System' (*Review of Economic Studies*, vol. 27, 1959–60, pp. 78–98) and the mathematical appendix to L. R. Klein's *The Keynesian Revolution* (Macmillan, 1952). Both are excellent examples of the facility with which apparently complex arguments can be expounded through the use of mathematics: in both cases the original sources are difficult to read yet the basic structure of the arguments can be seen through the mathematics to be quite simple.

Today the use of mathematics in economics require no apology. Simply, it has become an important means of expressing ideas and communicating them to other people. The contemporary student cannot expect to progress far in economic theory without at least a working knowledge of algebra and calculus.

The reasons why mathematics has come to be so accepted are not difficult to trace. First, there is the clarity and rigour that mathematics can bring to exposition, a good example of which is P. A. Samuelson's classic *Foundations of Economic Analysis* (Harvard U.P., 1947). This book demonstrates, as do the other references above, that economic theory readily translates into mathematical language. Moreover, much confusion and misunderstanding can be avoided if the theory is expressed mathematically in the first instance. A second reason why mathematics has become accepted is that its use gives a potential virility to the exposition of ideas. Through the mathematics the implications of generalisations, and relaxed or changed assumptions are often easy to discern and always in question. As other sciences have clearly shown, mathematics is a superb medium through which to develop the implications of a set of basic ideas.

Mathematical economics has its dangers, however. While the mathematical style is an excellent approach to developing ideas, it is not by any means the only approach to new ones. Indeed there may be some conflict. The quest for a conceptual framework within which the problems of underdeveloped countries can be better understood is every bit as likely to succeed if approached empirically than by abstract theorising. This is partly because there are strong temptations within the mathematical style to lose contact with economic reality by modifying or restricting assumptions so as to render the consequent mathematical problems more tractable. Thus the literature abounds with models in which constant returns to scale are assumed and capital is assumed to be homogeneous without reference to the sensitivity of results to such contentious propositions. Modern theory of economic growth contains few propositions which a government would be well advised to adopt as criteria for policy.

These dangers amount to no more than a warning that the mathematical approach to economic theory can be taken too far if the economist's concern is to remain with the realities of society. How far they should be taken is a matter of judgment. Every year it becomes possible and desirable to go a step further because meanwhile our understanding of how society works is developed in some respects. The danger is only in loss of contact with earth's gravity without having the means on board to effect re-entry from orbit.

Having expressed the dangers I can hasten to express also the great intellectual charm of the mathematical style. At its best mathematical economics is not simply a branch of applied mathematics: the economics is inextricably woven into the fabric of the argument, and it is as likely that economics will point the way to an answer as that the answer will be dictated by the mathematics. In this spirit it is not simply a matter of learning mathematics in order to become a mathematical economist: at each and every step the mathematics must be digested to the point where translation between economics and mathematics becomes second nature. Fluency in both languages is not enough since the greatest delights are reserved for the simultaneous translator and often derive from the translation process itself.

Textbooks

It follows from the above arguments that to become a mathematical economist requires a knowledge of both mathematics and economics, and that the best books to use are those which integrate the disciplines. Unfortunately there are not many that can be highly recommended according to this criterion, although there are several books on mathematics written for the economist. Many of these are referred to here, while mathematics books on the mathematics which an economist might find useful are not discussed.

Calculus and linear algebra are the two basic fields of mathematics with which an economist must be familiar. Differential equations are hardly less important, and the calculus of variations, set theory and topology must all be embraced by the mathematical economist who wants to contemplate contemporary work at the frontiers of the subject.

One of the earliest and best books written to explain the relevance and mysteries of the calculus is R. G. D. Allen, *Mathematical Analysis for Economists* (Macmillan, 1962). This was first published in 1938 and in some respects is now outdated. Applications are largely restricted to microeconomics and the selection of topics within mathematics could be improved in the light of subsequent developments. However, the degree of integration achieved surpasses most subsequent attempts and this pioneering work deserves to remain on every beginner's reading list.

An easier book than the above from the mathematical point of view is J. P. Lewis, *An Introduction to Mathematics for Students of Economics* (Macmillan, 1959). This volume is good for the student who needs to begin by being reminded what 'O-level' mathematics was about. The selection of mathematical topics is sensible, but the integration of economic topics is at best slight.

It has already been suggested that the range of mathematics

which is essential extends beyond the calculus to include linear algebra and some other topics. In recognition of this, R. G. D. Allen has produced a volume, *Basic Mathematics* (Macmillan, 1962) which introduces and develops to an extent the whole range of mathematics which economists now find most useful. The book is a very good exposition in these terms but is sadly lacking in reference to economics.

A volume which does cover application of 'the new math' (excluding calculus) and which is stimulating to the beginner as a result is J. G. Kemeny, J. L. Snell and G. L. Thompson, *Introduction to Finite Mathematics* (2nd edn, Prentice-Hall, 1966). Here the applications are drawn from across the social sciences and are not therefore exclusively economic. As a result the economic applications are not developed in any depth. However, for the beginner this book has much to commend it.

Some recent volumes attempt to cover much of 'the new math' as well as the calculus, and at the same time to integrate all this into the basic economic theory. Possibly the most successful of these is T. Yamane, *Mathematics for Economists: an Elementary Survey* (Prentice-Hall, 1962), although in some respects I have a preference for J. E. Draper and J. S. Klingman, *Mathematical Analysis: Business and Economic Applications* (Harper and Row, 1967) which covers less ground but in several ways to better effect.

All the above volumes are deficient to the extent that they treat mainly microeconomics and largely ignore macroeconomic problems. For this reason there is a case for adding G. C. Archibald and R. G. Lipsey, *An Introduction to a Mathematical Treatment of Economics* (Weidenfeld and Nicolson, 1967) to the initial reading list.

Once the student has progressed this far with his reading, the next step is to embrace texts on economics which utilise mathematics, and in parallel, to develop his understanding of mathematics with a continuing eye on its application to economics.

Several good books are available on microeconomics in which appropriate use of mathematics is made. J. M. Henderson and R. E. Quandt, *Microeconomic Theory: a Mathematical Approach* (McGraw-Hill, 1958) is deservedly well known, as is W. J. Baumol, *Economic Theory and Operations Analysis* (Prentice-Hall, 1961). These volumes are largely complementary and reading can usefully be extended by adding to them R. E. Kuenne, *Microeconomic Theory of the Market Mechanism: a General Equilibrium Approach* (Collier-Macmillan, 1968). Beyond these the field of choice is very wide, but there is a strong case for recommending the mathematical appendix of J. R. Hicks, *Value and Capital: an Enquiry into some Fundamental Principles of Economic Theory* (2nd edn, Clarendon Press, 1946) and that the student should eventually go further back in time to Samuelson's *Foundations of Economic Analysis* which was referred to earlier.

A very sound text on macroeconomics is G. Ackley, *Macroeconomic Theory* (Macmillan, 1961) although the use of mathematics here is not extensive. Generally the field is underdeveloped, and L. R. Klein, *The Keynesian Revolution* is one of the best books for the student who wishes to deploy his mathematical skills.

Knowledge of differential and difference equation methods becomes important in the development of macroeconomics at this point and the necessary skills are well expounded in W. J. Baumol, *Economic Dynamics: an Introduction* (2nd edn, Macmillan, 1959) and S. Goldberg, *Introduction to Difference Equations* (Wiley, 1958). Much of this ground is also covered in R. G. D. Allen, *Macroeconomic Theory: a Mathematical Treatment* (Macmillan, 1967) and this last stands alone as a serious attempt to express macroeconomics from a developed mathematical viewpoint. The book is deficient in its treatment of economic policy and on the monetary side, but there are no close substitutes for it. As a complement, but not covering the particular deficiencies referred to, J. R. Hicks, *Capital and Growth* (Oxford U.P., 1965) can be strongly recommended as a text on topics in advanced theory in which the use of mathematics facilitates the exposition.

It has already been said that linear algebra is an essential branch of mathematics for today's economic theorists. Beyond the extent to which this is covered in the introductory texts, the most popular volume is G. Hadley, *Linear Algebra* (Addison-Wesley, 1961). Through this the student can readily progress to one of the most important economics books in recent years: R. Dorfman, P. A. Samuelson and R. M. Solow, *Linear Programming and Economic Analysis* (McGraw-Hill, 1958).

There are in fact numerous books which cover linear algebra, linear programming and game theory. Many have considerable merit. On game theory some of the earlier volumes are still the best, such as J. C. C. McKinsey, *Introductory to the Theory of Games* (McGraw-Hill, 1952), and the pioneer work of J. von Neumann and O. Morgenstern, *Theory of Games and Economic Behavior* (Princeton U.P., 1953). On linear models generally D. Gale, *The Theory of Linear Economic Models* (McGraw-Hill, 1960) can be highly recommended and a less well known work, C. Almon, *Matrix Methods in Economics* (Addison-Wesley, 1967) is rewarding reading.

For the economist who wishes to go further, but first to take stock of the point now reached, a quite recent book, K. Lancaster, *Mathematical Economics* (Collier-Macmillan, 1968) meets the need. Half this volume is taken up with reviews of relevant mathematics and the remainder with its application. A graduate in mathematics might well begin reading economics at this point. But he should be warned of the need to retrace several more steps into the volumes discussed above and to read much other economics besides if the dangers discussed at the beginning of this chapter are to be avoided.

Other Reading

Through its developments immediately before, during and since the Second World War, mathematical economics has been closely linked with econometrics. The Econometric Society is the international society to which both mathematical economists and econometricians belong. Its journal, *Econometrica*, contains much of the most advanced work in the field. However as a journal of economic theory, that is to say, of advanced mathematical economic theory, *Econometrica* must currently be rated second to the *Review of Economic Studies*. Largely through its connection with Cambridge, England, this latter journal has been able to attract important papers from the world's leading theorists and to publish symposia on important and contentious topics. Within its pages many of the battles between Cambridge, England and Cambridge, Massachusetts have been fought, followed and sometimes won. Recently many contributions have tended to be written for the more exclusive consumption of mathematical economists and the *Review* has had only limited success in developing econometric contributions. Meanwhile *Econometrica* embraces many contributions of a management science nature while retaining much of its original emphasis. Most current articles in both journals are likely to be found difficult reading but many economists would hope to keep up with them, albeit with a time lag of a few years.

A third journal, the *International Economic Review*, first published in 1960, comprises papers which are mathematical or econometric in nature. A number of important contributions, especially from younger economists, have appeared in its pages. Further, yet another journal, the *Journal of Economic Theory* has been launched in 1969 to meet the growing demand for an outlet for research. This has attracted papers by some well known authors for its early issues and promises to be an important contribution to the literature.

Meanwhile, just about every journal in economics has articles with a mathematical flavour and the *Quarterly Journal of Economics* can perhaps be fairly picked out as one which a mathematical economist may find well suited to his tastes.

Most of the developments in mathematical economics have been published originally in journal articles or been made as contributions to symposia and conferences. For this reason collections of journal articles and conference papers provide an important source of reference. Important among such collections are *Readings in Mathematical Economics*, Vols. I and II, edited by P. K. Newman (Johns Hopkins Press, 1968), *Activity Analysis in the Theory of Growth and Planning*, proceedings of a conference of the International Economic Association, edited by E. Malinvand and M. O. L. Bacharach (Macmillan, 1967), and *Essays on the Theory of Optimal Economic Growth*, edited by K. Shell (MIT Press, 1967), all of which have been published in the last three years. Three earlier collections, all dating from the 1950s and containing papers that have retained importance are O. Morgenstern (editor) *Economic Activity Analysis* (Wiley, 1954), H. W. Kuhn and A. W. Tucker (editors) *Linear Inequalities and Related Systems* (Princeton U.P., 1956), and K. J. Arrow and others (editors) *Mathematical Methods in the Social Sciences*: Proceedings of the First Stanford Symposium on Mathematical Methods in the Social Sciences (Stanford U.P., 1960).

Among the books published on mathematical economics are three series which contain several important works and a new series which has made an auspicious start. The Cowles Commission Monographs contain highly significant contributions to mathematical economics as well as econometrics. Among them is a set of readings edited by T. C. Koopmans: *Activity Analysis of Production and Allocation* (Wiley, 1951), K. J. Arrow's important work: *Social Choice and Individual Values* (2nd edn, Wiley, 1963), and G. Debreu's *Theory of Value: an Axiomatic Analysis of Economic Equilibrium* (Wiley, 1959).

North-Holland publish two important series, Contributions to Economic Analysis, which is the older series, and Studies in Mathematical and Managerial Economics. Both contain much that is essentially econometric but the definitive works of J. Tinbergen, *On the Theory of Economic Policy* (2nd edn, North-Holland, 1963) and *Economic Policy: Principles and Design* (North-Holland, 1956) are included in the former, while the latter contains, for example, H. Theil's *Optimal Decision Rules for Government and Industry* (North-Holland, 1964).

The new series which is most promising is Oliver and Boyd's

Mathematical Economics Texts. Again econometrics and mathematical economics are combined. Four volumes have been published so far, three of which are accounted for by D. G. Champernowne: *Uncertainty and Estimation in Economics* (Oliver and Boyd, 1969).

All the texts referred to in this survey of the literature contain bibliographies which will direct further reading.

Mathematical economics has not yet become a field in which the literature is vast, and for those that work in it the references given above, plus occasional books, will be found to be an ample diet.

CHAPTER FIFTEEN

ECONOMETRIC THEORY AND METHOD

C. E. V. LESER

Introduction

Econometrics, in the words of the Econometric Society, is concerned with 'the advancement of economic theory in its relation
to statistics and mathematics'. As a discipline it originated in
attempts to give algebraic and numerical content to concepts of
economic theory such as the demand curve and the production
function, and later on to relationships between macroeconomic
variables. The main statistical tool employed for this purpose was
and still is regression analysis, which was originally developed for
application in the natural sciences.

However, the need for special methods to deal with economic
problems soon became apparent. To a large extent this is due to
the facts that a large part of the basic material analysed consists
of time series and that several relationships exist between the same
variables. These considerations led to the creation of a large body
of econometric theory, allied to mathematical statistics but with
emphasis on economic applications. The boundary between
statistical and econometric methods remains fluid, as is also the
boundary between econometric applications on one hand and
mathematical economics or economic statistics on the other, when
dealing with the specification of relationships and the use of
statistical data.

Textbooks of Econometrics

Before the 1960s, a scarcity of textbooks made the approach to the
subject difficult. This has now been remedied by the appearance in
print of a number of texts written for readers of different interests
and mathematical attainments. Accordingly, the emphasis given to
econometric methods and to applications respectively varies con-

siderably. The books briefly described here are arranged approximately in ascending order of mathematical difficulty and concentration on theoretical aspects.

An Introduction to Econometrics by L. R. Klein (Prentice-Hall, 1962) is written for the non-specialist. The approach is by field of application, and methodological problems are dealt with as they arise but are given quite a good deal of space.

Another book of the same title, *An Introduction to Econometrics* by A. A. Walters (Macmillan, 1968) is also written for non-specialists. The basic econometric methods are developed in considerable detail, followed by a discussion of applications.

Intermediate Economic Statistics by K. A. Fox (Wiley, 1968) may be described as an econometrics textbook although the word is not mentioned in the title. Emphasis is on application of regression analysis and allied methods to particular economic relationships including computation. It is suitable for students with some knowledge of economics and statistics.

Another book written for non-specialists with some knowledge of statistical concepts but also as introduction for students specialising in the subject is: *Econometric Techniques and Problems* by C. E. V. Leser (Griffin, 1966). Like the book by Walters, it deals with methods first and then with applications, but whilst the treatment is more concise, it covers more ground in methodology.

A standard text for students with a knowledge of basic statistical theory is *Econometric Methods* by J. Johnston (McGraw-Hill, 1963). The exposition of econometric methods is accompanied by numerical illustrations. Matrix algebra is taught in a separate chapter before being used in the latter part of the book.

Econometric Models and Methods by C. F. Christ (Wiley, 1966) provides a very detailed exposition, and as the title indicates, it deals at length with model formulation as well as estimation methods. It is suitable for students with knowledge of matrix algebra and basic statistical theory.

Originally written in French, *Statistical Methods of Econometrics* by E. Malinvaud (North-Holland, 1966) provides a very comprehensive text for final year honours and postgraduate students. It deals with a wide range of methodological problems, which are studied in relation to economic applications.

Finally, *Econometric Theory* by A. S. Goldberger (Wiley, 1964) is chiefly a textbook for postgraduate students with a good grounding in mathematics and statistics and a reference book for research workers. Written on the level of a mathematical statistics text, it starts off by revising the standard theory before branching out into the specific econometric field.

Two older textbooks are still likely to be extensively used for reference; they are: *Econometrics* by G. Tintner (Wiley, 1952) and *A Textbook of Econometrics* by L. R. Klein (Row, Peterson, 1953). The former is particularly useful on account of its full derivation of mathematical theorems and numerical results, the latter on account of its discussion of the problems encountered in simultaneous equation estimation. This topic is also covered in the monograph *Stochastically Dependent Equations: an Introductory Text for Econometricians* by P. R. Fisk (Griffin, 1967). Notwithstanding its title, this book is mainly suitable for postgraduate students.

Textbooks of Statistics

Before tackling econometrics, most students will have acquired a working knowledge of statistical sources and of analysing economic data by means of description and summarisation, including the principles of index number construction. These subjects are dealt with elsewhere in this book.

Students will normally also have followed a basic course in statistical theory and practice, and they will find it useful to refer back from time to time to one of the standard textbooks. Among these may be mentioned: *Statistics: An Introduction* by D. A. S. Fraser (Wiley, 1958); *Introduction to Mathematical Statistics* by P. G. Hoel (2nd edn, Wiley, 1954); *Introduction to the Theory of Statistics* by A. M. Mood and F. A. Graybill (2nd edn, McGraw-Hill, 1963); and *A First Course in Mathematical Statistics* by C. E. Weatherburn (2nd edn, Cambridge U.P., 1949). For a more detailed treatment, one can hardly do better than refer to *The Advanced Theory of Statistics* by M. G. Kendall and A. Stuart (Griffin, vol. 1, 2nd edn, 1963; vol. 2, 2nd edn, 1967; vol. 3, 1966). Originally assembled in two volumes, the material is now divided up in such a way that the first volume deals with frequency and probability distributions; the second with estimation, hypothesis testing, regression and correlation; the third with analysis of variance, design of experiments, sample surveys, multivariate analysis and time series.

Naturally, some parts of statistical theory are of greater interest to economists than other parts, and regression analysis in particular is the basic technique used in econometrics; hence, books specially devoted to this subject may be usefully studied. *Methods of Correlation and Regression Analysis* by M. Ezekiel and K. A. Fox (3rd edn, Wiley, 1959) gives a fairly elementary treatment but covers, besides ordinary least squares, some ground in simultaneous equation estimation. *Regression Analysis* by E. J. Williams (Wiley, 1959) deals with both standard techniques and a wide range of less well known ones, and it may be profitably read by economists even though the examples are chosen from other fields.

There are other statistical topics which are of interest to economists and which, though not extensively used so far in this context, are coming to assume greater importance. These include the theory of sample surveys, which are now being applied, for example, in studies of consumer behaviour; multi-variate methods such as principal components analysis and discriminant analysis, designed to study relationships between variables which are of a more complex nature than regression; and spectral methods which endeavour to give theoretical insight into the processes generating time series. A standard text dealing with the first of these topics is *Sampling Techniques* by W. G. Cochran (Wiley, 1963). The second topic is given a useful introduction in *A Course in Multivariate Analysis* by M. G. Kendall (Griffin, 1957). Spectral analysis with emphasis on economic applications is described in *Time Series Analysis* by E. J. Hannan (Methuen, 1960) and in *Spectral Analysis of Economic Time Series* by C. W. J. Granger and M. Hatanaka (Princeton U.P., 1964). This is not an exhaustive list of statistical topics which have a bearing on economics and econometrics, and others may become increasingly relevant in future.

Bibliographies

For the undergraduate reader, the existing textbooks of econometrics should be sufficient as far as the study of econometric theory and method is concerned. For additional reading, the emphasis is likely to be on econometric applications, and thus on monographs or articles in which econometric methods are used to tackle specific problems. The post-graduate student specialising in the subject will also want to go further in the methodological field, to learn how the relevant aspects of statistical theory have been derived and proved, and under which assumptions they are applicable.

All the econometrics textbooks quoted here have extensive bibliographies, be it as footnotes in the text, as references at the end of each chapter or as references at the end of the book. In most cases, both methodological and applied studies are covered. It should be noted that a number of studies are both, in the sense that new or modified methods of analysis are being developed in connection with specific applications.

In addition, there are a few surveys of the whole subject which quote a wide range of material for reading. Among these are *Methodology of Mathematical Economics and Econometrics* by G. Tintner (University of Chicago Press, 1968) and 'A Survey of Econometrics' by C. E. V. Leser (*J. Roy. Statist. Soc.*, ser. A, vol. 131, 1968, pp. 530–566). Their perusal may also be useful for students for reasons other than finding lists of references.

For material currently published, there are no indexes of econometric studies as such, perhaps largely on account of the difficulties inherent in drawing the boundary between econometrics on one hand and either statistics or economics on the other. Summaries of some among the theoretical studies can be found in the *Statistical Theory and Method Abstracts* (1960–), which appear at quarterly intervals. The material is arranged by section, and for the present purpose, sections 6 and 10, headed 'Relationships' and 'Stochastic Theory and Time Series Analysis' respectively, are particularly relevant.

A wider coverage of econometric studies is achieved in the *Journal of Economic Literature* (1963–), which prior to 1969 appeared under the name *Journal of Economic Abstracts*. From the very beginning on, it gives summaries of selected articles, and in addition it quotes references to others which are not summarised. Originally, the abstracted articles were arranged under the heading of the journal in which they appear, though with a subject index from January 1965 to March 1966; but since June 1966, the entries are classified by subject. This arrangement facilitates the identification of entries which are of interest to the reader, in this case found under the heading 'Statistical Methods; Econometrics; Social Accounting' until 1968 and from 1969 on under the heading 'Economic Statistics' and particularly the subheading 'Econometric and Statistical Methods'. Some applied econometric studies may be found under the subject of application. In addition, the journal under its new title contains survey articles, book reviews and a comprehensive annotated list of new books.

A Bibliography for Students of Economics (Oxford U.P., 1968) is also useful. One of its nine chapters is headed 'Statistics', and its subheadings include 'Econometric methods' and 'Econometric and statistical studies'.

Monograph Series

In the early days, there were no centres of econometric research as such. Research was initiated by pioneers such as H. L. Moore and H. Schultz in the field of demand analysis, P. H. Douglas in production function studies, J. Dean in cost function estimation and J. Tinbergen in the construction of macroeconomic models. Their work was then carried on by other individual investigators.

Criticism directed towards Tinbergen's method which individually estimated the equations forming part of a large interdependent system, led to the systematic study of simultaneous equation problems by the Cowles Commission for Research in Economics, originally in Colorado Springs and then in Chicago, later on becoming the Cowles Foundation for Research in Economics at Yale University. A valuable monograph series, containing both methodological and applied studies, was published by the Cowles Commission; particularly important are Monograph No. 10: *Statistical Inference in Dynamic Economic Models* edited by T. C. Koopmans (Wiley, 1950), and Monograph No. 14: *Studies in Econometric Method,* edited by W. C. Hood and T. C. Koopmans (Wiley, 1953). The former contains much of the statistical theory underlying simultaneous equation systems, whilst the latter is more directly concerned with estimation methods in this context.

In the post-war years, the Department of Applied Economics in the University of Cambridge became another centre of econometric research. The chief emphasis was an applied demand studies, but in the process much theoretical work on time series and autocorrelation was developed. Most of these studies were published in the form of journal articles but assembled by the Department of Applied Economics in its reprint series. Since many libraries collect reprint series, usually in boxes, it is thus easy for the student to lay hands on material otherwise scattered over various periodicals. This particular series includes, in reprints No. 36 and 43, the account and tabulation of the Durbin-Watson test, which has become a standard econometric technique. The original article is 'Testing for Serial Correlation in Least Squares Regression' by J. Durbin and G. S. Watson (*Biometrika,* vol. 37, 1950, pp. 409–428; vol. 38, 1951, pp. 159–178).

There is also a monograph series in which longer works of the Department of Applied Economics are published. It includes some econometric studies, notably No. 5: *The Lognormal Distribution* by J. Aitchison and J. A. C. Brown (Cambridge U.P., 1957). A more recently instituted series is *A Programme for Growth* (Chapman and Hall, 1962–), which incorporates work in progress on a planning model for the United Kingdom.

Another, and now perhaps the major, world centre of econometric research is the Econometric Institute at the Netherlands School of Economics in Rotterdam. Much of the centre's work is

219

of a methodological nature, first made available in an unpublished report series and later on published in learned journals. Many of the longer studies undertaken there are included in the numerous econometric publications of the North-Holland Publishing Company, together with results of work done elsewhere.

Most of the North-Holland books on economics and econometrics are arranged in series, the chief one being the Contributions to Economic Analysis. Publications in this series which are important for the student of econometric theory are: *Economic Forecasts and Policy* by H. Theil (2nd edn, 1961) and *Econometric Model Building: Essays on the Causal Chain Approach* edited by H. O. Wold (1964). Another more recently started series are the Studies in Mathematical and Managerial Economics, which include Malinvaud's textbook as well as other texts in disciplines allied to econometrics.

Periodicals

The one journal exclusively devoted to econometrics and its borderline disciplines is *Econometrica* (1933–) which was established by the Econometric Society soon after its foundation in 1930. It offers a major publication outlet for studies in econometric theory and applications as well as mathematical economics. About a dozen articles are at present contained in each quarterly issue.

Reference to *Econometrica* is indispensable for anyone studying recent advances in estimation techniques, particularly those dealing with simultaneous equations. Important articles on this subject are, among others:

'A Generalised Classical Method of Linear Estimation of Coefficients in a Structural Equation' by R. L. Basmann (vol. 25, 1957, pp. 77–83); 'Three-stage Least Squares; Simultaneous Estimates of Simultaneous Relations' by A. Zellner and H. Theil (vol. 30, 1962, pp. 54–78); and 'Efficient Estimation of Simultaneous Equation Systems' by T. J. Rothenberg and C. T. Leenders (vol. 32, 1964, pp. 57–76). An approach to the subject which has recently come into favour analyses the properties of alternative estimators by means of simulation studies. In this field, too, much of the work done has been published in *Econometrica;* 'A Capital-intensive Approach to the Small Sample Properties of various Simultaneous Equation Estimators' by R. Summers (vol. 35, 1965, pp. 1–41), deserves particular mention.

In addition to full articles and book reviews, *Econometrica* publishes the programme and summaries of papers read at

Econometric Society conferences which are normally held twice a year in North America, once a year in Europe and from time to time in other parts of the world. For the European conferences up to 1962, the custom was to publish summaries of the discussion as well as the paper, but this practice has now been abandoned. Since 1966, the conference reports have been assembled in an annual supplementary issue, the first one of these including an account of the society's First World Congress held in Rome in 1965. The conference papers are not automatically published as such, but many of them subsequently appear as articles in *Econometrica* or other journals.

Articles on econometric methods and applications also frequently appear in statistical journals, notably those emphasising government and economic statistics, such as the *Journal of the American Statistical Association* (1888–) and the *Review of the International Statistical Institute* (1933–), also known as *Revue de l'Institut International de Statistique,* which originally was its exclusive title. Econometric applications commonly find their way into economics periodicals. Some of these, for example the *International Economic Review* (1960–) and the *Review of Economics and Statistics* (1919–), also publish methodological studies to an increasing extent; and the last-named journal has, in particular, attracted many important articles dealing with theory and estimation of production functions.

Econometric Applications

It has already been pointed out that econometrics is a blend of statistical theory and economic applications, and that it is desirable for anybody studying econometric theory to make himself familiar with the main problems encountered in applying the techniques to actual problems. The difficulties in approaching econometric applications are, however, greater than in the case of theory, as there is less guidance available towards following a systematic path of study, the textbooks being less adequate in this respect. An attempt to provide a substantial amount of reading matter of this kind in one volume has been made in *Readings in Economic Statistics and Econometrics* edited by A. Zellner (Little, Brown, 1968).

A textbook specially designed to supplement the methodological treatises and to provide an approach with a view to applications is *Empirical Econometrics* by J. S. Cramer (North-Holland, 1969). Among the chief textbooks of econometrics mentioned earlier on, those by Klein, Walters and Leser give an introduction to problems encountered and actual studies in some major fields of applied econometrics such as production functions, demand analysis and macroeconomic models. Each of these fields deserves further study, but the difficulty is where to start.

In the first of the three fields mentioned, the position is perhaps a little easier than elsewhere. A valuable introduction to the problems concerned is provided by the article 'Production and Cost Functions: an Econometric Survey' by A. A. Walters (*Econometrica*, vol. 31, 1963, pp. 1–66), the monograph *On the Theory and Measurement of Technological Change* by M. Brown (Cambridge U.P., 1966), and the conference report *The Theory and Empirical Analysis of Production* edited by M. Brown (National Bureau of Economic Research, 1967).

There has been no recent comprehensive survey of econometric demand analysis, as distinct from surveys of demand theory. The approach to the subject is perhaps most readily made by reading a number of important monographs. *The Theory and Measurement of Demand* by H. Schultz (University Press of Chicago, 1938) surveys the early studies in the field and at the same time makes a pioneering contribution. *Demand Analysis: a Study in Econometrics* by H. Wold and L. Jureen (Wiley, 1953) deals with theoretical problems of regression analysis as applied to demand measurement, besides giving empirical results. *Econometric Analysis for Public Policy* by K. A. Fox (Iowa State U.P., 1958) is especially devoted to demand and supply relationships for agricultural commodities. A classical study of one aspect of demand measurement is *The Analysis of Family Budgets* by S. J. Prais and H. S. Houthakker (Cambridge U.P., 1955).

Econometric models of the economy as a whole are in most cases the products of substantial work and are generally published in the form of monographs, though accounts of some small-scale models are also published in article form. A classical study in model building, which may be a useful starting point, is *An Econometric Model of the United States, 1929–1952* by L. R. Klein and A. S. Goldberger (North-Holland, 1955). The model, containing 20 equations, is sufficiently large to illustrate the main problems encountered in model construction, and at the same time sufficiently small to permit intensive analysis of its properties. A description of several models and a discussion of model building methods and difficulties is found in *Models of Income Determination* edited by I. Friend (Princeton U.P., 1964).

Finally, mention may be made of the fact that econometrics, like statistics, is a subject which cannot be learnt from reading alone but demands practical work as well. Most textbooks provide exercises, but for the more ambitious, a small practical project may be appropriate. To this intent, study of the literature in the field of mathematically formulated economic theory and a knowledge of statistical sources and data may be equally important as familiarity with econometric theory and techniques.

CHAPTER SIXTEEN

ECONOMIC DEVELOPMENT, GROWTH AND PLANNING

S. K. NATH AND J. E. K. CORBETT

Economic development and economic growth are related subjects: indeed there is a great deal of overlap between them, so that some economists would want to consider them as one subject. They are both concerned with the causes and conditions of growth in income, wealth, and—ultimately and hopefully—welfare of a society. If the typical economy in mind is a relatively poor country, one is studying economic *development;* but if the typical economy is assumed to be a relatively developed country, one is studying economic *growth.* Differences between the two kinds of economies, particularly in terms of what can be taken for granted regarding the broader social and economic characteristics of a country, are large enough to make some theories applicable only to one of the two kinds. Even where the same theory can be applied to both kinds of economies, there may be a difference in the correct assumptions about the relevant empirical facts. For example, consider the simple theory of supply and demand: a rise in the price of a commodity is more likely in a poor country than in a developed one to lead to the expectation of a further price rise; therefore the predictions of what is broadly the same theory differ for the two kinds of economies.

The other object of this chapter is planning of the kind that is designed to promote the growth and development of a whole economy. However, growth of an economy rests on the growth of individual factories and farms (i.e. growth on a micro level); hence the literature planning at the level of an individual firm is also relevant to our field. Yet this field is often exclusively identified with planning at the *macro* level: one would perhaps be right in saying that in the theoretical literature too much attention is given to macro planning at the expense of micro planning.

Planning, especially in its applied aspect, is a derived subject: it uses tools developed in other parts of the subject of economics.

224

Some examples of these are: linear and other kinds of programming, input-output analysis, investment appraisal and cost-benefit analysis, and statistical techniques of prediction. Needless to say the last of these belongs to econometric theory, and the others to mathematical economics; hence for the reader who is interested in planning the chapters on these other two subjects are also relevant.

Again, a great many contributors to economic growth and development employ mathematical and econometric techniques. Hence the reader interested in growth and development must not exclude from his range of search periodicals whose titles make them sound mathematical or econometric. As for books, if their content is relevant to the field of economic development, growth and planning, the title would usually make this abundantly clear.

Reading Material

An excellent book giving a wide and yet detailed coverage of the field of development, growth and planning is *Economic Development: Theory, History, Policy* by G. M. Meier and R. E. Baldwin (Wiley, 1957). An analytical framework of the process of development is followed by the background to current problems, and in turn by theoretical and policy aspects of accelerating development in poor countries, and of maintaining growth in rich countries. In addition, three appendices contain bibliographies on the socio-cultural aspects of development, on development programmes and plans, and on case studies of development. Good supplementary reading to this book is provided by *Planning and Growth in Rich and Poor Countries,* edited by W. Birmingham and A. G. Ford (Allen and Unwin, 1967): this book starts by providing a theoretical framework for the appreciation of the problems of economic growth, and continues with a wide variety of case studies on individual countries in an attempt to highlight the contrast between rich and poor countries. It also contains a selected reading list. Another well-known book is *The Stages of Economic Growth,* by W. W. Rostow (Cambridge U.P., 1960), which looks at what the author describes as the five major stages of economic growth with illustrations from historical and contemporary experience.

There are a number of useful introductory books to the field of development economics. A broad coverage of the subject is given in *The Economics of Underdeveloped Countries,* by P. T. Bauer and B. S. Yamey (Cambridge U.P., 1957). Another textbook on the subject is *Principles of Development Economics,* by H. J. Bruton

(Prentice-Hall, 1965): this book also contains bibliographies at the end of each chapter pointing out historical aspects and development policies important to the subject. More recently, *The Economics of Underdeveloped Countries* by J. Bhagwati (Weidenfeld and Nicolson, 1966) gives a general description of these economies and the way in which they can be transformed within a planning framework. Note should also be taken of *International Development: Growth and Change* by H. W. Singer (McGraw-Hill, 1964) for a general approach to the many aspects of economic development.

Perhaps the most comprehensive and detailed book in this field is *Leading Issues in Development Economics,* by G. M. Meier (Oxford U.P., 1964). This consists of selected excerpts from conferences, government publications, journals and books. The excerpts are divided into nine parts and are integrated by means of connecting text notes; the editor is careful to include a variety of viewpoints on each issue. Recently this publication has been thoroughly revised and the new edition bears the title *Leading Issues in Economic Development,* by G. M. Meier (Oxford U.P., 1970). Whereas the first edition was principally concerned with the theoretical issues and conflicts of economic development, the second edition shifts the emphasis towards the more practical aspects of development policy. More than half of the readings of the first edition have been replaced by new material to reflect the shift in emphasis. The ten parts of the second edition still contain detailed bibliographies.

Another useful series of articles and papers is contained in *The Economics of Underdevelopment,* edited by A. N. Agarwala and S. P. Singh (Oxford U.P., 1958): the six sections of the book contain twenty-one items which have been selected on the basis of their overall approach to the various aspects of the subject. A book of thirty-three readings which attempts to reflect the recent drift of development economics is *Economic Development: Challenge and Promise,* edited by S. Spiegelglas and C. J. Welsh (Prentice-Hall, 1970). The survey article by H. B. Chenery 'Comparative advantage and development policy' in the *American Economic Review* of 1961 has a useful bibliography.

For the trade aspect of development a useful book is *International Trade and Development,* by G. M. Meier (Harper and Row, 1963). A revised and expanded edition of this concentrates more on the practical than the theoretical aspects of the subject and is entitled *The International Economics of Development,* by G. M. Meier (Harper and Row, 1968). This book assesses the effects of international trade and payments policies on development, and goes on to consider the conflict between gains from trade and gains from growth. There is an extensive 'Bibliographical Survey' at the end of the book.

Most of the important contributions to growth theory have appeared as articles in the various journals, and therefore an essential, and indeed superb book, is *Readings in the Modern Theory of Economic Growth*, edited by J. Stiglitz and H. Uzawa (MIT Press, 1969). This includes sections, amongst others, on basic aggregative growth models, technical progress, and Cambridge growth and distribution theory, and the list of contributors contains many names which are famous in the field of growth theory. The splendid survey article by F. H. Hahn and R. C. O. Matthews 'The theory of economic growth: a survey' in the *Economic Journal* of 1964 has a very good bibliography. For a more mathematical treatment of growth theory a useful book is *Macroeconomic Theory*, by R. G. D. Allen (Macmillan, 1967). Also of interest is the series of Radcliffe Lectures given at the University of Warwick in 1969 by R. M. Solow and published by Oxford U.P. in 1970 under the title *Growth Theory: an Exposition*, which also contains a selected bibliography of the modern theory of economic growth.

There are also a number of books of selected essays on the subject of economic growth, three of which deserve mention here: *Essays in Economic Stability and Growth*, by N. Kaldor (Duckworth, 1960), *Theories of Economic Growth* by B. F. Hoselitz and others (Free Press, 1960), and *Economic Growth and Structure*, selected essays by S. Kuznets (Heinemann, 1965).

Turning to the field of planning, there are once again a number of useful introductory books. Deserving particular mention is W. A. Lewis's *Development Planning* (Allen and Unwin, 1966), which gives an account of the basic techniques and the necessary policies for shaping a development plan; each section contains a list of further reading. Another interesting book is *Development Planning* by J. Tinbergen (Weidenfeld and Nicolson, 1967) which also contains an extensive bibliography. Two other books contribute to the theoretical approach to the problems of growth and planning: M. Dobb's *Economic Growth and Planning* (Routledge and Kegan Paul, 1960) and *Planning and Economic Growth*, by A. K. Dasgupta (Allen and Unwin, 1965) which draws on the Indian experience of planning.

A larger and more detailed book is *Developmental Planning* by R. L. Meier (McGraw-Hill, 1965) analysing the history of growth and planning and the recommendations which follow from this analysis. Most of the chapters contain an annotated list of works. A selection of readings edited by E. E. Hagen, *Planning Economic Development* (MIT Press, 1963) looks at the planning process in

227

various countries, eight of which are underdeveloped. Then follows a summary discussion of the difficulties encountered in planning and the remedies and machinery to overcome them. A more advanced and complex treatment is *Planning for Steady Growth,* by G. Mathur (Blackwell, 1965).

An important empirical contribution to the whole field of development is *Partners in Development,* the report of the Commission on International Development, chaired by L. B. Pearson (Praeger, 1969). The Commission looked into the whole question of international co-operation for economic development: recent history, indentification and analysis of the major obstacles which exist, and recommendations in such areas as international trade and assistance, population control and co-operation over the next two decades. There are two annexes to the report, on statistical materials and on the development situation in Latin America, Africa, South and West Asia, and East and South-east Asia, giving details of their various problems, policies and progress.

There are series of publications by various institutions, conferences, commissions, international organisations and governments. We can mention only a few of the more important here. The International Economic Association has devoted many conferences to various topics in economic development: the volumes containing the papers submitted to these conferences are often useful surveys of the relevant fields. The following are worth mentioning: *Capital Movements and Economic Development,* edited by J. H. Adler and P. W. Kuznets (1967), *Economic Consequences of the Size of Nations,* edited by E. A. G. Robinson (1960), *Economic Development for Africa South of the Sahara,* edited by E. A. G. Robinson (1964), *Economic Development for Eastern Europe,* edited by H. S. Ellis and H. C. Wallich (1962), *Economic Development with Special Reference to East Asia,* edited by K. Berrill (1964), *The Economics of Take-off into Sustained Growth,* edited by W. W. Rostow (1963), *International Trade in a Developing World,* edited by R. F. Harrod and D. Hague (1963), *Problems in Economic Development,* edited by E. A. G. Robinson (1965), *Stability and Progress in the World Economy,* edited by D. Hague (1958), *Activity Analysis in the Theory of Growth and Planning,* edited by E. Malinvaud and M. Bacharach (1967), and *Economics of International Migration,* edited by T. Brinley (1958). (All are published by Macmillan and the dates are of publication of the conference proceedings.)

Three volumes of the new Penguin Modern Economics Series are related to this subject: *Regional Analysis,* edited by L. Needleman (Penguin, 1968), an excellent book of articles, *Foreign Aid,*

228

edited by J. Bhagwati (Penguin, 1970) and *Growth Economics*, edited by A. K. Sen (Penguin, 1970). The Society for International Development holds a conference each year, the papers of which are published as *International Development ...*: they are also useful surveys of topical problems in the theory and practice of economic development. Several series of working papers are devoted to development economics (*see* p. 69).

Official Publications

Economic development plans are published in many of the underdeveloped countries, and these can be a useful source of statistical information. In developed countries these are fewer, but those for the United Kingdom are worth noting: *The National Plan* (Cmnd. 2764, HMSO, 1964) and *The Task Ahead: Economic Assessment to 1972* (HMSO, 1969) were issued by the Department of Economic Affairs. The Economic Development Committees for various industries are now publishing more detailed assessments to 1972 for their own industries.

The most important international source of development literature is the United Nations and its agencies. Some of the more important publications in this subject are *Pattern of Industrial Growth, 1938–58* (UN, 1960), *The Growth of World Industry, 1938–61* (2 vols, UN, 1963 and 1967), for statistical source material; and for planning techniques: *Planning for Economic Development* (2 vols, UN, 1963 and 1965), *Manual on Economic Development Projects* (UN, 1958), and *Planning and Plan Implementation* (UN, 1967). (*See* also pp. 109–119).

Two sections of the OECD have produced useful reports on economic development subjects: the Economic Policy Committee's *Growth and Economic Efficiency* (an unpublished report of 1964), *Policies for Economic Growth* (OECD, 1962) and *Multidisciplinary Aspects of Regional Development* (OECD, 1969). The Organisation's Development Centre has issued a *Manual of Industrial Project Analysis* (2 vols, OECD, 1968 and 1969).

Other international organisations publishing material regularly in this field are the International Monetary Fund, International Labour Office, International Bank for Reconstruction and Development, and the United Nations Conference on Trade and Development. For the publications of these and other international organisations (*see* Chapter 9).

229

Bibliographies

Bibliographies, often extensive, appear in many of the books mentioned so far. There are also some specialised lists. We have first *The Economics of 'Underdeveloped' Areas*, compiled by A. Hazlewood (2nd edn, Oxford U.P., 1959): an annotated list of books, articles and official publications, making an excellent bibliography, easy to use, comprehensive in coverage yet discriminating in selection. However, the trouble with the Hazlewood bibliography is that it is of use only for publications up to 1958. A recent bibliography is J. Brode's *The Process of Modernization* (Harvard U.P., 1969) which includes only such publications as cover the sociocultural aspects of economic development: one may say that it covers the sociology of development. Though this is an important field it leaves out the more technical aspects of development problems. Another specialist bibliography is *Human Resource and Economic Growth,* edited by M. C. Alexander-Frutschi (Stanford Research Center, 1963). This bibliography concentrates on the role of education and training in economic and social development. A publication which covers the general field of development in a very selective way is *Selected Readings and Source Materials on Economic Development;* this is a list of books, articles and reports recommended as reading material for the general development course of the Economic Development Institute during 1965–66, and is published by the International Bank for Reconstruction and Development, Washington. A similar selective bibliography is *Selected Bibliography on Financing of Development and Related Fields,* prepared by Mohammed Eweida and others, and published by the Institute of National Planning, United Arab Republic, March 1968. A guide to information sources concerning the economic, political, technical and social problems of the developing countries is *The Developing Nations* by E. G. Requa and J. Statham (Management information guides series, Gale Research Co., 1965).

For Latin American countries specifically, there are *Economic Development in Latin America,* by J. R. Wish, an annotated bibliography published by Praeger, 1965, and *Periodicals for Latin American Economic Development, Trade and Finance,* by M. H. Sable; this is also annotated and is published by the Latin American Center, University of California, Los Angeles, 1965.

Journals

There are a couple of journals which deal exclusively with economic development. The first is *Economic Development and Cultural Change* (University of Chicago Press, quarterly, 1952–). The second such periodical is the *Journal of Development Studies* (Cass, quarterly, 1964–). Then, there is the *Economic and Political Weekly* (Bombay, Sameeksha Trust, 1967–).

Finally, important articles about economic growth and development can appear from time to time in almost any journal of economics, e.g. the *Economic Journal,* or the *American Economic Review.* However, journals published in the developing countries or by institutions specially dealing with development problems more usually include papers on these topics. There is a very large number of these journals, and we present below a list of those which are of general interest.

Artha Vijnana (Gokhale Institute of Politics and Economics, quarterly, 1959–).

Asian Economic Review (Indian Institute of Economics, quarterly, 1966–).

Developing Economies (Tokyo, Institute of Asian Economic Affairs, quarterly, 1962–).

East African Economic Review (Kenya, semi-annually, 1954–).

Economic Bulletin for Asia and the Far East (UN, quarterly, 1966–).

Economic Bulletin for Latin America (UN, semi-annually, 1956–).

Economic Development (Washington, monthly).

Economic Review of the Arab World (Bureau of Lebanese and Arab Documentation, monthly, 1961–).

Finance and Development (IMF and IBRD, quarterly, 1964).

Indian Economic Journal (Indian Economic Association, quarterly, 1953–).

Intereconomics (Hamburg Institute for International Economics, monthly, 1966–).

International Development Review (Society for International Development, quarterly, 1959–).

International Monetary Fund Staff Papers (IMF, 3 p.a., 1950–).

International Review Service, Special Services, Trade and Economic Development (International Review Service, monthly, 1956–).

Journal of Asian Studies (Duke University, 5 p.a., 1941–).

Journal of Developing Areas (Western Illinois University, quarterly, 1966–).

Middle East Economic Papers (American University of Beirut, 1954–).

231

Overseas Development (Ministry of Overseas Development, bi-monthly, 1966–).
South East Asia Treaty Organisation Economic Bulletin (Bangkok, SEATO, quarterly, 1963–).
We also include a list of journals which are concerned more with local issues, and should be of interest for area studies:
African Development, 1966–
Bank of Ghana Quarterly Economic Bulletin, 1965–
Caribbean Monthly Bulletin, 1963–
Central Bank of Jordan Quarterly Bulletin, 1965–
Chile: Economic Notes, 1967–
Colombo Plan, 1954–
Economic Affairs (Calcutta), 1965–
Economic Bulletin of Ghana, 1957–
Economic Studies (Calcutta), 1959–
Economic Times (Bombay), 1961–
Economic Weekly (Bombay), 1949–
Far Eastern Economic Review, 1946–
Hawaii Economic Review, 1955–
Indian Economic Review, 1952–
Indian Journal of Economics, 1916–
Israel Economic Indicators, 1955–
Israel Economist, 1945–
Kashmir Affairs, 1959–
Malayan Economic Review, 1956–
Mysore Economic Review, 1915–
Nigerian Institute of Social and Economic Research Information Bulletin, 1965–
Nigerian Journal of Economic and Social Studies, 1959–
Pakistan Development Review, 1961–
Pakistan Economic Journal, 1951–
Phillipine Economic Journal, 1962–
Phillipine Economy Bulletin, 1966–
Review of Economic Conditions (Ankara), 1954–
Situation in Argentina, 1963–
Tata Quarterly (Bombay), 1946–
Turkish Economic News Summary, 1960–
United Malayan Banking Corporation Economic Review, 1965–
West Africa (London) 1917–

CHAPTER SEVENTEEN

BUSINESS CYCLES, SHORT-TERM ECONOMIC STABILISATION, PRICES AND INCOMES

DAVID R. CROOME

Changes in the levels of economic variables over time may be divided into movements which take place over a long period, reflecting the underlying trends of the growing economy, and fluctuations around these trends which occur over a much shorter period. These are often contrasted as 'secular' and 'cyclical' movements and it is with the latter that this chapter will be concerned.

The short-term cycle in economic activity, typically spanning five to seven years, dominates government economic policy. Although the economic planners have become increasingly interested in stimulating long-term growth rates, their immediate concern is to stabilise the behaviour of various economic variables as close as possible to some target values. The most important of these variables are the level of income, the level of prices, the unemployment rate and the balance of payments. This chapter will look especially at prices and income stabilisation.

Business Cycles

A rapid introduction to the development of business cycle study can be obtained by reading the articles under this title in *The Encyclopaedia of the Social Sciences* (New York, Macmillan, 1931) and *The International Encyclopaedia of the Social Sciences* (Macmillan and The Free Press, 1968). The articles by Wesley C. Mitchell in the first and Arthur F. Burns and T. Haavelmo in the second, give a concise summary of pre-Keynesian and post-Keynesian work respectively and contain useful introductory bibliographies.

Other bibliographies are published as appendices to the following books: *Business Fluctuations, Growth and Economic Stabilization: A Reader* edited by John J. Clark and Morris Cohen

233

(Random House, 1963). This bibliography extends to 46 pages but is difficult to use since it is unclassified. More useful are the 'Guides to Further Reading' at the end of each section of articles reprinted in the book. *Business Cycles and National Income* by Alvin H. Hansen (Allen and Unwin, 1964): the bibliography, compiled by R. V. Clemence, contains about 350 references to books and articles and supplements this revised edition of Hansen's book which is one of the classic texts in business cycle analysis. *Readings in Business Cycle Theory* selected by a committee of the American Economic Association (Allen and Unwin, 1950): the bibliography is intended 'to be useful not only for teaching purposes, but also a reference list for the expert'. It has a well-arranged selection of several hundred items, classified into sixty sections, with a short note discussing the use of the references introducing each section. Unfortunately, only articles published before 1944 are listed.

Most of the books written about various aspects of the business cycle have bibliographies based on the works referred to by the author. Other references may be found in the *Index of Economic Journals* prepared under the auspices of the American Economic Association (Irwin) which is brought up to date in the *Journal of Economic Literature* (formerly the *Journal of Economic Abstracts*) also published by the American Economic Association. In the *Index* the most useful references are given under Class 12, 'Economic Fluctuations, Stabilization, Growth and Employment Policy'.

Apart from these bibliographies, the best and most convenient way of gathering information about the subject of business cycles is to work through some of the books of readings where articles and excerpts from books have been selected and reprinted to illustrate various aspects that have been studied. Two of these readers have already been noted; other important collections are: *Readings in Business Cycles* edited by Robert A. Gordon and Lawrence R. Klein (Irwin for the American Economic Association, 1966): Gordon and Klein's selection is a successor to the earlier AEA volume. In the introduction they note the change in emphasis illustrated by comparing the 1966 selection with the 1946 choice, especially the development of business-cycle studies into the field of non-linear models and attempts to integrate cyclical and growth processes. The readings are divided into sections on Theory, Methodology, Econometric Models, Models of Particular Variables, Long Cycles, International Aspects, Forecasting and Policy. *Readings in Business Cycles and National Income* edited by A. H. Hansen and R. V. Clemence (Allen and Unwin, 1953) is an excellent collection 'intended primarily for undergraduates' and 'arranged in the order of the topics covered in many undergraduate courses'. The drawback with this volume is that it only contains material published before 1951.

Similar to these collections is an important volume of papers and discussions at the International Economic Association 1952 conference entitled *The Business Cycle in the Post-War World*, edited by Erik Lundberg (Macmillan, 1955). The papers include descriptions of the cycle in eight European countries, the United States and Japan and discuss developments in business-cycle theory and testing.

By far the most important collection of literature on business cycles is the series *Studies in Business Cycles* published by the National Bureau of Economic Research. In 1969 there were nineteen volumes in this series, ranging from *Business Cycles: the Problem and its Setting* (1927) by Wesley C. Mitchell, to *The Business Cycle in a Changing World*, a collection of essays by Arthur F. Burns, one of the 'deans' of business-cycle research whom President Nixon appointed head of the US Federal Reserve System in 1969. This series is complemented by other NBER books, occasional papers and annual reports. The best guide to this literature is the 1967 catalogue of *Publications of the National Bureau of Economic Research* and its 1968 supplement where many of the publications are described by short paragraphs. (The NBER offers a special annual subscription rate to students which in 1969 allowed them to receive all the Bureau's publications in that year for $10, and to buy previous years' publications at a much-reduced rate; address: 261 Madison Ave., New York, 10016.

The major research tools needed for the study of business cycles are, of course, statistical series of economic variables. A detailed account of statistical source materials is given in Chapter 10; however, the following references are to sources which may be particularly useful to a student of short-term economic fluctuations.

The World Economy

The major difficulty the research worker faces here is that different countries define macroeconomic variables in different ways so that it becomes meaningless to aggregate or compare data between countries. The most accessible and comprehensive collections are found in *The United Nations Statistical Year Book* and the publications of other, more specialised international organisations such as FAO, the World Bank and the IMF. In particular *International Financial Statistics* (IMF, monthly) publishes the 40 to 50 most important economic series for each of the member countries of the

IMF on a quarterly basis, and includes statistics from the national income and expenditure accounts as well as the financial sector.

The 'developed economies'

The business cycle has mostly been studied in the context of countries with developed economies and the most comprehensive statistical accounts of this are found in the publications of the OECD, the EEC, etc. In particular *Main Economic Indicators* published by OECD is very useful.

The United States

As noted previously, the business cycle has been studied in greatest depth as it has occurred in the USA. The best statistical sources which are relatively easily available to students outside America are: *The Economic Report of the President with The Report of the Council of Economic Advisers* (US Government Printing Office, annually) which in its appendix gives an excellent selection of the major statistical series, and the *Federal Reserve Bulletin* (Board of Governors of the Federal Reserve System, Washington, monthly) where most attention is given to financial statistics. (Note also the *Chartbook of Historical Statistics*, also published by the FRB where many of the series are graphed.)

The United Kingdom

For long runs of economic statistics, the only comprehensive source is *Abstract of British Historical Statistics* edited by B. R. Mitchell and P. Deane (Cambridge U.P., 1962). However, since the business cycle is usually completed in less than eight years, most econometric studies need quarterly data to generate sufficient observations to allow significant relations to be brought out. This data has to be collected from a range of publications, either official like the *Annual Abstract* and *Monthly Digest of Statistics, Economic Trends,* the *Board of Trade Journal, Financial Statistics* and the *Bank of England Quarterly Bulletin,* or non-official, such as the *National Institute Economic Review* (quarterly), the *London and Cambridge Economic Bulletin* which is published quarterly in *The Times* (note also *The British Economy: Key Statistics 1900–1966* by this same group, which is a convenient abstract of most of the

236

useful economic series), and the statistical sections of some of the bank reviews (i.e. *Midland Bank Review, Barclays Bank Review*).

Stabilisation Policy

Over the last 50 years the business cycle has increasingly become the object of economic management, as the government has endeavoured to offset the fluctuations of economic activity by using economic policy instruments to pull or push the system back to its long-run growth path.

The literature of business cycles inevitably includes schemes for controlling this behaviour. Other research has examined the theoretical and empirical relation between economic policy and the behaviour of the economy. It has even been claimed that government action is one of the major causes of economic fluctuation, and there have been studies to test whether the presence of a government taking discretionary economic action is stabilising or de-stabilising.

Thus, much of the material referred to in the first section is relevant for this aspect of economic study. The following are bibliographies which give additional useful references especially in the field of stabilisation policy. *Readings in Fiscal Policy* selected by a committee of the American Economic Association (Allen and Unwin, 1955), includes an extremely comprehensive bibliography compiled by W. A. Steger and divided into more than 35 sections, many of which pertain directly to the stabilisation aspects of fiscal policy. The major drawback to the bibliography is that it only includes items written before 1953. *Studies in Economic Stabilization* edited by Albert Ando and others (Brookings Institution, 1968): the seven pages of 'selected references' at the end of this collection of essays is useful for bringing the AEA bibliography up to date. For the British economy the best sources of references to published studies of stabilisation policy are the list of works quoted in *The Management of the British Economy 1945–60* by J. C. R. Dow (Cambridge U.P. for the NIESR, 1968) and the references given in the footnotes to various chapters in *Britain's Economic Prospects* edited by R. E. Caves (Allen and Unwin for the Brooking Institution, 1968).

The books and collections of articles which have been mentioned in this section and the previous one as sources for bibliographies are also amongst the most important references if stabilisation policies are being studied. In particular, the AEA volumes of readings give a wide coverage of the major articles in this field and the collection of essays edited by Ando includes several studies which represent the most modern research approaches.

The US *Economic Report of the President* gives a comprehensive annual account of the progress of stabilisation policy in that country, which might be compared with the commentary in the *Federal Reserve Bank of St. Louis Review*, where the 'monetarist' view of short-term fluctuations is especially emphasised.

The British situation is well covered by the Dow and Caves volumes, both essential readings for any student of recent UK economic developments. These may be supplemented by *The British Economy 1945–50* and *The British Economy in the 1950s*, both edited by G. Worswick and P. Ady (Oxford U.P., 1952 and 1962), *The British Economy: a Manual of Applied Economics* edited by A. Prest (Weidenfeld and Nicholson, 2nd edn, 1968), and *Output, Inflation and Growth*, by D. C. Rowan (Macmillan, 1968). The British equivalent of the *Economic Report of the President* is the annual *Economic Survey* published before the Budget. This should be used in conjunction with articles in *Economic Trends*, the *National Institute Economic Review*, the *Bank of England Quarterly Bulletin*, and the *London and Cambridge Economic Bulletin*.

Prices and Incomes Policy

An important aspect of stabilisation policy in the 1960s has been the adoption by several governments of measures which reflect the belief that the balance of the economy between employment and price stabilisation targets can only be maintained by allowing total money income to grow at the 'natural growth rate' of the economy, which is based on the long-term expansion of factor inputs and increases in factor productivity. This has led to the application of 'guide lines' or 'norms' to the growth of wage rates, prices and dividends, based on projections of the anticipated expansion.

Because prices and incomes policy is a fairly recent addition to the arsenal of macroeconomic weapons (and, some writers would claim, one that may soon be abandoned) there is no good bibliography to its literature. The best research strategy would be to use the AEA *Index of Economic Journals* and the *Journal of Economic Literature*, which have a special section covering this subject, to collect references. The following books and pamphlets are useful as introductions to the field and as sources for further readings:

Guidelines, Informal Controls and the Market Place edited by George P. Schultz and Robert Z. Aliber (University of Chicago Press, 1966) is the report of an American conference where papers on all aspects of government informal action against various sectors of the economy were read and discussed; *Inflation* edited by J. Ball and P. Doyle (Penguin, 1969) is an excellent compendium of important articles about price-level aspects of the business cycle and short-term stabilisation policy.

There is an extremely useful chapter on 'Incomes policy in the United Kingdom' in the Brookings volume on the British economy edited by R. E. Caves referred to in the previous section; the footnotes give some guide to the literature. Another useful commentary is *Incomes Policy: Problems and Prospects* by J. Corina (2 vols, Institute of Personnel Management, 1966). This study, published as two pamphlets, places British experience in the context of incomes policy in other countries and summarises recent developments. Finally, two publications by Prof. Frank Paish review and criticise UK incomes policy: *Policy for Incomes* by F. Paish and J. Hennesey (Institute of Economic Affairs, Hobart Papers, No. 29, 3rd edn, 1967) and *The Rise and Fall of Incomes Policy* by F. Paish (Hobart Papers, No. 47, 1969). Both these pamphlets contain a short list of further readings.

The definitive account of government action against wage and price changes has yet to be written. When it is, it will draw heavily on the publications of the official bodies charged with administering this policy. The most important of these are the reports of the National Board for Prices and Incomes (PIB) which give the results of over one hundred investigations into proposed price and wage increases. The PIB have also published three annual reports dealing with general aspects of prices and incomes policy. The PIB is to be discontinued in its present form, but it is likely that some similar body will be producing a commentary on the progress and problems of this policy instrument. The other source which may be particularly useful for research workers is the fortnightly magazine *Incomes Data* published in London by Incomes Data Services Ltd. which gives details of all the major wage negotiations in progress and the settlements arrived at.

CHAPTER EIGHTEEN

LABOUR ECONOMICS AND INDUSTRIAL RELATIONS

GEORGE SAYERS BAIN and GILLIAN B. WOOLVEN

The labour economist is particularly interested in contributing to an understanding of labour markets and their relationship to product markets, the economy as a whole, and the work-place and social environments. But he does not enjoy a monopoly position: anthropologists, historians, industrial relations specialists, lawyers, personnel specialists, political scientists, psychologists, sociologists, and others have similar interests. Opinions differ as to who has the most to contribute, but there is general agreement that all have at least something to offer. The result is that much of the writing in this field is multi-disciplinary and, at its best, inter-disciplinary.

This means that it is undesirable and, in any case, difficult to treat the literature on labour economics separately from that of the other disciplines. But, unfortunately, there is not room here to deal adequately with them all. Hence the main emphasis is placed on the literature of labour economics, industrial relations, and, to a lesser extent, labour history, labour law, and personnel management. The relevant literature in industrial pyschology, industrial sociology, political science, and social anthropology receives very little attention. This deficiency is remedied to some extent with respect to industrial sociology by Chapter 24 on 'Economic Sociology'. In general, the objective is to deal with those aspects of the subject which are of most interest to the labour economist and to treat the relevant literature adequately from his point of view but not necessarily from that of any of the other contributing disciplines.

Limitations of space also demand some geographical restrictions. To begin with, only sources in the English language are considered. Most of these have been published in the United States and Great Britain, and hence these countries get the major emphasis. But the literature of Australia, Canada, India, and a few other countries

240

also receives some attention. In addition, publications of an international nature are included.

The inter-disciplinary nature of the literature makes it very difficult to classify by subject. The only practicable plan is to classify it by type of publication and function, namely: learned journals; bibliographies, indexes, and literature surveys; abstracts, reporting services, and current affairs information services; government publications; dictionaries, directories, handbooks, and yearbooks; publications in series; unpublished material and research in progress.

Learned Journals

The literature in this field is published in the journals of a wide variety of disciplines and also by a multitude of organisations. Virtually every major union and national and international federation of unions publishes its own journal as do some employers and employers' associations. In addition, there are a large number of 'popular' journals. These publications are not dealt with here. The discussion is generally restricted to 'learned' journals. The major exception is the inclusion of personnel management journals which generally deal with the subject from the practitioner's rather than the academic's point of view. Moreover, only those learned journals specifically concerned with labour economics and industrial relations widely defined are included here. But it should not be forgotten that many of the most important articles in labour economics and industrial relations appear in general economics and sociology journals. Although these are not mentioned here because of limitations of space, the serious student should make himself familiar with the more important of them (*see* Chapter 5) and scan them regularly.

The *Industrial and Labor Relations Review* (1947–) is the major journal in the field in the United States and perhaps the world. It contains articles, communications from readers, original documents, book reviews, and informational items on most aspects of the subject. In addition to the annual index in each volume, there is a cumulative index for the period October 1947–July 1960 and October 1960–July 1967. *Industrial Relations* (1961–) includes 'articles and symposia on all aspects of the employment relationship' with special attention being given 'to pertinent developments in the field of labor economics, sociology, psychology, political science, and law'. The *Journal of Human Resources* (1966–) 'emphasises the role of education and training ... in enhancing productive skills, employment opportunities, and income. It also includes articles on more general manpower, health, and welfare policies, as they relate to the labor market and to economic and social development'. *Labor History* (1960–) carries articles, book reviews, bibliographical guides, notes on archives and sources, and informational items relating to American labour history. 1. The *Labor Law Journal* (1949–) concentrates on arbitral and legal industrial relations, but it also includes more general articles. 2. The psychological aspects of the subject are covered by the *Journal of Applied Psychology* (1917–), *Personnel Psychology* (1948–), and the *Journal of Industrial Psychology* (1963–).

There are also a few less substantial but nevertheless useful American journals in the industrial relations field. The *Industrial and Labor Relations Forum* (1964–) contains papers written by the students of the New York State School of Industrial and Labor Relations at Cornell University. The School also published *ILR Research* between 1954 and 1967. It contained short articles on current industrial relations problems, brief bibliographies, and useful informational items. This publication was replaced in 1969 by *Issues in Industrial Society*, each number of which is devoted to a single subject and covers 'contemporary problems of interest to laymen, practitioners, academics, and students' in the industrial relations field. The most useful of the personnel management journals include: *Personnel* (1919–), *Personnel Journal* (1922–), *Personnel Administration* (1938–), *Public Personnel Review* (1940–), *Personnel Administrator* (1948–), and *Management of Personnel Quarterly* (1961–).

The *British Journal of Industrial Relations* (1963–) is the major journal of its kind in the United Kingdom. It focuses 'on the entire field of employmental relationships and the environment in which they are shaped'. A particularly useful feature of the journal is the 'Chronicle' of recent British industrial relations events which appears in each issue. The *Industrial Relations Research Bulletin* (1969–) published by the Research Department of the Engineering Employers' Federation brings together 'fact and opinion, findings and conclusions, and information and advice, deriving from the general field of industrial relations research'. A new journal, the *Industrial Relations Journal* (1970–), 'is intended to provide a forum for the reflections of those involved in the day-to-day practice of industrial relations', and 'the means by which contributions from academic teachers and researchers, whose work has important practical significance, can be brought to a wider audience'. The *Bulletin of the Society for the Study of Labour History* (1960–) views itself as 'a working journal', a 'tool of the trade'. Consequently, it does not publish full-scale articles, but only carries conference reports, hitherto unpublished documents, short notes, book reviews, bibliographies, notes on archives and sources, and information on both British and foreign labour history. *Bulletin* No. 15 contains a cumulative index of the contents of Nos. 1 to 14. The Marx Memorial Library's *Quarterly Bulletin* (1957–) is also a useful source of information on labour history. The legal aspects of the subject are covered by the *Modern Law Review* (1937–), a general legal journal, which has frequently carried important case notes and articles on labour law in recent years; the *Industrial Law Review* (1946–1960) which primarily reviewed recent legislation in Great Britain and other countries, but also contained a few articles and book reviews; and the *Bulletin of the Industrial Law Society* (1968–) which carries articles, reports of meetings and conferences, and details of recent cases, statutes and other developments in labour law. The psychological aspects of industry are dealt with by *Occupational Psychology* (formerly *The Human Factor* and earlier still the *Journal of the National Institute of Industrial Psychology*, 1922–). The issue for July 1954 contains a cumulative index for the period 1938–1953. The major personnel journals are *Industrial Society* (fomerly *Industrial Welfare*, 1918–) and *Personnel Management* (1920–) which in 1969 absorbed *Personnel and Training Management* (formerly *Personnel Magazine* and earlier *Personnel Management and Methods*, 1945–).

The major Australian periodical is the *Journal of Industrial Relations* (1959–) which carries articles and notes, book reviews, and information on most aspects of labour economics and industrial relations. A particularly useful feature of the journal is the series of regular articles which review recent developments in trade unionism, industrial relations, and labour law in Australia. *Labour History* (1962–) contains articles, notes on bibliographies and sources, and book reviews relating primarily but not exclusively to Australian labour history.

For a developing country, India has a surprising number of industrial relations journals. The *Indian Journal of Labour Economics* (1958–) carries general articles on labour economics concerned particularly but not exclusively with India and other developing countries. The *Indian Journal of Industrial Relations* (1965–) publishes articles, book reviews, communications, and information on most aspects of industrial relations.

In Canada *Relations Industrielles-Industrial Relations* (formerly the *Bulletin des Relations Industrielles*, 1945–) publishes articles in English and French on most aspects of the subject. A cumulative index for the period 1945–1963 is contained in the issue for October 1963. The *Canadian Personnel and Industrial Relations Journal* (1954–   ) deals with the more practical aspects of personnel administration.

The national journals described above tend to a greater or lesser extent to concentrate on developments in their respective countries. There are only two journals of a truly international nature. The *International Labour Review* (1921–   ) contains articles, book reviews, bibliographies and abstracts, and informational items dealing with industrial relations in virtually every country of the world. Volume 21 contains a cumulative index covering Volumes 1 to 20. The International Institute for Labour Studies was formed in 1960 in Geneva, and in 1966 it began publishing a *Bulletin* which carries articles and reports on the Institute's activities and research programme.

Bibliographies, Indexes, and Literature Surveys

Bibliographies can be divided into two basic categories: those of an international nature and those which deal with the literature of only one country or geographical area.

There are three major sources of international bibliographical information on labour economics and industrial relations. The first is the International Labour Office. Between 1949 and 1954 the Central Library and Documentation Branch of the ILO issued a *Daily Reference List* of journal articles selected from the numerous periodicals it received. The periodicity of the list was changed from daily to weekly in 1954, and the service was renamed *International Labour Documentation*. A cumulative subject index was begun in 1957, and the *Subject Index to International Labour Documentation 1957–1964* (G. K. Hall, 1968) contains the references accumulated during the first eight years of the service. Subsequent cumulations will be issued on microfiche, the first one covering the years 1965–67. A new but allied ILO service is an information retrieval system whereby a search in the bibliographical records can be made for all items recorded in a particular subject field. The ILO also publishes *Bibliographical Contributions* (1949–   ) which contains a large and growing number of bibliographies on various aspects of industrial relations. The *Subject Guide to Publications of the International Labour Office 1919–1964* (ILO, 1967) provides a subject index to the vast amount of material published by the ILO, and a supplement published in 1968 supplies a geographical index. ILO material still in print is listed in its annual catalogue of publications.

Published library catalogues provide the two other major sources of world-wide bibliographical references on labour economics and industrial relations. In addition to the subject catalogues produced by the United States Library of Congress, the British Museum, and other general libraries, there is *A London Bibliography of the Social Sciences* (London School of Economics and Political Science, 1931–) which lists the holdings of certain London libraries, particularly the British Library of Political and Economic Science which is very rich in industrial relations material. An even richer source is the *Library Catalog of the New York State School of Industrial and Labor Relations, Cornell University* (G. K. Hall, 1967–) which lists over 78 000 volumes and bound periodicals and 80 000 pamphlets from the late eighteenth century to the present. Author and subject entries for selected articles from 150 periodicals have been included since 1952.

There are also a number of smaller international bibliographies. Much of the early literature on wages and other aspects of labour economics can be found in *A Select Bibliography of Modern Economic Theory 1870–1929* compiled by Harold E. Batson (Routledge, 1930; reissued in 1967). *History and Theories of Working-Class Movements: A Select Bibliography* compiled by Charles A. Gulick *et al.* (Berkeley, University of California, Bureau of Business and Economic Research and the Institute of Industrial Relations, 1955) lists sources on nearly every area of the world as does the *International Bibliography of Trade Unionism* compiled by V. L. Allen (London, Merlin Press, 1968). *Personnel Management: A Bibliography* compiled by Carole Faubert (London, Institute of Personnel Management, 1968) contains a lengthy list of primarily British and American items on personnel management and industrial relations. The most up to date source of international bibliographical information is the list of 'Recent Publications' which is classified by subject and published in each issue of the *Industrial and Labor Relations Review*. Each issue of *Relations Industrielles-Industrial Relations* and the *International Labour Review* contains similar but less extensive lists. Much of the literature in English published between the late 1940s and 1965 on automation is listed and annotated in three volumes published by the School of Labor and Industrial Relations at Michigan State University under the main title *Economic and Social Implications of Automation*. Volume 1 was compiled by Gloria Cheek and published in 1958, while Volumes 2 and 3 were compiled by Einar Hardin *et al.* and published in 1961 and 1967 respectively. Another useful source of information on automation is the series of bulletins published by the ILO under the main title *Labour and Automation* (1964–   ). 3.

A few surveys and critical appraisals of labour economics and industrial relations literature have been published. They give particular attention to America, but many deal with the literature of other countries as well. Most of the important literature of the 1930s and early 1940s is reviewed by Lloyd G. Reynolds in 'Economics of Labor', a chapter in *A Survey of Contemporary Economics* edited by H. S. Ellis (Blakiston, for the American Economic Association, 1948). Three volumes sponsored by the Industrial Relations Research Association—*A Decade of Industrial Relations Research, 1946–1956: An Appraisal of the Literature in the Field* edited by Neil W. Chamberlain *et al.* (Harper, 1958), *Research in Industrial Human Relations: A Critical Appraisal* edited by Conrad M. Arensberg *et al.* (Harper, 1957), and *Employment Relations Research: A Summary and Appraisal* edited by H. G. Heneman *et al.* (Harper, 1960)—contain a series of bibliographical and critical essays which start approximately where Reynolds left off. The literature published during the past decade or so will be surveyed by two volumes which the Industrial Relations Research Association is planning to publish in 1970 and 1971. *Research Needs in Industrial Relations* by K. F. Walker (2nd edn, Melbourne, Cheshire, 1964) provides an excellent bibliography and a useful 'critical assessment of current trends and needs in research in industrial relations generally' with particular reference to Australia. *Research in Labor Problems in the United States* by Milton Derber (Random House, 1967) discusses much of the outstanding American industrial relations literature.

There are a number of international bibliographies which although not specifically intended for students of labour economics and industrial relations are nevertheless of use to them. The most comprehensive are the four bibliographies published by the International Committee for Social Sciences Documentation: the *International Bibliography of Sociology* (1952–   ) covering the literature from 1951 (the first four volumes formed part of *Current Sociology which is described below*), the *International Bibliography of Economics* (1955–   ) covering the literature from 1952, the *International Bibliography of Political Science* (1954–) covering the literature from 1953, and the *International Bibliography of Social and Cultural Anthropology* (1958–   ) covering the literature from 1955. These bibliographies are published annually and include the most important scholarly publications relating to each discipline regardless of country of origin or language in which they are written. The *Population Index* (1935–) performs a similar function for demography and has useful sections on such topics as the labour force. Some useful references on the labour force and the distribution of income are contained in the *Bibliography on Income and Wealth* (1952–) covering the literature from 1937. The *Index of Economic Journals* (1961–) lists by author and subject English language articles in major professional economic journals from 1886. From 1964 onwards this publication has been indexing articles published in such collective volumes as conference reports, festschriften, collected essays, and books of readings. A specific section of the *Index* is devoted to labour economics. *Current Sociology* (1952–) is a series of bibliographies and trend reports on subjects of particular importance in sociology. No. 2 of volume 12 (1963–64) on 'Industrial Sociology, 1951–62' is particularly useful.

Most of the major industrialised countries of the world have bibliographies which are specifically devoted to their industrial relations literature. The United States has so many that it is not possible to list them all here. Those who wish to get some idea of the American bibliographies should begin by consulting two publications of the Institute of Labor and Industrial Relations at the University of Illinois: *Industrial Relations Bibliographies: A Check List* compiled by George F. Mundle (1965) and the *Exchange Bibliography Series* (1947–), sponsored by the Committee of University Industrial Relations Librarians and compiled at the University of Illinois, which so far includes over 1500 separate bibliographies. Bibliographical series are also published by the Institute at the University of Illinois (1952–), the Industrial Relations Section of the Department of Economics at Princeton University (*Bibliographical Series*, 1939–1958; *Selected References*, 1945–), and the New York State School of Industrial and Labor Relations at Cornell University (1952–). *A Representative Bibliography of American Labor History* by Maurice F. Neufeld (Cornell University, New York State School of Industrial and Labor Relations, 1964) provides the best guide to its subject. *Labor History* publishes an 'Annual Bibliography of Periodical Articles on American Labor History'. *Trade Union Publications* by Lloyd G. Reynolds and Charles C. Killingsworth (3 vols, Johns Hopkins Press, 1944–45) provides a useful guide to trade union records for the period 1850–1941. *Index to Labor Articles* (1926–53) published by the Rand School of Social Science in New York indexed industrial relations articles in labour union publications and general periodicals. *The Michigan Index to Labor Union Periodicals* (1960–69) indexed the contents of fifty major American trade union publications. *American Labor Union Periodicals: A Guide to Their Location* by Bernard G. Naas and Carmelita S. Sakr (Cornell University, New York State School of Industrial and Labor Relations, 1956) gives information on where over 1700 union periodicals can be found.

In spite of the maturity of the British industrial relations system and the size of the literature dealing with it, there are few bibliographical guides. *Industrial Relations in Wartime: Great Britain, 1914–1918* compiled by Waldo Chamberlin (Stanford University Press, 1940) contains an annotated list of British materials in the Hoover Library on War, Revolution, and Peace. *An Interim Bibliography of the Scottish Working Class Movement* edited by Ian McDougall (Edinburgh, Scottish Committee of the Society for the Study of Labour History, 1965) gives a detailed list of Scottish labour material. 4. The Society also publishes an annual bibliography on British labour history as well as bibliographies on special topics from time to time in its *Bulletin. The History of British Trade Unionism: A Select Bibliography* by R. and E. Frow and M. Katanka (London, Historical Association, 1969) gives a list of the more important trade union histories. *British Industrial Relations: An Annotated Bibliography* by A. W. Gottschalk *et al.* (University of Nottingham, Department of Adult Education, 1969) is an extremely useful annotated guide to much of the most important recent industrial relations literature.

The Industrial Relations Centre at Queen's University in Canada publishes a series of bibliographies. The most useful of these is *Industrial and Labour Relations in Canada: A Selected Bibliography* (1965) compiled by A. F. Isbester *et al.* which lists over 1100 items on Canada and, in addition, gives a list of trade union newspapers and journals. There is also a comprehensive bibliography on Canadian labour economics and industrial relations in *Labour Policy and Labour Economics in Canada* by H. D. Woods and S. Ostry (Toronto, Macmillan, 1962). 5. Much of the important periodical literature on Australia has been listed in the bibliographies published in *Australian Labour Relations: Readings* (Melbourne, Sun Books, 1966) and *Australian Labour Economics: Readings* (Sun Books, 1967) both edited by J. E. Isaac and G. W. Ford. A considerable number of references on New Zealand are contained in *Labour Legislation in New Zealand: A Bibliography* compiled by H. O. Roth (University of Auckland Press, 1964).

A substantial literature exists on industrial relations in developing countries. Many of the most important sources are listed in *A Brief Annotated Bibliography on Labor in Emerging Societies* by S. C. Sufrin and F. E. Wagner (Syracuse University, Maxwell

Graduate School of Citizenship and Public Affairs, Center for Overseas Operations, 1961), and *Industrial Relations and Economic Development* edited by A. M. Ross (Macmillan, 1966), pp. 321-406. In 1968 the International Institute for Labour Studies in Geneva started an *International Educational Materials Exchange* which contains, among other things, curricula, syllabuses, lectures, source material, case studies, and bibliographies on labour problems and related fields, with particular emphasis on developing countries. The Indian Ministry of Labour and Employment publishes *Documentation of Labour* (1957–) which is a monthly classified index to the periodical literature received in the Ministry's library. This is cumulated annually and published as *Labour Literature: A Bibliography* (1957–) which forms part of a wider *Bibliographical Series* (1957–). The *Indian Journal of Industrial Relations* (vol. 1, 1966, pp. 490–510) gives a list of books, journals, and periodicals on industrial relations in India. In addition, each issue of the journal contains an index of current periodical articles in this field. *Bibliography of Industrial Relations in Latin America* by James O. Morris and Efrén Córdova (Cornell University, New York State School of Industrial and Labor Relations, 1967), *Bibliography on Trade Union Movements in Latin America 1950–1964* (International Institute for Labour Studies, 1965), and *Unions, Labor and Industrial Relations in Africa: An Annotated Bibliography* (Cornell University, Center for International Studies, 1965) give most of the important sources for Latin America and Africa.

Abstracts, Reporting Services, and Current Affairs Information Services

Of the very few abstracting services which deal specifically with labour economics and industrial relations, *Industrial and Labor Relations Abstracts and Annotations* (1948 1957), *Employment Relations Abstracts* (formerly *Labor-Personnel Index*, 1951–), *Personnel Management Abstracts* (1955–), *Occupational Safety and Health Abstracts* (1963–), and *Poverty and Human Resources Abstracts/PHRA* (1966–) are the most useful. Also of use are the more general social science abstracting services: the *Journal of Economic Literature* (formerly the *Journal of Economic Abstracts*, 1963–), *International Political Science Abstracts* (1952–) covering the literature from 1951, *Sociological Abstracts* (1953–), and *Psychological Abstracts* (1927–) which has a cumulative index for the period 1927–59.

There are numerous law reporting services, some of which also provide facts and comment on current events in industrial relations. The most important in the United States are those provided by the Bureau of National Affairs, Washington, and Commerce Clearing House, Inc., Chicago. BNA publishes *Labor Relations Reporter* (1937–) covering the period from 1935, a most comprehensive service which includes legal information on industrial relations; *Collective Bargaining Negotiations and Contracts* (1945–), in which 'thousands of current contract clauses' are 'quoted and analysed for basic patterns'; the *Daily Labor Report* (1946–) which 'provides overnight notification of major labor relations developments'; the *BNA Policy and Practice Series* (1946–) which 'analyses more than 5000 case histories of labor-management disputes'; the *Union Labor Report* (1951–) which provides information of particular interest to union officials; and the *Manpower Information Service* (1969–) which includes information on the effective utilisation and training of human resources. The Bureau also publishes a series of reports covering specific areas of employment. These include: the *Retail Labor Report* (1949–), the *Construction Labor Report* (1955–), *Government Security and Loyalty* (1955–), the *White Collar Report* (1957–), and the *Government Employee Relations Report* (1963–).

CCH publishes weekly *Labor Law Reports* (1934–) covering most aspects of industrial relations, the current issues of which subscribers can file by subject in a series of loose-leaf volumes entitled *Labor Law Reporter*. Past federal and state court decisions are recorded in bound volumes of *Labor Cases*, covering the period from 1934, and digests of decisions of the National Labor Relations Board are given in a similar series *CCH NLRB Decisions* (1960–). *Labor Law Guide* (1947–) reports weekly on 'labor relations and wage-hour rules' and is 'designed for use on everyday problems'; *Labor Arbitration Awards* (1961–) publishes weekly the texts of 'current awards settling labor relations disputes' and a series of bound volumes is available; the twice monthly *Employment Practices Guide* (1965–) provides coverage of developments in employment practices 'with explanations and official texts covering federal and state fair employment rules'; and the *Personnel Guide* (1969–) discusses and explains practical problems and solutions.

Relevant legal reports in Great Britain are to be found in *Industrial Court Awards* (1920–) and *Industrial Tribunals Reports* (1966–), both published by HMSO, and *Knight's Industrial Reports* (1966–). Current information and comment are to be found in *Labour Research* (London, Labour Research Department

Publications Ltd., 1917–), *Industrial Information Service* (Stow-market, Thames Bank Publishing Co. Ltd., 1946–67), *IRIS News* (London, Industrial Research and Information Services Ltd., 1956–), *Incomes Data* (London, Incomes Data Services Ltd., 1966–), and the *Bulletin of the Institute for Workers' Control* (Nottingham, The Institute, 1968–).

The major Indian law reporting services include the following: *Industrial Court Reporter* (Bombay, Commissioner of Labour and Director of Employment, 1948–); the *Labour Law Journal* (Madras, R. Krishnaswamy, 1949–); *Digest of Labour Cases* (Madras Book Agency, 1960–); *Labour Law Journal Digest* (Madras, Veegee Mohan, 1968–) covering decisions from 1949; and *Awards Digest* (New Delhi, Indian Institute of Labour Studies, 1969–). There is also the *Current Central Labour Code* (Delhi, Central Law House, 1962–March 1965, June 1967–), a loose-leaf service which keeps central government legislation on labour up to date.

In Canada, Commerce Clearing House Canadian Ltd., Don Mills, Ontario, provides a current legal reporting service in its *Labour Law Reporter* (1946–), and past decisions from 1944 are recorded in a series of casebooks. Australian labour law cases are reported in the *Industrial Information Bulletin* (Melbourne, Commonwealth Department of Labour and National Service, 1946–) and the *Australian Industrial Law Review* (Sydney, E. G. Lambert, 1959–; title varies).

Government Publications

There is a voluminous quantity of government material on labour economics and industrial relations. There is not room here to discuss it in any detail. All that can be done is to indicate the major official labour journals in each country and any useful guides to official literature. The reader should refer to Chapters 7, 8, and 9 for a fuller discussion of the sources of official material.

The government of almost every country publishes a journal containing articles, informational items, and statistical series relating to labour economics and industrial relations. Great Britain's is the *Employment and Productivity Gazette* (formerly the *Ministry of Labour Gazette* and earlier still the *Labour Gazette*, 1893–), Canada's is the *Labour Gazette* (1900–), Australia's is the *Personnel Practice Bulletin* (1945–). The United States government publishes the *Monthly Labor Review* (1915–) and *Manpower* (1969–), while the Indian government publishes the *Indian Labour Journal* (for-

251

merly the *Indian Labour Gazette*, 1943–) and *Manpower Journal* (1965–). Many of the state governments in federal countries such as the United States and India also publish labour journals, but there is not room here to deal with these.

A list of the major Australian official sources is contained in *Australian Labour Relations: Readings* by J. E. Isaac and G. W. Ford. *Government Publications of India: A Survey of their Nature, Bibliographical Control and Distribution Systems* by M. Singh (Delhi, Metropolitan Co., 1967) provides a guide to Indian official sources. For Great Britain, *see* the section on 'Labour' in the *Select List of British Parliamentary Papers 1833–1899* by P. and G. Ford (Blackwell, 1953) and *A Breviate of Parliamentary Papers* by the same authors (Blackwell, 1951–61) which covers the period 1900–1954 in three volumes. 6. See also *Government Information and the Research Worker* edited by Ronald Staveley and Mary Piggott (Library Association, 1965), particularly the chapter on 'The Ministry of Labour' by P. D. Ward. There would appear to be no recent guides to American and Canadian official industrial relations sources.

Dictionaries, Directories, Handbooks, and Yearbooks

In addition to the general economics dictionaries referred to in Chapter 4 there are a few which deal specifically with labour economics and industrial relations. The *Dictionary of Labor Economics* by Byrne Joseph Horton (Public Affairs Press, 1948), *Labor Terms* (Commerce Clearing House, 1955), and the *Dictionary of Personnel and Industrial Relations* by Esther R. Becker (Philosophical Library, 1958) are useful but somewhat dated. 7. The most comprehensive and up-to-date glossary is *Roberts' Dictionary of Industrial Relations* by Harold S. Roberts (Bureau of National Affairs, 1966). All these dictionaries tend to be primarily concerned with North American terminology, custom and practice. 8.

The *Directory of National and International Labor Unions in the United States* (Bureau of Labor Statistics, 1943–) lists the names and addresses of most of the various unions operating in the United States. *Labour Organizations in Canada* (Ottawa, Department of Labour, Economics and Research Branch, 1911–) performs the same function for Canada as does the *List of Trade Unions in India* (Simla, Ministry of Labour and Employment, Labour Bureau, 1956–) for India. In Great Britain, the loose-leaf volume, the *Directory of Employers' Associations, Trade Unions, Joint Organisations, Etc.* (HMSO, 1960–) lists the names and addresses of the kinds of organisations mentioned in its title. In Australia, the *Industrial Information Bulletin* (1946–) includes in its January issue a directory of union and employer organisations registered in the federal jurisdiction.

The Bureau of International Labor Affairs of the United States Department of Labor publishes several useful international labour directories: the loose-leaf publication, the *Directory of World Federation of Trade Unions* (1955 and 1959); the *Directory of International Trade Secretariats* (1954 and 1961); the *Directory of International Confederation of Free Trade Unions* (1954, 1956, 1958, and 1963), and the *Directory of International Federation of Christian Trade Unions* (1955 and 1963). It also publishes the *Directory of Labour Organizations,* a loose-leaf publication with a separate volume on Asia and Australasia (1958–60 and 1963–); the Western Hemisphere excluding the United States (1955, 1957, 1960, and 1964); Europe (1955, 1959, and 1965–); and Africa (1958, 1962, and 1966–). Each volume contains 'the best available data and information on the structure, composition, membership, and international affiliations of labor organisations in the area covered'.

Several handbooks and yearbooks give useful information on labour organisations and industrial relations. Most of these are devoted primarily to the United States although they also generally give some information on other countries and international developments. They include the following: the biennial publication, *Labor Fact Book* (New York, International Publishers for the Labor Research Association, 1931–1965); the *Labor Dictionary: A Concise Encyclopaedia of Labor Information* (Philosophical Library, 1949); the *International Labor Directory and Handbook* edited by Jack Schuyler (Praeger, 1950 and 1955); *Handbook of Personnel Management and Labor Relations* by Dale Yoder *et al.* (McGraw-Hill, 1958); the *Labor Relations Yearbook* (Bureau of National Affairs, 1965–); and the *Personnel Director's Handbook* by W. E. Scheer (Dartnell Corporation, 1969).

The *Industrial Relations Handbook* (HMSO, 1944, 1953 and 1961) gives an account of the most important aspects of the British industrial relations system, while the first issue of what is planned to be an annual series, *Trade Union Register* edited by Ken Coates *et al.* (Merlin Press, 1969) provides a diary and review of the major industrial relations events of the previous year, articles on trade unionism in Great Britain and other countries, texts of important agreements, and key statistics. Two annual publications of the Labour Bureau of the Indian Ministry of Labour and Employment, *Indian Labour Yearbook* (1946–) and *Indian Labour Statistics* (1960–), provide a great deal of statistical data as well as information relating to labour legislation, awards, and judgements in India. Also of use are the *Handbook of Labour Laws and Industrial Relations* by R. N. Rose and S. R. Mukherjee (2nd edn, Calcutta, Nalanda's Press and Publications, 1965), and the *Handbook of Employer-Employee Relations in Canada* by A. C. Crysler (Don Mills, Ontario, Commerce Clearing House Canadian Ltd., 1969). *Labour Report* (1912–), an annual publication of the Commonwealth Bureau of Census and Statistics, gives comprehensive quantitative and qualitative information on all matters affecting employment, prices, wages, industrial disputes, and labour organisations in Australia.

The *Yearbook of the International Free Trade Union Movement* edited by J. Braunthal and A. J. Forrest (London, Lincolns-Prager, 1957 and 1961–62), and the *Yearbook of the International Socialist Labour Movement* edited by J. Braunthal (Lincolns-Prager, 1956–57 and 1960–61) provide a great deal of useful information on the non-Communist labour movement.

Publications providing statistical information are being dealt with in Chapter 10, but the main international source for labour statistics ought to be mentioned here. The first volume of the International Labour Office's *Year Book of Labour Statistics* covered 1935–36. Previously, statistical information had been included in the *ILO Yearbook* (1930–1939/40). The *Year Book of Labour Statistics* 'presents a summary of the principal labour statistics in more than 170 countries or territories', wherever possible, for the last ten years. This information is supplemented and kept up to date by the quarterly *Bulletin of Labour Statistics* (1965–), whose predecessor was the monthly *International Labour Review: Statistical Supplement* (1952–64), and before that the statistics section in the *International Labour Review*. The statistical data in the *Bulletin* are, in turn, brought up to date by a *Supplement* which is published in each month that the *Bulletin* does not appear and whose information is then incorporated into the next issue of the *Bulletin*.

There are a large number of national and international societies which bring together the professionals engaged in the various fields under review here. A list of members can be obtained from most of these societies by writing to their secretaries. A few of them publish their membership lists. In the United States the Industrial Relations Research Association periodically publishes a *Membership Directory* (the latest is for 1966) which gives, among other things, the research interests of the members. *Who's Who in Industrial Relations* by Harold S. Roberts (2 vols, University of Hawaii, Industrial Relations Center, 1966–67) gives the names and positions of some of the leading figures in industrial relations and personnel management in the United States. The Canadian Industrial Relations Research Institute publishes a *Membership Directory* (the latest is for 1968). In Great Britain the membership lists of the Society for the Study of Labour History and the Industrial Law Society are published in their *Bulletins.*

Publications in Series

Labour economics and industrial relations are characterised by a large number of publications in series. One of the most useful series is that of the Industrial Relations Research Association. Each year it generally publishes the *Proceedings* of its annual winter meeting (1948–), the *Proceedings* of its annual spring meeting (1958–), and a volume on a special research topic (1949–). An index to its publications for the period 1948–60 is contained in the *Proceedings of the Thirteenth Annual Winter Meeting,* and for the period 1961–65 in the *Proceedings of the Eighteenth Annual Winter Meeting.* Another useful series is the *Proceedings of the National Academy of Arbitrators* which has been published since 1955 by the Bureau of National Affairs in Washington. The *Wertheim Publications in Industrial Relations* series (1927–) published by Harvard University Press contains several classic studies. The *Random House Studies in Labor* (1965–), the *Industrial Relations Monograph* series (1939–) of the Industrial Relations Counselors of New York, and the *Studies in Personnel Policy* (1937–) of the National Industrial Conference Board of New York are also worth consulting.

In Great Britain, the *Broadsheets* (1943–1965) and *Occasional Papers* (1951–1965) of the Institute of Personnel Management contain a number of valuable studies. Although these series have been discontinued as such, the Institute continues to publish numerous studies in this field, details of which can be found in its *Publications Catalogue.* The British Institute of Management also has a wide range of publications, including some series which contain several personnel and industrial relations studies. These are listed in its catalogue *Management Information.* The Engineering Employers' Federation has recently begun a *Federation Research Paper Series* (1968–) and a series of occasional papers (1969–) which contain a number of useful studies.

Several academic institutions in the United States publish research series, conference series, lecture series, reprint series, and bibliographical series. Institutions publishing bibliographical series have been mentioned above. Those publishing other kinds of series include the following: the Institute of Industrial Relations, University of California at Berkeley (*Reprint* series, 1947– ; *California Public Employee Relations Series*, 1969–); the Institute of Industrial Relations, University of California at Los Angeles (*Reprint* series, 1948–); the Industrial Relations Center, California Institute of Technology (*Bulletin*, 1940– ; *Circular Series*, 1945– ; *Lecture Series*, 1956– ; *Benefits and Insurance Series*, 1956–61); the Industrial Relations Center, University of Chicago (*Reprint Series*, 1950–; *Occasional Papers*, 1953–); the New York State School of Industrial and Labor Relations, Cornell University (*Bulletin*, 1948– ; *Reprint Series*, 1952–); the Institute of Labor and Industrial Relations, University of Illinois (*ILIR Bulletin*, 1947– ; *Research Report*, 1948– ; *Lecture Series*, 1948– ; *Reprint Series*, 1949–); the Center for Labor and Management, University of Iowa (*Research Series*, 1951– ; *Conference Series*, 1953– ; *Reprint Series*, 1953– ; *Information Series*, 1959–); the Institute of Industrial Relations, Loyola University of Chicago (*Research and Reprint Series*, 1958–); the Labor Relations and Research Center, University of Massachusetts (*Reprint* series, 1967– ; *Monograph* series, 1967–); the Bureau of Industrial Relations, University of Michigan (*Bulletin*, 1936–1961; *Report* series, 1937–); the School of Labor and Industrial Relations, Michigan State University (*Reprint Series*, 1957–); the Institute of Labor and Industrial Relations, University of Michigan–Wayne State University (*Reprint Series*, 1957–); the Industrial Relations Center, University of Minnesota (*Bulletin*, 1945– ; *Research and Technical Reports*, 1948–1960; *Reprint Series*, 1949– ; *Special Releases*, 1959–); the Institute of Labor Relations, New York University (*Proceedings of the Annual Conference on Labor*, 1948–); Department of Economics, University of Notre Dame (*Annual Union-Management Conference* series, 1953–); the Labor Education and Research Service, Ohio State University (*Reprint Series*, 1964– ; *Occasional Publication Series*, 1964–); the Industrial Relations Section, Department of Economics, Princeton University (*Report*, 1926–1939; *Research Report Series*, 1940– ; *Industrial Relations Digests*, 1941–43); the Institute of Management and Labor Relations, Rutgers University (*Labor-Management Conference* series, 1949– ; *Bulletin*, 1952– ; *Reprint from Rutgers* series, 1958– ; *Occasional Papers*, 1963–); the Industrial Relations Research Institute, University of Wisconsin (*Reprint Series*, 1955–).

A few Canadian institutions publish similar series. They include the following: the Industrial Relations Center, McGill University (*Annual Conference* series, 1949–); the Industrial Relations Center,

Queen's University (*Bulletin*, 1938–1960; *Reprint Series*, 1961– ; *Research Series*, 1964–). The *Studies* (1957–) and the *Conference and Other Reports* (1957–) of the Institute of Public Affairs, Dalhousie University, contain several industrial relations publications. The Department of Industrial Relations at Laval University publishes the papers given at its annual Industrial Relations Conference which has been held since 1946.

The following international organisations also publish series in industrial relations: the International Labour Organisation (*Legislative Series*, 1919– ; *Studies and Reports*, 1920– ; *Labour-Management Relations Series*, 1957–); the International Society for Labour Law and Social Legislation (*Proceedings of Congress*, 1951–); and the International Association of Personnel in Employment Security (*Proceedings of the Annual Convention*, 1913–). The International Institute for Labour Studies publishes a *Reprint* series (1963–) and an *International Educational Materials Exchange* series (1968–) referred to earlier.

Most governments also issue a large number of publications in series in labour economics and industrial relations. Those dealing primarily with statistical data are for the most part not listed here partly because of limitations of space and partly because the more important of these are discussed in Chapters 7, 8 and 9. The United States Bureau of Labor Statistics publishes the numbered *BLS Bulletin* series (1895–), *Wages Chronologies* (1949–), the numbered *BLS Report* series (1953–), and *Special Labor Force Reports* (1960–). The Office of Foreign Labor and Trade of the Bureau of Labor Statistics has issued monographs on labour in selected countries since 1955. From 1955 to 1960, general monographs were issued in the *Foreign Labor Information Series* (*FLI*); from 1961 to 1964, such studies were in the Bureau's numbered series of reports and were entitled 'Labor in ...'. In 1961, the Office began to issue monographs in the *Labor Law and Practice Series* (*LLP*); each monograph in this series is entitled 'Labor Law and Practice in ...'. A numerical listing of *Publications of the Bureau of Labor Statistics* (1886–), including a subject index beginning in 1915, is published periodically in the numbered *BLS Bulletin* series. Finally, the United States Department of Labor publishes a series of *Manpower Research Bulletins* (1963–).

In Canada the Economics and Research Branch of the Department of Labour publishes a *Labour-Management Research Series* (1961–) and an *Occasional Paper* series (1964–). The Dominion Bureau of Statistics publishes a *Labour Force Studies* series (1967–), and *Special Labour Force Studies* (1966–). In addition, there are the *Proceedings of the Canadian Association of Admini-*

strators of Labour Legislation (Department of Labour, 1938–)
which contain the papers and discussions of those concerned with
administering Canadian labour legislation. The Manpower
Research Unit of the Department of Employment in Great Britain
publishes a *Manpower Studies* series (1964–) and a *Manpower
Papers* series (1968–). The Indian Ministry of Labour and Employment publishes a *Pamphlet Series* (1959–).

Unpublished Material and Research in Progress

American and Canadian doctoral dissertations in all fields are listed
annually in *American Doctoral Dissertations* (formerly *Doctoral
Dissertations Accepted by American Universities*, 1933–). Those
accepted between 1933 and 1953 in labour economics and
industrial relations have been brought together in *Doctoral Dissertations in Labor and Industrial Relations, 1933–1953* by Ned
Rosen and Ralph E. McCoy (University of Illinois, Institute of
Labor and Industrial Relations, 1955). The Institute of Industrial
Relations at the University of California at Berkeley and later the
Industrial Relations Research Institute at the University of Wisconsin have compiled at irregular intervals a list of *Industrial
Relations Theses and Dissertations Accepted at Universities*
(1949–) arranged by subject. A very large proportion of these theses
can be obtained on microfilm from University Microfilms Inc.,
Ann Arbor, Michigan. *Dissertation Abstracts International*
(1938–) lists the doctoral theses, and *Masters' Abstracts* (1962–)
the Masters' theses, available from this source. A useful but unfortunately out-of-date list of Canadian dissertations is contained
in *Canadian Graduate Theses in the Humanities and Social
Sciences, 1921–1946* (King's Printer, 1951) and *A List of Theses
Accepted by Canadian Universities in 1952* (Queen's Printer, 1953).
9. From time to time, *Relations Industrielles–Industrial Relations*
publishes a list of theses in labour economics and industrial relations accepted at Laval University and the University of Montreal.

*Index to Theses Accepted for Higher Degrees in the Univer-
sities of Great Britain and Ireland* (1950–) lists all theses and
dissertations accepted for higher degrees in the United Kingdom.
Many of the theses submitted to Indian universities are listed in
the *Bulletin of Research Theses and Dissertations* (New Delhi,
National Archives of India, 1955–), and the *Bibliography of
Doctorate Theses in Arts and Science Accepted by Indian Universities* (New Delhi, Inter-University Board of India, 1935–62). 10.
Australian Social Science Abstracts (1946–54) listed, among other

258

things, unpublished theses accepted by Australian and New Zealand universities.

The 'Research Notes' section contained in each issue of the *Industrial and Labor Relations Review* is the major source of information on research under way in labour economics and industrial relations. Over a period of two to three years (eight to twelve issues) all the major American, Canadian and international centres of industrial relations research are covered as well as some in Great Britain, Australia, India, and other places. *Labor History* and the *Bulletin of the Society for the Study of Labour History* periodically publish articles on research in progress. The *Journal of Industrial Relations* periodically publishes a list of industrial relations research in Australia. *Labour and Industrial Relations Research in Canada* (Department of Labour, 1968–) performs a similar service for Canada. The *Indian Journal of Industrial Relations* periodically publishes reports of research under way at the Shri Ram Centre for Industrial Relations in New Delhi. The *Register of Research in the Human Sciences Applied to Problems of Work and Directory of Relevant Research Institutions* (OECD, 1958 and 1962) 'provides a guide to research on the human problems of work undertaken in European Member countries of the OECD'. The *International Educational Materials Exchange* of the International Institute for Labour Studies described above also covers research in progress.

Finally, there are a number of useful sources of information on such things as forthcoming conferences, seminars, lectures, and research grants. These include the following: the *ILR Newsletter* (1967–) and the *Industrial and Labor Relations Report* (1964–), both published by the New York State School of Industrial and Labor Relations at Cornell University; and *IRRA Newsletter* (1959–) published by the Industrial Relations Research Association; the *Newsletter* (1962–) published by the School of Labor and Industrial Relations at Michigan State University; the *Labor Historians Newsletter* (1967–) which, since the autumn of 1968, has been published in *Labor History* as 'The Labor Historians Newsnotes'; and the *Review* (1966–) published by the Industrial Relations Centre of McGill University. The *Bulletin of the Society for the Study of Labour History* and Australia's *Labour History* and *Journal of Industrial Relations* carry news and notes regarding the activities of various professional societies in the industrial relations field. Each issue of the International Institute for Labour Studies, *Bulletin* carries information concerning the activities of the International Industrial Relations Association.

259

Notes

1. A cumulative index to volumes 1–10 of *Labor History* appeared in the issue for Fall, 1970.

2. Also worth noting is *Arbitration Journal* (1937–42, 1946–) which was suspended from 1943 to 1945 and replaced by *Arbitration Magazine* and *International Arbitration Journal*.

3. A large part of the literature on manpower planning is discussed and listed in *Manpower Planning: A Bibliography* edited by C. G. Lewis (English Universities Press, 1970).

4. A new edition of McDougall's bibliography should be published late in 1971.

5. *Bibliographie des Relations Industrielles au Canada, 1940–1967* by Louis-Marie Tremblay (Presses de l'Université de Montréal, 1969) lists both published and unpublished material on the subject.

6. The latest list is *Select List of British Parliamentary Papers, 1955–64* by P. and G. Ford and D. Marshallsay (Irish Universities Press, 1971).

7. *Dictionary of Arbitration and its Terms* by Katherine Seide (Oceana, 1970) covers one area of industrial relations.

8. This cultural limitation will be removed to some extent by a *Dictionary of Industrial Relations* being compiled by A. I. Marsh and E. O. Evans to be published by Hutchinson, probably in 1971.

9. A list of all Canadian theses in economics, business and industrial relations since 1919 is in *Canadian Graduate Theses, 1919–1967: An Annotated Bibliography* by D. W. Wood, L. A. Kelly and P. Kumar (Industrial Relations Centre, Queen's University, 1970).

10. For Australia there is the *Union List of Higher Degree Theses in Australian University Libraries* by M. J. Marshall (University of Tasmania Library, 1959).

CHAPTER NINETEEN

INDUSTRIAL ECONOMICS

J. R. CABLE

Subject Matter

Industrial Economics is a rather broad area of applied economics concerned with the behaviour of firms and industries. Its boundaries are by no means well defined. What follows is a personal view of the subject, hopefully not too idiosyncratic.

To the present writer there are four main areas of interest: industrial structure, in a wide sense; individual areas of decision making and behaviour; the evaluation of behaviour as 'performance'; and government intervention and policies touching on these matters. The first traditionally includes, e.g. the size and spatial distribution of firms, industries, and activities; market concentration; a good deal of institutional material, etc., but can also be seen to extend into econometric work on cost, demand and production functions, and input-output analysis of structure. Examples of the areas of behaviour covered would be market strategy of all kinds, location, innovation, investment, co-operative behaviour and collusion, etc. For the most part 'performance' is evaluated from the community viewpoint, as in conventional welfare economics. The strands of public policy most directly involved would include monopoly control, location policy, state ownership or regulation of particular industries, manipulation of industry structure and productivity, and the like.

In the main industrial economics is, at least to the present writer, primarily a positive rather than normative area. Thus it excludes the mainly normative content of business studies and management science. Certain other areas, distinct and substantial enough to stand alone, may be included or excluded at will, namely transport and agricultural economics; banking; labour economics and industrial relations; and the economics of public enterprise. As it happens the writer finds himself excluding all but the last.

Relationship with Theory

Much of the subject matter delineated can be investigated in a way relatively divorced from economic theory. The theory, if present at all, is implicit; there is no explicit testing of hypotheses; and the empirical work is not brought directly to bear to modify existing theories or formulate new ones. Much of the British industrial economics literature of the 1950s was of this kind, e.g. P. Sargent Florence's *The Logic of British and American Industry* (Routledge & Kegan Paul, 1953) and *Ownership Control and Success of Large Companies* (Sweet and Maxwell, 1961); the three books by C. F. Carter and B. R. Williams on innovation, *Industry and Technical Progress* (Oxford U.P., 1957); *Investment in Innovation* (Oxford U.P., 1958), and *Science in Industry* (Oxford U.P., 1959); and R. S. Edwards' and H. Townsend's two books *Business Enterprise* (Macmillan, 1958), and *Business Growth* (Macmillan, 1966).

However, the character and content of contemporary industrial economics has been much influenced by theory. One extremely influential development has been the structure-conduct-performance hypothesis, developed at Harvard under the leadership of E. S. Mason and now linked most closely with the name of J. S. Bain, *Barriers to New Competition* (Harvard U.P., 1956), and *Industrial Organisation* (Wiley, 1959). This has profoundly influenced the scope and content of much undergraduate, graduate and research work in the US and more recently in the UK also: a trend confirmed by the recent publication of D. Needham's *Economic Analysis and Industrial Structure* (Holt, Rinehart & Winston, 1969), which, however, shows the approach capable of further refinement.

Secondly, firms' price behaviour is an area of natural overlap between industrial economics and pure theory, and this is reflected in an overlap in the literature, notably that following the famous article by R. L. Hall and C. I. Hitch 'Price Theory and Business Behaviour', *Oxford Economic Papers*, vol. 2, May 1939, pp. 12–45, and involving the names of F. Machlup 'Marginal Analysis and Empirical Research', *American Economic Review*, vol. 36, No. 4, September 1946, pp. 19–54, P. W. S. Andrews' *Manufacturing Business* (Macmillan, 1949), and *On Competition in Economic Theory* (Macmillan, 1964), Lester, Gordon, Earley, Barback and others. Thirdly, the most striking current links between theory and industrial economics centre on the 'new' theories of the firm, which are propounded with a closer eye on the observed motivations and organisational characteristics of firms and managers. Two recent strands in this development of especial interest to industrial economists are, on the one hand, the 'managerial' theories of W. J. Baumol 'On the Theory of Oligopoly', *Economica*, vol. 25, No. 99, August 1958, and *Business Behaviour Value and Growth* (Macmillan, 1959); R. Marris *The Economic Theory of Managerial Capitalism* (Macmillan, 1964); and O. E. Williamson *The Economics of Discretionary Behaviour: Managerial Objectives in a Theory of the Firm* (Prentice-Hall, 1964), and on the other hand the behavioural models of H. A. Simon 'A Behavioural Model of Rational Choice', *Quarterly Journal of Economics*, vol. 69, 1965, pp. 99–118, and R. M. Cyert and J. G. March *A Behavioural Theory of the Firm* (Prentice-Hall, 1963). These developments provide new hypotheses to be tested, and fresh guidelines for the analysis of the subject matter outlined earlier.

Empirical Techniques

One of the things making industrial economics hard to define is that it has no distinctive methodology. However, the case study approach at the level of the firm, and especially the industry, has long been much favoured. Indeed at one time it seemed as if the subject might devolve into an industry by industry breakdown of the subject matter which has been discussed. What the writer has especially in mind here are the countless books on individual industries of the 1940s and 1950s, and in particular, say, the work of G. C. Allen, especially his *British Industries and Their Organisation* (4th edn, Longmans, 1959), and the Duncan Burn symposium *The Structure of British Industry: A Symposium* (Cambridge U.P. for National Institute of Economic and Social Research, 1958). Currently a rather different general trend is apparent. Individual industry studies continue to appear (many adopting the Bain approach as a framework, both the UK and the US) and case study work is still vigorous. But there appears now to be a greater emphasis on individual problems and topics, and on the testing of specific hypotheses. This tends to involve the use of industry or firm cross-section data, and so operates counter to any tendency for industrial economics to resolve into an industry-by-industry pattern. An important factor contributing to this development is the fact that industrial economics is sharing in the general extension of quantitative techniques in empirical work. A natural area for the application of econometric techniques is in the empirical testing of the structure-conduct-performance hypothesis and of the 'new' theories of the firm. To the present writer it seems inevitable that the application of quantitative methods will continue to expand in industrial economics (hopefully intertwining with the case study approach, since the combination seems potentially extremely fruit-ful), and as it does so substantially shape and structure its subject matter in the future.

Influence of Public Policy

It may be that the development of various strands of public policy relevant to industrial economics has been influenced by advances in the subject. Certainly the subject has in return been influenced by policy developments—the introduction of policy measures play-ing an attention, focusing role, and the application of policies throwing up large quantities of primary data. Noteworthy in the US in this context would be the life of the Temporary National Economic Committee (described by E. S. Mason as 'as fecund in literary output as it was abortive in action'; E. S. Mason, *Economic Concentration and the Monopoly Problem* (Harvard U.P., 1959)) and the work of the Anti-Trust-Division and the Federal Trade Commission; the holding of various House and Senate Investiga-tions on concentration, price discrimination, mergers, etc., and the work of the various bodies set up to deal with the regulated industries. In the UK, one could cite the setting up, work and reports of the Monopolies Commission, Restrictive Practices Court, Nationalised Industries, NBPI, IRC, NEDO and the little Neddies and so on.

The Literature in General

In view of the rather broad area of interest of industrial economics, and the overlaps with other areas like microeconomic theory, econometrics, management science, etc., it is not surprising that the literature of the subject matter should be a widely scattered one. As always the key to a successful approach to the literature is a firm delineation of subject matter. As will be by now apparent, the present writer's view is that this should be on a topic basis. A supplementary approach is via the names of particular authors, since there is a fairly well-defined group of important contem-porary contributors. The names of some though by no means all of these are mentioned herein; a more comprehensive list is quickly acquired as familiarity with the literature grows. Almost certainly the industrial economist will find himself spending most of his time with the better-known, academic, economics journals. The remainder of this contribution is divided into two sections dealing with journals and books respectively. References to the various abstracting and indexing services, etc., are made *en passant*.

Journals

The only journal with an industrial economics title is the (British) *Journal of Industrial Economics*. Avowedly intended for an academic and business readership it is probably of greater interest to the former in practice. Not a prestige journal, its contents are of somewhat mixed quality, though they have, during the 1960s, reflected the increasingly quantitative character of the subject. Of other professional UK journals, the author finds himself most frequently referring to *Oxford Economic Papers*, mainly on account of its continuing, if rather traditional concern with pricing and oligopoly models, and good coverage of the industrial area of applied economics (notably, e.g. the 1966 symposium on restrictive practices). The *Economic Journal* is of interest mainly for its survey articles (also the occasional symposium, as on restrictive practices in 1960), but otherwise is certainly no richer a store for the industrial economist than others, e.g. the *Manchester School*.

None of the UK journals really compare with their American counterparts, however, in terms of the frequency of appearance of relevant material or of its quality. Among US journals the *American Economic Review* is probably of paramount importance in this field, as in many others. It has been especially important in recent theoretical advances, was deeply involved in the earlier marginalist controversy, and is a steady supplier of important contributions on many topics central to industrial economics. Next in importance in this area are probably the *Journal of Political Economy*, and the *Review of Economics and Statistics*, the latter, especially, in the context of the application of quantitative techniques. The *Quarterly Journal of Economics* is perhaps less regularly relevant, but when it does contribute it is usually with importance (e.g. it had the first presentation of R. Marris's growth maximising models, 'A model of the Managerial Enterprise', vol. 77, May 1963, pp. 185–209). Also worth mentioning is the *American Journal of Agricultural Economics*, formerly the *Journal of Farm Economics*, mainly on account of the interest agricultural economists have shown in the structure-conduct-performance hypothesis.

These are the journals the author finds it necessary to keep in constant touch with. For systematic search, the AEA *Index of Economic Journals* is as usual invaluable. The most relevant subject classifications are Business Organisation and Managerial Economics (14) and, more especially, Industrial Organisation and Public Policy (15). The latter is the longest and most detailed of any subject and has some useful sub-classifications, e.g. Market Structure and Behaviour, and Government Policy towards Monopoly and Competition. However, most of the sub-classifications are in terms of industries, which is not so helpful as the subject moves more to a topic basis. The other snag is, of course, the publication delay, usually at least four years.

Alongside the learned journals are other useful periodicals. The British commercial bank Reviews (especially *Lloyds Bank Review*) frequently contain articles on various policy issues. Though often written by academic economists, they tend to be somewhat lightweight on account of the readership, but they are nevertheless useful. The *Midland Bank Review* provides one unusual service, which is the regular section on 'Government and Business', which briefly notes all major policy developments (including, e.g. brief details of budgets and farm price reviews, changes in export quotas and regulations, as well as monopoly policy, measures for structural reform of industries, etc.). In the context of keeping up with current developments the *Research Index* published by Business Surveys Ltd. is worth mentioning. This is a fortnightly list giving headline, subject and reference to press and periodical reports on matters 'of financial interest' meaning, roughly, covering the same ground as UK newspaper financial pages and business sections. Insertions are classified under both subject and Company headings, and the whole thing amounts to the next-best thing to a personal newscutting service. *Business Ratios*, now in its fifth year, has produced some useful articles on productivity, as well as supplying statistical data, and is important in the general area of performance and efficiency. To some extent it has taken on the mantle of the earlier, excellent OECD publication *Productivity Measurement Review*, which sadly demised in 1965. Finally, there should be mention of *The Times Review of Industry* and *Fortune*, especially for their lists of the top 500 largest firms, along with some key statistical data for each.

A persistent problem in keeping track of the literature of industrial economics is the overlap in subject matter with management science, operational research, accounting, finance. Given the mainly normative emphasis of these, it is of only occasional relevance and interest to the industrial economist. But the problem of there being occasionally an important article is sufficiently great to make ignorance of this literature potentially costly. In this regard it is a comfort that the *Index of Economic Journals* covers journals like *Harvard Business Review*, the *Journal of Business* and the *Journal of Finance*, though this will not permit scanning of current and more recent issues. The natural step is of course to turn to abstracting and indexing services. But these tend to be less than convenient, since the classifications seem to be tailored mainly to business and business-school users. One of the most helpful is probably the *Anbar Documentation Service Index*, which has a good coverage of British, American and West European journals and books, and features an alphabetical classification, permitting fairly narrow subject areas (e.g. 'R & D' and 'simulation') to be picked out. The *Business Periodicals Index* published by H. W. Wilson Co. also features a subject classification, and is very comprehensive. But while a possibly useful tool for a specific project, it has never commended itself to the author as a scanning device. The same can be said, though with somewhat less force, for *Anbar*.

Books

Some typical or seminal titles in industrial economics have already been listed, in outlining the subject. Picking on individual authors and titles is inevitably an arbitrary process and an invidious task, but there are a number which the present author would like to mention. These are A. A. Berle and G. C. Means *The Modern Corporation and Private Property* (Macmillan, 1932); E. S. Mason *The Corporation in Modern Society* (Harvard U.P., 1959); J. Schumpeter *Capitalism, Socialism and Democracy* (Allen and Unwin, 1943); and J. K. Galbraith *American Capitalism* (Hamish Hamilton, 1952), and *The New Industrial State* (Hamish Hamilton, 1967). All of these can be regarded as either provocative or seminal, and important among the more general and background books relevant to industrial economics. Finally, G. J. Stigler has been the author of many significant contributions to industrial economics, many of which are collected in his *The Organisation of Industry* (Irwin, 1968).

As has been suggested, it is journals rather than books with which the industrial economist is likely to spend most of his time. However, there are sorts of services which books can more easily provide than journals. Two important ones would be to point up the key issues in a particular area of interest, and to draw together and organise the literature on a particular topic. Two areas come to mind where something of this sort exists. Thus, in the general area of technical progress and innovation we have, *inter alia*, W. G. Salter *Productivity and Technical Change* (2nd edn, Cambridge

267

U.P., 1966); Murray Brown *On the Theory and Measurement of Technological Change* (Cambridge U.P., 1966); D. Hamberg *R & D: Essays in the Economics of Research and Development* (Random House, 1966); and E. Mansfield *The Economics of Technological Change* (Norton, 1968). Then, in the field of anti-trust economics we have a number of good books providing this sort of service, e.g. C. Kayser and D. F. Turner *Anti-Trust Policy: An Economic and Legal Analysis* (Harvard U.P., 1959); A. D. Neale, *The Anti-Trust Laws of the U.S.A.* (Cambridge U.P. for NIESR, 1960); E. M. Singer *Anti-Trust Economics* (Prentice-Hall, 1968); R. B. Stevens and B. S. Yamey *The Restrictive Practices Court* (Weidenfeld and Nicolson, 1965); C. K. Rowley *The British Monopolies Commission* (Allen and Unwin, 1966); A. Hunter *Competition and the Law* (Allen and Unwin, 1966); and also his *Monopoly and Competition: Selected Readings* (Penguin, 1969). (The monopoly issue is one where this sort of service is especially needed, on account of the frequency of new developments from Court decisions, etc. However, this dynamism also obviously means that the books providing the service tend rapidly to become out of date).

In general, however, industrial economics is not particularly fortunate with books providing this sort of service. At the time of writing there is a glaring need for a good book on recent developments in the theory of the firm: J. W. McGuire's *Theories of Business Behaviour* (Prentice-Hall, 1964) is now far from up to date and in any case too broad in scope to be entirely adequate in its particular parts. We also have no adequate teaching text nor comprehensive collection of readings: R. B. Heflebower and G. W. Stocking *Readings in Industrial Organisation and Public Policy* (Irwin for AEA, 1958) being now out of date.

In searching for individual titles the usual tools display some limitations. The annual volumes of the *British National Bibliography* have sub-divisions (under the most relevant main heading 338: Economic Organisation) which are largely on an industry-by-industry basis, with some other categories. The *Cumulative Book Index*, being listed alphabetically by subject and author, makes for an easier search on a topic basis. However, a precise definition of the subject area is, of course, crucial. The Library of Congress Catalogue has some useful sub-headings under economics, e.g. 'competition', 'monopoly', 'cost', 'Government ownership', 'risk', etc. Then there is the *Subject Index* of the British Museum which, however, the present author has never been so desperate as actually to use.

CHAPTER TWENTY

AGRICULTURAL ECONOMICS

K. E. HUNT

Scope of the Subject

The boundaries of the subject of agricultural economics are not unequivocably defined, but one might include the following areas of interest without arousing much dissent; the supply of the resources of land, labour and capital and the demand for them, production, economic concepts applied to the farm firm and to the firms engaged in the distribution of farm products, marketing and distribution viewed as services, the interrelationships between supply, demand and prices of agricultural and food products, finance and credit for farm operations, co-operation as applied to the production and distribution of farm products, agricultural policy (including income policy, agrarian reforms, regional planning, etc.), international trade, including international commodity problems and agreements, development problems in low income countries, aspects of agricultural education and training. In practice the boundaries are tending to become less well-defined as, for example, where the agricultural production sector has integrated with the distribution sector to a considerable degree.

A comprehensive history of the development of the subject in the United States is given in *The Story of Agricultural Economics in the United States. 1840–1932: Men, Services, Ideas* by Henry C. and Anne Dewees Taylor (Iowa State College Press, 1952). A guide to the evolution of the subject in more recent years can be obtained by glancing through the contents lists of the journals referred to below, particularly American *Journal of Farm Economics*, the *Journal of the Proceedings of the Agricultural Economics Society* in Great Britain (both these Journals later changed their names somewhat) and the *Proceedings of the Conferences of the International Association of Agricultural Economists*. The main areas of interest in the subject have varied from country to country and from time to time. Farm accounting had a central place in the early days in most countries, farm income problems and commodity supply control issues were of active concern quite early and they became much in evidence after the slump in the 1930s. It might be said that, broadly speaking, up to the end of the 1920s, with the exception of fairly straightforward costing and accountancy studies, the bulk of the work was in qualitative terms. Increasingly through the 1930s and the subsequent years quantitative techniques were applied to the solution of agricultural economic problems with a particular surge in mathematical model building after the Second World War. A notable feature of these later periods has been the increased concern for the identification of problems in the field and the direction of research to their solution.

Abstracting and Indexing Services

The earliest published venture in this field was the *Agricultural Economics Literature* published by the US Department of Agriculture during the period 1937–1942. This began as an internal document for the American Government Bureau of Agricultural Economics and was gradually formalised. At this time a number of national abstracting and indexing services included some agricultural economics publications (e.g. the Experimental Station Record) but the coverage of agricultural economics material was not comprehensive. From 1932 the *International Bibliography of Agricultural Economics* was published as a supplement to the *Berichte über Landwirtschaft*. This ceased in 1938. From 1938 the International Institute of Agriculture in Rome published its *Bibliographie Internationale d'Agriculture*. *The Agricultural Index* (now the *Biological and Agricultural Index* of Wilson & Co.) has always listed a certain amount of agricultural economics material.

There are five major bibliographic services currently available for agricultural economists. The *Bibliography of Agriculture* published by the US Department of Agriculture provides a listing embracing both biological and economic fields. It is published monthly in English and is probably the most comprehensive of the group though the variation in academic level of the material listed is greater than in the others. It includes not only original research publications of the highest academic standing but also secondary reviews and articles designed for the popularisation of the results of research.

The World Agricultural Economics and Rural Sociology Abstracts (WAERSA) is one of a large group of abstracting journals in the agricultural fields published by the Commonwealth Agricultural Bureaux. The Bureaux are financed by contributions from the Governments of British Commonwealth countries and the Republic of Ireland but the scope of the literature abstracted by the several organisations is world-wide. *WAERSA* now provides the main abstract service in English for agricultural economics, covering some 5000 publications, journal articles, bulletins and books, a year. The abstracts are classified and grouped by subject, and subject, geographical and author indexes are provided.

The Bibliothek des Instituts für Weltwirtschaft an der Universität Kiel also provides a title service in German covering all agricultural sciences, including a section on agricultural economics.

The remaining two services provide abstracts on cards of primarily agricultural economic material. The more comprehensive *Informations dienst Kartei* (Dokumentationsstelle für Marktwesen und ländliche Soziologie, Bonn) in its earlier stages included mainly material of German origin, but it is now world-wide. The other prepared in East Germany is *Dokumentationsdienst Agrarökonomik* (Institut für Landwirtschaftliche Information und Dokumentation, Deutsche Akademie der Landwirtschaftswissenschaften zu Berlin, Berlin).

Apart from these services for dealing with current publications numerous substantial publications containing bibliographies for sectors of the agricultural economic field have been published. Many on specific subjects (e.g. food aid, land tenure, etc.) have been prepared by FAO. Others provide lists of publications by particular organisations or in particular areas. For example: *Economics of Agriculture: Reports and publications of USDA's Economic Research Service*, 1961–65 (Washington, USDA Economic Research Service ERS 350, 1967); the Stanford Food Research Institute studies are listed in their *Publications, 1954–59* (1959), and for 1959–65 in *Food Research Institute Studies*, vol. 6, No. 1, 1966, pp. 95–113; *An Australasian Bibliography of Agricultural Economics, 1788–1960* by J. L. Dillon and C. C. McFarlane (University of Sydney, Department of Agriculture, 1967); and India, Ministry of Food and Agriculture: *Agricultural Economics: a Bibliography* (New Delhi, Government Press, 1961).

Substantial bibliographies may be included in research, for example studies issued by the Agricultural Development Council, New York, on developing areas: *Research on agricultural development in North Africa* by P. W. Foster (1967); *Research on agricultural development in Central America* by H. A. Lombardo (1969); and *Research on agricultural development in South-east Asia* by C. R. Wharton (1965).

271

Journals

One might broadly separate periodicals of interest to agricultural economists into two groups on the basis of their main subject matter. The core of the research material on agricultural economics is to be found in the journals specifically devoted to this subject which now appear, sponsored mainly by local associations of agricultural economists, university departments or occasionally by government agricultural economics departments, in most of the major countries of the world.

Among the main journals in the United Kingdom are the *Journal of Agricultural Economics* (Reading, 1954–) (formerly *Journal of Proceedings of the Agricultural Economics Society*, 1928–); *Farm Economist* (Oxford, 1933–); *Scottish Agricultural Economics* (Edinburgh, Department of Agricultural Economics, 1950–); and *Farm Management Notes* (Sutton Bonington, University of Nottingham, 1949–).

As is noted below, many of the university departments of agricultural economics in Great Britain publish bulletin series rather than journals.

In the USA the best known are the *American Journal of Agricultural Economics*, formerly the *Journal of Farm Economics* (1919–), *Agricultural Economics Research* (US Department of Agriculture, 1949–), and the *Food Research Institute Studies* (Stanford University Food Research Institute, 1960–).

A number of agricultural economics departments of Universities publish journals, e.g. *Illinois Farm Economics*, but the bulk of their work is likely to be found in their bulletins. The academic content of journals depends on whether they are channels for primary publication or are intended for popularising the results of research published elsewhere.

It is rarely possible to judge the scope of agricultural economic studies in a particular country from one or two periodicals because each may be specialised by the nature of its origin. However, the following selection would provide an introduction to the work of the countries or areas listed.

Africa
Agricultural Economics Bulletin for Africa (UN Economic Commission for Africa and FAO, 1962–)
East African Journal of Rural Development (Kampala, Makerere University College, Department of Rural Economy and Extension, 1968–)

Australia
Australian Journal of Agricultural Economics (Sydney, etc., 1957–)

Canada
Canadian Farm Economics (Ottawa, Department of Agriculture, 1966–)
Canadian Journal of Agricultural Economics (Toronto, 1953–)

France
Economie Rurale (Paris, 1949–)

Germany, West
Agrarwirtschaft (Hannover, 1952–)

Holland
Landbouw voorlichting ('s-Gravenhage, 1947/8–)

India
Indian Journal of Agricultural Economics (Bombay, 1946–)

Ireland
Irish Journal of Agricultural Economics and Rural Sociology (Dublin, 1967–)

Nigeria
Bulletin of Rural Economics of Sociology (Ibadan, 1964–)

Pakistan
Pakistan Development Review (Karachi, Institute of Development Economics, 1961–)

USSR
Ekonomika sel'skogo khozyaistva (Moscow, 1957–)

West Indies
Social and Economic Studies (Mona Jamaica, 1953–)

Generally speaking the bulk of the papers to be found in these periodicals are concerned with the situations and problems in the country of publication. However, agricultural economic studies are now so firmly international in character, and so many workers have been on assignments, or undergone training, in countries other than their own that studies of international problems or of

273

conditions abroad may be found in any of these national journals. *The International Journal of Agrarian Affairs* (published by Oxford U.P. on behalf of the International Association of Agricultural Economists) is explicitly concerned with problems common to a number of countries.

Apart from the central core, a second group of material of interest to agricultural economists is to be found in journals whose main concern is either with the economics of the economy in general, rather than with the agricultural sector alone, or in other disciplines touching agricultural science or the rural social scene. Many periodicals concerned with general economics contain an occasional paper on an agricultural subject. *Economica* (1921–), *Econometrica* (1933–), *Economic Journal* (1891–), and *American Economic Review* (1911–) might be quoted as examples, but others could be found in the economics journals of most countries, especially those whose economics have a large agrarian sector.

Among associated disciplines whose periodicals may yield, if only occasionally, material of interest to agricultural economists are the agricultural sciences, sociology, business management, geography, town and country planning, land use studies, etc. The agricultural sciences might be expected to be the most fruitful but though periodicals vary, papers in which specifically economic techniques of analysis are used tend to be rare in agricultural science periodicals. On the other hand, many studies reported in such journals provide results which are of very distinct value to agricultural economists (e.g. *see* Aberdeen University School of Agriculture *Index of Scientific and Economic Studies of Particular Significance to the big Industry in the United Kingdom*: 7 separate parts published at intervals between 1963 and 1969). The main periodicals in agricultural science are listed for their respective fields in the abstract journals published by the Commonwealth Agricultural Bureaux.

The list of periodicals in other associated disciplines which might from time to time contain papers of agricultural economic interest might be long and diverse. However, as illustration, one might quote *Sociologia Ruralis* (1960–), *Economic Geography* (1925–), *Land Economics* (formerly *Journal of Land and Public Utility Economics*, 1925–), *Journal of Development Studies* (1964–), and *Agricultural History Review* (Reading, British Agricultural History Society, 1953–).

There are also a number of journals concerned with business management and marketing which, though not necessarily containing papers specifically concerned with the agricultural sector, nonetheless deal with problems which find their rather close parallels

274

there: e.g. *Journal of Industrial Economics* (1952/3–) and *Journal of Marketing* (1936–).

The searchers for journals outside those mentioned here which might have articles on agricultural economics subjects are likely to find useful the list of journals scanned by the Commonwealth Bureau of Agricultural Economics. This is published in vol. 10, No. 1, 1968, and vol. 11, No. 4, 1969, of *WAERSA* with supplements in subsequent issues.

When forming a view about the most useful journals for studies in particular subject matter fields, it would be useful to look up these subjects in the index of a number of issues of this abstract journal and to note the sources from which the individual abstracts have been drawn. Similarly, guidance on journals serving particular geographical areas can be obtained by using the geographical index of the Abstracts.

Among other sources of periodical names are: *Ulrich International Periodicals Directory*, 12th edn. Periodicals of interest to agricultural economists may be found both in vol. 1, Arts, Humanities, Social Science, or vol. 2, Scientific, Technical and Medical: *List of Agricultural Press and Periodicals in OEEC Member Countries* (OEEC, 1960); *Library List of Current Periodicals Received in the FAO Library* (FAO, 1959); *Library Catalogue of Annuals Currently Received by the Library* (FAO, 1968); and *Current Agricultural Serials* by D. H. Boalch (2 vols, Oxford, International Association of Agricultural Librarians and Documentalists, 1965).

Other Publications

Books originating in a great variety of disciplines may have an interest to workers in agricultural economics but, generally speaking, the principal books can be located through libraries or abstract journals without great difficulty. From the viewpoint of the user, it is much more noteworthy that a substantial amount of important material appears in separate bulletins of some substance: say, of 50 to 100 pages, issued by a great diversity of sources.

One important group of sources is the university agricultural economics departments in Great Britain, North America and many other countries. Some of their bulletins appear in numbered series; however, a series may include publications on both agricultural sciences and agricultural economics. Other bulletins may appear as occasional publications and it may consequently be extremely difficult to know of their existence.

Similar bulletins are published by non-university research institutions, among them government departments or government sponsored institutes, independent units and occasionally institutes run by industrial or commercial firms.

Much valuable material may appear in the reports of special committees and commissions: sometimes appearing in a series such as the British 'Command' papers, sometimes in isolation.

Amongst the government publications are several very useful series, between them including a large variety of subjects, issued by the United States Department of Agriculture including *Agriculture Handbooks, Agriculture Information Bulletins, Foreign Agriculture Reports, Foreign Agricultural Service* series and the *Marketing Research Reports, Agricultural Economics Reports* and the *Foreign Agricultural Economic Reports* of the USDA Economic Research Service.

Information on Current Research

Routine sources of information on current research include the Aslib *Index to Theses Accepted for Higher Degrees in the Universities of Great Britain and Ireland.* American theses appear in *Dissertation Abstracts: The Humanities and Social Sciences.*

Current research in Great Britain is listed in *Scientific Research in British Universities and Colleges, vol. 3, Social Sciences* prepared by the Department of Education and Science. However, lists of current research activities usually provide only general pointers to the areas of interest in particular departments. The same entry may continue over several years.

Reviews of Major Publications

Review articles on specific subjects in agricultural economics are regular features of *WAERSA*. Many of the larger agricultural economics journals provide reviews of current publications of substance. English-speaking readers are likely to look first to the American *Journal of Agricultural Economics*, the English *Journal of Agricultural Economics* and the *Indian Journal of Agricultural Economics*.

Problems of Use

Apart from the problems of language and difficulties concerned with the availability of statistical information, probably the main problems which agricultural economists meet are concerned with (a) finding out what work has been published which would be useful to them, (b) locating copies for consultation and (c) over-coming problems of definition.

The development of title and abstract services in recent years has considerably eased the difficulty of knowing what is available. A student or research worker beginning work on a new field should consult the subject indexes in each volume of *WAERSA* and make a detailed search for any relevant specialist bibliographies as a first step before casting more widely. Though the bulk of the published material may be found through the bibliographic sources there is, unfortunately, a significant margin which may escape. Some consists of articles and bulletins on agricultural economic matters which appear amongst a body of material on other subjects and escape notice in consequence. Others consist of 'working' papers, and papers circulated for discussion which may or may not later be revised for more general publication; still others consist of substantial documents prepared for general information (e.g. various series on the European Common Markets). Accessions lists of the FAO library, the library of the Ministry of Agriculture, Fisheries and Food (Whitehall Place, London) and of other libraries specialising in the field are often valuable in bringing such items to the attention of research workers.

A second difficulty is the actual location of the desired publi-cation. If *WAERSA* has abstracted it, the Bureau will usually be able to assist. A good deal of inter-library lending is often needed before a worker's reading is complete. Unfortunately there is no central lending library for the subject. Among the libraries with a considerable body of agricultural economic material are those of the Ministry of Agriculture, Fisheries and Food; the Institute for Agricultural Economics, University of Oxford; Wye College, University of London; the Departments of Agricultural Science and of Land Economy, Cambridge. Libraries in a number of other university agricultural economics departments and research institutes whose staff are publishing studies in particular fields are likely to be well supplied too.

Finally, problems of terminology and definition are hampering in certain fields though perhaps not more than in other sectors of the social sciences. Two examples might be quoted as illustrations: first, before incorporating the data in analyses all definitions of statistical material relating to agricultural production and distri-bution and of farm financial and labour records should be studied closely. If possible, the form used for the collection of the raw data and the instructions for its use should be scrutinised. In a quite different field unlike the biological and physical world, economic institutions vary from place to place. Consequently a feature found only in, say, Brazil or the USSR may have no equivalent in Great Britain and no suitable term in English may be available. Terms used by different authors for the same concept may then need careful comparison. A useful glossary of terms relating to Soviet agricultural organisation is given in *WAERSA*, vol. 12, No. 1, March 1970.

CHAPTER TWENTY-ONE

MONETARY ECONOMICS

G. E. WOOD

The volume of work on monetary economics, both theoretical and empirical, is currently increasing at an increasing rate. It would be impossible in the length here permitted to list every study of importance; rather we shall attempt to suggest works, whether books or articles, that will open up views of what fields are available, and provide guidance on where more details of these fields can be found.

Many **textbooks** have sections on monetary economics contained in them: at an introductory level, A. A. Alchian and W. R. Allen's *University Economics* (2nd edn, Wadsworth, 1967) has three very useful chapters on the demand for money and its relation to national income, and the supply of money. Unfortunately it is, like many books in this field, American, so its institutional material is not of immediate interest to British students. Martin J. Bailey's *National Income and the Price Level* (McGraw-Hill, 1962) is a macroeconomics text for students who have at least a first-year course in macroeconomics behind them; though not on monetary economics it does lay great stress on the importance of money for macroeconomic theory and policy. It would be useful reading for those who wish to see more clearly why monetary economists are trying to refine the theory and empirics of the demand for, and, supply of, money.

Two very useful short books are *Theory of Money*, by Walter T. Newlyn (Oxford U.P., 1962) and *Money and the Balance of Payments*, by Tibor Scitovsky (Unwin University Books, 1969). The first considers money supply both theoretically and practically, and in a British institutional context. It approaches the demand for money in a traditionally Keynesian (*General Theory*) sort of way, and contains a very useful examination of the concept of liquidity. Scitovsky's short book is half monetary theory, and in addition to examining both the theoretical and empirical work on money supply and demand theory, he has an admirable chapter on how disequilibrium in the money market affects the real sector.

Probably the best text available is *The Demand for Money*, by David E. W. Laidler (International Textbook Co., 1969). This is slightly more advanced than the two mentioned previously, and is designed for students who have taken (or are taking) an intermediate macroeconomics course. The first chapters set up a macroeconomic framework for the problems dealt with in the rest of the book; both classical and modern theories of the demand for money are then surveyed in some detail, and empirical work is also discussed. The theory of the supply of money is not, of course, mentioned. There is an admirable collection of references.

Another good, considerably longer, text is *Macroeconomics: Income and Monetary Theory*, by J. Aschheim and Ching-Yao Hsieh (Merrill, 1969): this book has a long and extremely good section on the history of monetary theory. For those who would read the originals, two classics from earlier years are Alfred Marshall's *Money, Credit and Commerce* (Macmillan, 1923) and Irving Fisher's *The Theory of Interest* (Macmillan, 1930). There are numerous American textbooks on monetary economics: all are handicapped from the British point of view by being set very definitely in an American institutional context, and frequently have very long sections on financial institutions. A. G. Hart, P. B. Kenen and A. D. Entine's *Money, Debt and Economic Activity* (4th edn, Prentice-Hall, 1969) is a good example of the genre. They are all very much longer than Laidler's book.

We now move from textbooks to **treatises** and **journal articles**. Most treatises deal with particular aspects of monetary theory, but two, well worth mentioning, do not: *Money*, by M. L. Burstein (Schenkman, 1963), and *An Introduction to the Theory of Interest*, by Joseph W. Conard (California U.P., 1959). Burstein's book deals with the theory and practice of commercial and central banking, the choice of monetary standards, the demand for money and national income theory, and with institutional aspects of monetary theory. Despite its length it is a very concisely written book, and at times very tough. Conard's title is misleading, for it does not imply that the book is an introduction to the subject, but rather the first step in his theoretical and empirical study of the determinants of interest rate level and structure. Non-monetary and monetary theories of the interest rate level are surveyed at considerable length, and there is a very useful survey of theories of the term structure of rates. D. Meiselman's book *The Term Structure of Interest Rates* (Prentice-Hall, 1962) should also be noted in this context.

Before we deal with works on particular aspects of monetary economics, we should make explicit the division of monetary economics we are using. For our present purpose we should, I think, divide monetary economics into four sections: the role of **money in national income determination**, the implications of non-bank financial intermediaries for theory and policy, the role of money in economic growth, and the role of money in general equilibrium. The classic text on the first is, of course, J. M. Keynes' *The General Theory of Employment, Interest and Money* (Macmillan, 1936). A modern magnificently scholarly and analytical work by A. Leijonhufvud *On Keynesian Economics and the Economics of Keynes* (Oxford U.P., 1968) carries on the tradition of that work which it regards as an extension of Keynes' earlier work *Treatise on Money* (2 vols, Macmillan, 1930). Both of these books are hard, but are essential reading for the serious student of monetary economics. The lowest estimate of this branch of monetary economics is represented by the *Report of the Committee on the Working of the Monetary System* (Cmnd. 827) (HMSO, 1959), the 'Radcliffe Report', wherein is contained the view that money is, because of the infinite variability of the velocity of circulation, quite unimportant for economic management. Though there is considerable description of the institutions of the money market, there is no econometric evidence in the volume, and no *explicit* economic theory. The complete opposite of this volume is *Studies in the Quantity Theory of Money* by Milton Friedman (Chicago U.P., 1956). The introductory essay by Friedman is the classic statement of the approach to the demand for money which uses the tools of microeconomics to analyse the demand for money as we would analyse the demand for any other durable good. There follow four studies of the demand for money, all in this tradition, which aim to show that, while velocity is variable, it varies in a systematic way, and that asset holders move along a stable demand for real cash balances function.

This field contains a great deal of work, both theoretical and applied, on the demand for money. Much of it is in the form of journal articles: three worth noting as leading examples of different approaches to the same problem are, 'The Demand for Money: Some Theoretical and Empirical Results' by Milton Friedman (*Journal of Political Economy*, vol. 67, 1959, pp. 327–351), 'Liquidity Preference as Behaviour towards Risk' by James Tobin (*Review of Economic Studies*, vol. 25, 1957–58, pp. 65–86), and 'The Transactions Demand for Cash: an Inventory Theoretic Approach' by W. J. Baumol in *Quarterly Journal of Economics*, vol. 66, 1952, pp. 545-556. These, and many other articles on this

281

aspect of monetary theory (and on money in general equilibrium), are contained in an admirable collection of readings *Monetary Theory and Policy* edited by R. S. Thorn (Random House, 1966). Indeed books of readings and the proceedings of conferences abound in monetary economics. A policy-oriented book of readings is *Monetary Economics* edited by Alan D. Entine (Wadsworth, 1968), whilst another book of readings *Readings in Monetary Theory* edited by F. A. Lutz and L. W. Mints for the AEA (Allen and Unwin, 1952) contains many classic articles on this topic, as well as on the integration of money and value theory. A very recent conference, *The Radcliffe Report: Ten Years After* has had its proceedings published in *Money in Britain, 1959–1969* edited by David R. Croome and Harry G. Johnson (Oxford U.P., 1970). Like the original report, it is concerned with the workings of the financial system and the stability of the demand function for real cash balances. Unlike the original report it contains some econometrics, some theory (in an admirable survey by Harry G. Johnson) and discussion and criticism of the views expressed in the papers. The book also contains a lengthy bibliography of theoretical and empirical material of relevance to analysis of the UK monetary system.

Turning now to the importance of **financial intermediaries**, the work of J. G. Gurley and E. S. Shaw in both articles and in their book, *Money in a Theory of Finance* (Brookings Institution, 1960) must be mentioned. Their work is important for analysing how the institutions affect the supply of money, for disputing the proposition that once-for-all changes in the stock of money are neutral, and for its implications for the role of money in economic growth. The book is not easy. Their results on money supply theory have implications for macroeconomics, as has too a collection of papers edited by Donald D. Hester, *Financial Markets and Economic Activity* (Wiley, 1967). The import of this volume is that the money supply should not be taken as exogenous, but is, rather, endogenous to the system, and determined by the profit maximising behaviour of banks and other institutions and the utility maximising behaviour of asset holders. Whenever we recognise the importance of financial intermediaries we are forced to consider what is and what is not money. One approach has been to define as money everything which has to be included in the demand for money function. There have also been theoretical attempts, turning on the long-run neutrality or otherwise of changes in its stock (L. B. Yeager, 'Essential Properties of the Medium of Exchange' in *Kyklos*, vol. 21, 1968, pp. 45–69), or on whether or not it is a part of the country's net wealth (*Money, Wealth and*

Economic Theory, by B. P. Pesek and T. R. Saving, Collier-Macmillan, 1967). There is a survey of this field in the *Journal of Economic Literature* (vol. 7, No. 1, March 1969, pp. 27–56) entitled 'Money, Intermediation and Growth' by Allan H. Meltzer. That survey also deals with our next topic, the role of **money in economic growth**. There are as yet no books on this subject, but two path-breaking articles are 'Wealth, Saving and the Rate of Interest' by Lloyd A. Metzler (*Journal of Political Economy*, vol. 59, 1951, pp. 93–116) and 'A Dynamic Aggregative Model' by James Tobin (*Journal of Political Economy*, vol. 63, 1955, pp. 103–115). Neither are there as yet any collections of articles on money and growth, but the proceedings of a conference on the subject were published in a supplement to the *Journal of Political Economy* for July/August, 1968. Allan H. Meltzer's above-mentioned survey is again useful, both to provide a framework for what has been written, and as a bibliography.

Our final subject is **money in general equilibrium**. This work originates with J. R. Hicks' *Value and Capital* (2nd edn, Oxford U.P., 1946) (and of course his earlier 'Suggestion for Simplifying the Theory of Money' in *Economica*, New Series, vol. 2, 1935, pp. 1–19) was continued by O. Lange in *Price Flexibility and Employment* (Principia Press, 1944) and reached its peak of development in D. Patinkin's *Money Interest and Prices* (2nd edn, Harper and Row, 1965). Robert W. Clower has been the leading critic of this approach: a collection of articles around this theme is his book of readings *Monetary Theory* (Penguin, 1969). Every article here is well worth reading in detail, but particularly relevant to our present theme are Clower's introduction and part three of the volume. Clower's article 'The Keynesian Counter-revolution: a Theoretical Appraisal' (first published in the Hahn and Brechling volume noted below, and reprinted in part in the Penguin volume) is fascinating in that it pioneered the modern, microeconomic approach to Keynesian economics that was further developed in Leijonhufvud's book noted above. Another book which fits best into this section is *The Theory of Interest Rates*, the proceedings of an International Economics Association conference edited by F. H. Hahn and F. P. R. Brechling (Macmillan, 1965). This is a collection of theoretically very sophisticated papers on theories of asset preference, money in general equilibrium, and the use of interest rates for intertemporal allocation.

There remain three items to mention. The first is Harry G. Johnson's masterly survey of the whole field of monetary theory excluding only balance of payments policy, first published in *American Economic Review* in 1962, then reprinted in the American Economic Association/Royal Economic Society, *Surveys of Economic Theory* (Macmillan, 1965), vol. 1. No serious student should omit to read this (it should be noted that its great compression makes it heavy going unless the reader has some knowledge of the subject) and to use its massive bibliography. Second is a collection *Critical Essays in Monetary Theory* by J. R. Hicks (Oxford U.P., 1967) which embodies that great economist's views on a wide range of monetary topics.

Our final word is on journals: the *Journal of Money, Credit and Banking* (1968–), is the first journal to be devoted exclusively to monetary topics, and is well worth following. Articles on monetary economics are to be found in all the other major economics journals; of these the *Journal of Political Economy* has traditionally laid more emphasis on monetary economics than have the others. Many studies can be found in the publications of the Federal Reserve Bank of St. Louis, and a good bibliography is the US Board of Governors of the Federal Reserve System, *Monetary Theory and Policy: a Bibliography: part 1, Domestic Aspects* (The Board, 1965).

CHAPTER TWENTY-TWO

PUBLIC FINANCE

ALAN WILLIAMS

The boundaries of 'public' finance' as a branch of economics have become very unclear since about 1950, with the great upsurge of academic interest in public expenditure analysis, and the growing importance of the budget as a tool of economic management. This is reflected in the increasing use of terms like 'public sector economics' or simply 'public economics' to describe this field of inquiry more accurately than is implied by the term 'public finance', with its traditional connotation of legal-administrative 'institutional' bias, and the concentration on tax problems.

This extension of coverage and shift of emphasis is well illustrated by comparing with earlier works the Proceedings of the Biarritz Conference of the International Economic Association on *Public Economics* edited by J. Margolis and H. Guitton (Macmillan, 1969) which (significantly) was subtitled *An Analysis of Public Production and Consumption and Their Relations to the Private Sector*. It is a far cry from earlier compendia, such as the American Economic Association's *Readings in Fiscal Policy* edited by A. Smithies and J. K. Butters (Allen and Unwin, 1955) which was mostly concerned with stabilisation policy problems, or the AEA *Readings in the Economics of Taxation* edited by R. A. Musgrave and C. S. Shoup (Allen and Unwin, 1959) which was even more narrowly contrained to the tax side of the budget, partly because the general fiscal policy areas had been covered in the earlier volume, but also because 'the economics of taxation appeared the most appropriate topic for the present series of *Readings*, since it represents the area of public finance in which the major body of economic analysis has developed'. This view also implicitly underlies one other important compendium *Readings on Taxation in Developing Countries* edited by R. Bird and O. Oldman (Johns Hopkins Press, 1964), an offshoot of Harvard's International Program in Taxation. But curiously enough, if one

285

goes back much further in time, for instance to the period 1880 to 1930 covered in the IEA compendium *Classics in the Theory of Public Finance* edited by R. A. Musgrave and A. T. Peacock (Macmillan, 1958), the material is far more wide ranging, and comes closer in coverage (though it is still far removed in spirit and technique) to *Public Economics*. Plus ça change....

But this extension of the subject matter of 'public finance' creates great difficulties from the viewpoint of literature searching, because one can no longer be sure that all important items in the field will be classified as 'public finance' (or even so cross-referenced). This difficulty is particularly acute in the field of public expenditure analysis, where a vast and burgeoning literature of great significance manifests itself as 'welfare economics', the 'economics of education', or of health, defence, social security, transport, etc. For instance, about a third of the selections in the recent AEA *Readings in Welfare Economics* edited by K. J. Arrow and T. Scitovsky (Allen and Unwin, 1969) fall clearly within the field of 'Public Economics' as do virtually all the selections in the Penguin Modern Economics Readings on *Public Enterprise* edited by R. Turvey (Penguin, 1968) *Transport* edited by D. Munby (Penguin, 1968), *Economics of Education* edited by M. Blaug (2 vols, Penguin, 1968–69) and to a lesser extent *Regional Analysis* edited by L. Needleman (Penguin, 1968).

Inevitably these changes are reflected rather slowly in the standard textbooks, and although the various compendia mentioned earlier serve a useful purpose as a starting point, they are inevitably somewhat out of date, and are likely to reflect selection criteria which do not accord fully with the needs and interests of any particular investigator. For more comprehensive bibliographies, the earlier AEA *Readings* (Smithies and Butters, 1955; and Musgrave and Shoup, 1959) each contained extensive classified lists of references, but 'in view of the availability of the *Index of Economic Journals*' (*see* p. 185) Arrow and Scitovsky decided to dispense with one in their *Readings in Welfare Economics* volume.

If one turns to the public finance (and associated) sections of the general bibliographies, their main weakness is the one already mentioned, namely that the subject matter of 'Public Finance' has changed so much, and is still changing so rapidly, that the conventional classifications that are still commonly used are not very helpful. For instance, the *American Economic Review* included in each quarterly issue a classified list of titles of new books, and in one issue (picked at random) none of the following titles appeared under the heading 'Public Finance; Fiscal Policy' but only under some other classification: *Metropolitan America: Challenge to*

Federalism; Metropolitan America: Fiscal Patterns and Governmental Systems; Open Space, Land Planning and Taxation: a Selected Bibliography; Should Pensioners Receive Unemployment Compensation; Normative Evaluation of a Public Health Program; and *State Public School Finance Programs 1966–7.* Similarly, abstracting services which are aimed at the general economist tend to be rather inadequate for the specialist in any one field, for example, several of them do not cover articles published in the journal *Public Finance.*

If we then turn to more specialised bibliographies, they tend to suffer from being rather sporadic phenomena, possibly cropping up in a rather out-of-the-way context (e.g. the very useful *Annotated Bibliography of Benefits and Costs in the Public Sector* of 2700 entries, published by Research for Better Schools Inc. Philadelphia, in November 1968); or being restricted in coverage to subjects of topical interest in the country of origin (e.g. the rather slim 'Research Bibliographies' produced by the Tax Foundation in New York, or the bibliographies produced by the House of Commons Library for the benefit of M.P.s).

The best specialised regular bibliographical service I have come across is that contained in the *Public Affairs Information Service Bulletin.* It is by no means perfect, and I will outline some of its faults, but in my experience it has yet to be beaten. Let us work our way into it gently through the entry 'FINANCE, PUBLIC'. We are immediately cross-referenced to 16 other heads, and some further sub-heads under specific countries. However, by this route we would *not* reach any of the following relevant headings, which I found accidentally and without exhaustive search, so there may well be others that I have not tracked down : Cost-Benefit Analysis; Decentralisation in Government; Defence Contracts; Federal Aid; Government Accounting; Government Business Enterprises; Government Loans and Grants; Government Ownership; Government Trading; Industry and State; Municipal Accounting; Nationalisation; Performance Budgeting; Public Buildings; Public Lands; Public Utilities; Public Welfare; Social Insurance. Indeed, under the very important entry 'Cost-Benefit Analysis' we are not cross-referenced to any other entry at all, and as far as I can see this entry itself is not referred to under any other heading (it is certainly not mentioned under any of the obvious points of contact elsewhere, such as 'Efficiency' or 'Investment, Decision-making'). Literature search is hard work in Public Economics!

The next, and major, source of material to be considered is the journals themselves. Here again the situation is difficult because relevant material is scattered not only throughout the *general* journals, but also throughout a lot of 'specialist' journals which are *not* (on the face of things) 'public finance' journals. The *Journal of Finance* is obviously fairly close, but how much public finance would one expect to find in the *Journal of Law and Economics*, or the *American Journal of Economics and Sociology*, or *Land Economics*? Yet each of these contains a great deal of 'public finance' material, as do many others. Of the more specialised journals, *Public Finance* has already been mentioned, and the *National Tax Journal* is another important source. Although rather more biased towards the legal side, the *British Tax Review* often contains some economic analysis. *Local Government Finance* and *Public Administration* also contain material of a more traditional public finance kind, but neither of them can hold a candle to the US *Public Administration Review* as regards the academic power and range of some of the public economics contained therein. The various British bank reviews also often contain material of interest, though at a more popular level, hence better for teaching purposes than as research material.

In my view the most important single centre for current research into public sector economics is the Brookings Institution in Washington D.C. and their publications in the series *'Studies of Government Finance'* though US oriented, represent collectively a major contribution to the field. They vary greatly in style, approach, pitch, content and methodological interest, but at worst they always constitute a good source of bibliographical material in their respective subject areas, and at best bring one right up to the important and stimulating intellectual frontiers of the subject. Several of them are symposia based on conference proceedings, and have the important merit of being published with a much shorter time lag than is usually the case for such volumes. The Brookings Institution has a Reprint Series also which includes material in the same field. Reprint Series are a useful way of keeping up with work in the field, and the University of York has one which includes a large proportion of 'Public Economics' simply because of the special interests of its economists in that field. Besides the Registers of Theses (which suffer the usual classification snags), there is also a growing volume of working papers and memoranda distributed in an organised way by some institutions which are available to scholars in the field, but here it is important to know the interests of the people concerned if one is not to be bombarded with masses of irrelevant and bulky typescript.

Keeping informed of what other work is currently going on in any field is one of the major problems for anyone doing or directing or encouraging or sponsoring research. Titles of ongoing dissertations are some help, as are the reports of research-financing bodies like the SSRC (which publishes an annual register of titles of research projects it is supporting, classified by institution, and indexed both by names of researchers and by titles). A more comprehensive register—*Scientific Research in British Universities and Colleges: Volume III—Social Sciences (including Government Departments and Other Institutions)* is produced annually by the Department of Education and Science. This is listed (within 'Economics') by institution, but there are also separate name and subject indices. There is no subject classification within Economics, hence no easy way of locating 'Public Economics' or even 'Public Finance' topics quickly, and indeed in the 1966–7 issue (which I happen to have to hand) the only two mentions of 'cost-benefit analysis' in the subject index led us *not* to the Economics section at all, but once to 'Industrial Administration' (for *'Cost Benefit Investigation of Rheumatoid Arthritis'*) and once to 'Information Science' (for *'Cost-Benefit Study of University Libraries'*). Information Science? We've a long way to go yet!

Let us turn to slightly more informal channels of communication. The Treasury Economics Section has adopted the admirable practice of sending out scouts to universities and similar institutions, visiting each one every two or three years or so, talking to as many economists as can be contacted on the day in question, then collating and circularising the information so collected. All rather casual and unsystematic, and sometimes difficult to interpret (the statement that 'X is interested in taxation problems' may mean that he is about to burst forth with a book on the subject which will be the culmination of a lifetime's work, or that he recently emerged unsuccessfully from an argument with a colleague, or with his tax inspector, about the impact of Capital Gains Taxation, and has decided to look into it a bit more deeply). However, despite these obvious flaws, it does scatter straws in the wind for those to clutch at who are anxious to establish contact with others of like interests. A sort of lonely hearts club! It is classified with the following areas: Mathematical Economics, Econometrics, and Economic Statistics; Models of the UK Economy; Agriculture; Growth and Development; Regional Economics; Money, Banking and Financial Institutions; Public and Local Government Finance; Private Investment and Company Finance; Industrial Economics; Nationalised Industries and Public Enterprises; Transport Economics; Social Economics; Labour Economics; and International Economics. There is no cross-referencing, but some borderline items are repeated so that they appear in each relevant section.

289

The final informal channel of communication is the personal network, which is an important one for me, despite its acknowledged defects (it will be evident from the foregoing that all the other channels have defects too!). The personal network is built up through conferences, mutual friends, correspondence about published work, seminar visits, informal exchange of working papers, joint supervision or examining of graduate work, visiting scholarships, etc. It can be used in a multitude of ways, from the fairly formal request for offprints or unpublished material, to the casual telephone call seeking out suitable graduates to hire as research assistants on particular projects in fields of common interest. An active researcher who is also a conscientious teacher can be a valuable source of bibliographies, for his 'course reading list' at graduate or even advanced undergraduate level may embody a highly skilled (and sometimes tersely annotated) selection of the important and relevant material distilled from a great deal of reading. A good and active contact can also often tell you who, in an unfamiliar field, is the best person to contact even if he is not, hence certain people become 'telephone exchanges' in the system. It does, however, require restraint on the part of the inquirers, because it is a system that is open to abuse, and an excessive volume of relatively trivial but time-consuming inquiries can lead to severance of the links!

There are other important problems facing the economist interested in the Public Sector on which I have not dwelt because they are treated elsewhere in this volume. Official publications of one kind or another are usefully crucial to his work, and the problems entailed in tracking them down, and in digging out items of information from them, are extremely forbidding. The same is true of much of the statistical material required. Nor have I mentioned historical research in this field, because I do not do it and have no first-hand experience of the difficulties, but it doubtless throws up literature-search problems of its own.

Samuel Johnson long ago observed that 'Knowledge is of two kinds. We know a subject ourselves, or we know where we can find information upon it.' The trouble nowadays seems to be that until you yourself know the subject fairly well, you cannot know what information you need, and without knowing other people who know the subject even better, you are unlikely to find it!

CHAPTER TWENTY-THREE

INTERNATIONAL ECONOMICS

A. G. FORD and G. E. WOOD

The study of international economics has produced a vast mass of literature in terms of both analytical and empirical work. Furthermore, the theoretical work has usually divided itself up into the pure theory of international trade as distinct from the monetary theory of international trade. The former has concerned itself with explaining flows of trade and patterns of trade, and seeking to demonstrate the gains from trade, while it has abstracted from problems of the balance of payments and its adjustment, and international monetary systems. These have been the province of the latter. Links between the pure and monetary approaches have indeed been few until recently when interest in economic growth problems in an international context has involved both approaches to a greater extent.

The volume of the literature has forced the authors to omit almost completely reference to empirical work and to concentrate on key analytical works which are highly important in themselves in the development of the theories or which are useful in terms of introducing the student to themes together with follow-up suggestions for further reading. This has meant that books alone are mentioned by name and articles are not cited. Hence some famous economists who have contributed mightily to the subject are not mentioned since their valuable work has been in article form.

Fortunately these omissions can be justified because of the existence of some excellent surveys of the subject which vary in difficulty and to some degree are complementary. On a general level *A Survey of International Trade Theory* (Princeton Special Paper in International Economics, No. 1) by G. Haberler (rev. edn, Princeton U.P., 1961) and *Recent Developments in the Theory of International Trade* (Princeton Special Paper in International Economics, No. 7) by W. M. Corden (1965) provide excellent introductions for the non-specialist. More acquaintanceship with international economics is required to benefit from J. Bhagwati, 'The Pure Theory of International Trade: A Survey', *Economic Journal*, vol. 74, 1964 (reprinted in *Surveys of Economic Theory*, vol. 2, Macmillan, 1965) which is essential reading for the specialist, is non-mathematical, and possesses a good selective bibliography. Finally, mathematical skills are required to benefit from J. S. Chipman, 'A Survey of the Theory of International Trade, Part 1: The Classical Theory', *Econometrica*, vol. 33, 1965; 'Part 2: The Neo-classical Theory', *Econometrica*, vol. 33, 1965; 'Part 3: The Modern Theory', *Econometrica*, vol. 34, 1966.

For the graduate or finalist undergraduate with little acquaintanceship with international economics, who regrettably is not infrequently met, there can be suggested *International Economics* by S. J. Wells (Allen and Unwin, 1969), or *International Economics* by Sir Roy Harrod (rev. edn, Cambridge U.P., 1957), or *The International Economy* by P. T. Ellsworth (4th edn, Macmillan, 1969), or *International Economics* by C. P. Kindleberger (4th edn, Irwin, 1968). These provide comprehensive introductions, are largely non-mathematical, and mostly have useful suggestions for further reading. If this stage has already been attained, much benefit will be gained from *Theoretical Issues in International Economics* by M. O. Clement, R. L. Pfister, and K. J. Rothwell (Houghton-Mifflin, 1967) which deals with selected topics in the pure and monetary branches and provides lengthy bibliographies on each topic covered. Again, it is non-mathematical, but certain points could be made better if some calculus had been used. Likewise, *International Trade Theory and Empirical Evidence* by H. R. Heller (Prentice-Hall, 1968) provides a short, non-mathematical approach to the problems of the pure theory with little space devoted to evidence.

For those graduates who are seeking a rigorous approach to the theory of international economics and who have a mathematical grounding, little better can be found than *The Pure Theory of International Trade* by M. C. Kemp (Prentice-Hall, 1964) and *The Pure Theory of International Trade and Investment* by M. C. Kemp (Prentice-Hall, 1969). The latter is essentially the former so extensively rewritten and with such additions and deletions that both can be read with great profit. The reader must be prepared to work hard through these books and their mathematical methods. Coupled with Kemp can be recommended *Trade and Economic Structure* by R. E. Caves (Harvard U.P., 1960) which provides a comprehensive non-mathematical discussion of international trade theories and a selective bibliography.

Perhaps the most influential and important international economics treatise of the twentieth century is *Interregional and International Trade* by B. Ohlin (Harvard U.P., 1933) which initiated much theoretical development and tended to supersede such famous works as *International Trade* by F. W. Taussig (Macmillan, 1927). Other distinguished works of this period which are very well worth reading are *The Theory of International Trade* by G. Haberler (Hodge, 1936) and *Studies in the Theory of International Trade* by J. Viner (Harper, 1937). The latter provides a superb exposition of the historical evolution of international trade theory and is essential reading to understand the development of doctrine.

Amongst the many works of the post-1945 period one must surely single out for mention the massive taxonomic contributions (each with separate mathematical appendices) in the theory of international economic policy by J. E. Meade. Volume 1, entitled *The Balance of Payments* by J. E. Meade (Oxford U.P., 1951) is a vital contribution to the monetary theory, while Volume 2, entitled *Trade and Welfare* (Oxford U.P., 1955) provides a thorough treatise on the pure theory. Both are very lucid, but are most profitably used as reference books in which to investigate particular topics.

Important contributions to theory of trade and growth have been made in *International Trade and Economic Growth* by H. G. Johnson (Allen and Unwin, 1958), in *Money, Trade and Economic Growth* by H. G. Johnson (Allen and Unwin, 1962), and in *International Trade and Development* by G. M. Meier (Harper and Row, 1963). It should be noted that there are also contributions to the static pure theory of trade in the Johnson books, while *Economic Policies Towards Less Developed Countries* by H. G. Johnson (Brookings Institution, 1967) examines these problems in a more practical way in the cases of poor countries.

International finance has provided many useful books of which the non-specialist will find *International Monetary Policy* by W. M. Scammell (2nd edn, Macmillan, 1961) a useful introduction, while those with a liking for a historical treatment will enjoy *International Monetary Relations* by L. B. Yeager (Harper and Row, 1966) with its blend of history, analysis and policy. Other important books for the specialists are *The World Dollar Problem* by Sir Donald MacDougall (Macmillan, 1957) and *Sterling-Dollar Diplomacy* by R. N. Gardner (Oxford U.P., 1956), while all will find valuable *International Currency Experience* by R. Nurkse (League of Nations, 1944), and *Equilibrium and Growth in the World Economy* by R. Nurkse (Harvard U.P., 1961).

In the post-1945 period great interest has been developed in the theory of Customs Unions, to which notable contributions have been made by *The Customs Unions Issue* by J. Viner (Carnegie Endowment for International Peace, 1950), *The Theory of Customs Unions* by J. E. Meade (North-Holland, 1955), *Economic Theory and Western European Integration* by T. Scitovsky (Allen and Unwin, 1958), and *The Theory of Economic Integration* by B. Balassa (Allen and Unwin, 1962).

Western economists are often apt to forget that trade also takes place amongst communist countries and they will find *Communist International Economics* by P. J. D. Wiles (Blackwell, 1968) a very useful book which appears set to become the definitive work.

Although it was earlier mentioned that much important work by distinguished economists would not be cited because it appeared in journals, nevertheless these contributions have become more accessible because the authors have published collections of their articles in reprint or because editors have presented various collections of important work. In the first category are *International Monetary Economics* by F. Machlup (Allen and Unwin, 1966), *International Economics* by R. A. Mundell (Collier-Macmillan, 1968), and *Trade, Tariffs, Growth* by J. Bhagwati (Weidenfeld and Nicolson, 1969), which are all essential reading for the specialist. P. A. Samuelson's distinguished contributions will be found in *Collected Scientific Papers of Paul A. Samuelson vol. 2*, edited by J. Stiglitz (M.I.T. Press, 1967).

In the second category the American Economic Association has earned much gratitude by sponsoring two highly important collections. The first is *Readings in the Theory of International Trade* edited by H. S. Ellis and L. A. Metzler (Allen and Unwin, 1949) which has an invaluable bibliography of material up to 1947. The second is *Readings in International Economics* edited by R. E. Caves and H. G. Johnson (Allen and Unwin, 1968) which has no bibliography. As the authors say, the American Economic Association's *Index of Economic Journals* should now be consulted. *Foreign Trade and Finance* edited by W. R. Allen and C. L. Allen (Macmillan, 1959) has selected articles arranged to form a useful textbook, while *International Finance* edited by R. N. Cooper (Penguin Books, 1969) and *International Trade* edited by J. Bhagwati (Penguin Books, 1969) provide very helpful and complementary collections of articles.

Other useful collective contributions are to be found in *Maintaining and Restoring Balance in International Payments* edited by W. Fellner *et al.* (Princeton U.P., 1966) and *Monetary Problems of the International Economy* edited by R. A. Mundell and A. K. Swoboda (University of Chicago Press, 1969).

No specialist journal devotes itself entirely to international economics although *The International Monetary Fund Staff Papers* has a high international content. Students should not be misled by the 'international' adjective in *International Economic Review, Economia Internazionale,* and *Kyklos, An International Review of the Social Sciences.* This does *not* refer to content, but to authorship and distribution of readership. International economic articles appear frequently in all the main non-specialist journals and they must be searched persistently.

Special mention must be made of the pamphlet publications of the International Finance Section, Department of Economics, Princeton University, which have made an invaluable contribution to the monetary side of international economics in particular. These are issued irregularly in three series (i) *Princeton Essays in International Finance*; (ii) *Princeton Studies in International Finance* (more substantial in length than (i)); and (iii) *Princeton Special Papers in International Economics.*

CHAPTER TWENTY-FOUR

ECONOMIC SOCIOLOGY

A. F. HEATH

Economic sociology has been defined as 'the application of the general frame of reference, variables, and explanatory models of sociology to that complex of activities concerned with the production, distribution, exchange, and consumption of scarce goods and services' (N. J. Smelser, *The Sociology of Economic Life,* Prentice-Hall, 1963, p. 32). In fact, however, economic sociology is much more amorphous and heterogeneous than this definition implies, and there is considerable disagreement among sociologists on its scope and nature. Frequently, too, the terms 'industrial sociology' or 'the sociology of work' are used rather than that of 'economic sociology'.

Nevertheless, in practice a fairly restricted number of specific topics (most of them relating to the so-called advanced societies) are included under the heading of economic sociology. They can be roughly divided into the following six main groups. First, there is a group of what might be called 'macro-sociological' topics. These deal with such matters as the interrelationship between the type of economy or the level of economic development on the one hand and the kinship system or the system of stratification on the other. Second, there are a number of topics dealing with the internal structure and functioning of economic organisations. These deal, for example, with the relationship between the type of technology and the system of management, and with that between supervisory styles, incentive schemes, morale and productivity. This group of topics overlaps to a large extent with what is often called 'organisation theory'. A third group of topics is that which covers what is sometimes called 'the sociology of occupations'. This includes discussions of the professions and of occupational associations, occupational mobility and attitudes to work. Fourth, there are the sociological discussions of industrial relations and industrial conflict. These are dealt with in Chapter 18.

296

and I shall not deal with them further in this chapter. Fifth, there is a group of topics connected with the sociology of leisure and of consumption behaviour. And, sixth, there are the discussions of the sociological aspects of economic development.

Usually books on economic sociology can be expected to cover the whole range of subjects, while those on industrial sociology or the sociology of work will cover a more limited range (concentrating primarily on the second, third, and fourth groups of subjects). However, this division is not kept to at all strictly. In addition, sociologists have not researched equally extensively (or equally successfully) into all the groups of subjects. For example, relatively little work has been carried out on the sociology of leisure, while discussions of some of the 'macro-sociological' topics seem to generate more heat than light. Organisation theory, on the other hand, is probably the most developed and theoretically advanced of the main groups of subjects.

Introductory Works

Brief guides to the main issues of economic sociology can be obtained from most introductory textbooks on sociology. An up-to-date one is *Sociology: An Introduction* edited by N. J. Smelser (Wiley, 1967). T. Burns 'The sociology of industry' in *Society: Problems and Methods of Study* edited by A. T. Welford (Routledge, 1962) is also an excellent brief review.

Possibly the best short textbook which deals exclusively with the issues of economic sociology is *The Sociology of Economic Life* by N. J. Smelser (Prentice-Hall, 1963). Like most textbooks in sociology it is American and uses mainly American material. A short British work which covers more or less the same ground and makes extensive use of British material is *The Sociology of Industry* by S. R. Parker and others (Allen and Unwin, 1967). In addition it gives a brief but useful guide to the literature.

There are also a large number of detailed and lengthy American textbooks (usually with extensive bibliographies). One of the most sophisticated of these is *Industrial Sociology* by E. V. Schneider (2nd edn, McGraw-Hill, 1969). Other useful texts are:

The Sociology of Work by T. Caplow (University of Minnesota Press, 1954)

Work and Society by E. Gross (Crowell, 1958)

Industrial Sociology: The Sociology of Work Organizations by D. C. Miller and W. H. Form (2nd edn, Harper & Row, 1964).

Monographs

The character and quality of monographs in economic sociology varies enormously, and this is particularly evident among those which deal with the 'macro-sociological' topics. One of the most noted, and most ambitious, of these is *Economy and Society* by Talcott Parsons and N. J. Smelser (Routledge, 1956). This largely fact-free work tries to integrate economic and sociological theory, but whether it has more than curiosity value remains to be seen. Another ambitious and much noted work is *Industrialism and Industrial Man* by C. Kerr and others (Heinemann, 1962). This is known particularly for its (highly speculative) claim that there is a 'logic of industrialism' such that all fully industrialised societies will come to share certain specified characteristics. More empirically based, and more limited in their objectives, are *World Revolution and Family Patterns* by W. J. Goode (Collier-Macmillan, 1963) and *Power and Privilege: A Theory of Social Stratification* by G. E. Lenski (McGraw-Hill, 1966). These two works examine the relationship between industrialisation and the family and between industrialisation and stratification respectively. A useful critical survey of empirical and theoretical work in these two areas and an extensive bibliography is also to be found in *Comparative Sociology* by R. M. Marsh (Harcourt, Brace and World, 1967).

As mentioned above, there has been a great deal of work on economic organisations, and as a result there are a very large number of specialist monographs in this area. *Formal Organizations* by P. M. Blau and W. R. Scott (Routledge, 1963) contains a comprehensive survey and bibliography of this work. Two other monographs which contain extensive critical reviews of the literature in their particular fields are *The Business Enterprise in Modern Industrial Society* by J. Child (Collier-Macmillan, 1969) and *Industrial Democracy: The Sociology of Participation* by P. Blumberg (Constable, 1968). These two books are mainly useful as guides to the literature. Of those, on the other hand, which make individual contributions to their field, two outstanding examples are *Industrial Organization: Theory and Practice* by J. Woodward (Oxford U.P., 1965) and *The Management of Innovation* by T. Burns and G. M. Stalker (Tavistock, 1961). The former presents some important findings on the relationship between technology, organisational structure and business success while the latter examines the relationship between market conditions, organisational structure and business success.

On occupations an excellent general work is *Occupations and the Social Structure* by R. H. Hall (Prentice-Hall, 1969). There are also a large number of monographs on specific occupational groups, of which some of the more useful are *The Industrial Manager* by D. G. Clark (Business Publications, 1966), *Scientists in Industry* by W. Kornhauser (University of California Press, 1962), and *The Affluent Worker: Industrial Attitudes and Behaviour* by J. H. Goldthorpe and others (Cambridge U.P., 1968). Another extremely useful work which should probably be included here is *Ownership, Control and Ideology* by Theo. Nichols (Allen and Unwin, 1969). This is primarily concerned with the social role and ideology of the modern businessman and reports some new empirical material as well as providing an excellent survey of the existing literature.

Finally, the sociology of leisure and that of economic development have produced relatively little work of any stature. In the former field a standard work is *Work and Leisure* by N. Anderson (Routledge, 1961) and in the latter a standard one is *Modernization: Protest and Change* by S. N. Eisenstadt (Prentice-Hall, 1966).

Articles

New material on economic sociology appears both in article form and in specialist monographs, although the contents of a monograph will often have been summarised in an earlier article. There are a large number of general sociological journals, and almost all of them contain material on economic sociology. The following is a list of the main British and American journals (although it is far from exhaustive):

British Journal of Sociology (1950–)
Human Relations (1947–)
Sociological Review (1908–)
Sociology (1967–)
American Journal of Sociology (1895–)
American Sociological Review (1936–)

The *Sociological Review* also publishes Monographs at approximately yearly intervals. These contain collections of articles on specific topics, and of them Monograph No. 8 *The Development of Industrial Societies* edited by P. Halmos is a particularly important one.

In addition to the general sociological journals listed above there are a number of more specialist journals which are important sources for many of the topics covered by economic sociology. They include:

Administrative Science Quarterly (1956–)
British Journal of Industrial Relations (1963–)

299

Industrial and Labor Relations Review (1947–)
Industrial Relations (1961–)
Sociologie du Travail (1959–).

Two specialist journals which carry articles on the sociological aspects of economic development are:

Economic Development and Cultural Change (1952–)
Explorations in Entrepreneurial History (1949–).

The former of these has a useful annotated index covering the first fifteen volumes.

The general psychological journals also sometimes carry articles on such topics as job satisfaction or workers' needs or motivation, and these topics also frequently appear in *Occupational Psychology* (1922. Originally this was called the *Journal of the National Institute of Industrial Psychology*. The name was changed to *Human Factor* in 1932 and then to *Occupational Psychology* in 1938.)

Another important source of original material are the papers presented at the world congresses of sociology and a selection of these are published after each congress by the International Sociological Association. The contributions range widely over sociology but include a number on economic sociology. Similarly, *Current Sociology* (1952–) contains lengthy review articles and bibliographies on various sociological topics but from time to time will cover an area relevant to economic sociology. The major abstracting and indexing services also deal with sociology in general but have sections relevant to economic sociology. Thus the annual UNESCO publication *International Bibliography of Sociology* (1951–) indexes published books and articles of sociological interest generally but has a section on economic institutions, while *Sociological Abstracts* (1953–) covers some unpublished as well as published material and has a section on industrial sociology.

Finally, many of the key articles in economic sociology are reprinted in the *Bobbs-Merrill Reprint Series in Sociology*. The series is biased towards American sources, but is nevertheless an excellent starting-point for a bibliography. The British suppliers are Eurospan Ltd., 44 Hatton Garden, London, E.C.1.

Readers

Important articles in sociology are frequently collected in readers and there are a large number of such collections ranging from general introductory readings on sociology to specialised sets on particular theoretical issues. One which covers the field of economic

300

sociology generally is *Readings on Economic Sociology* edited by N. J. Smelser (Prentice-Hall, 1965). Rather more limited in scope, but quite useful, are *Man, Work and Society* edited by S. Nosow and W. H. Form (Basic Books, 1962) and *Readings in Industrial Sociology* edited by W. A. Faunce (Appleton Century Crofts, 1967).

Of the more specialised collections two good ones on organisation theory are *Handbook of Organizations* edited by J. G. March (Rand, McNally, 1965) and *A Sociological Reader on Complex Organizations* edited by A. Etzioni (2nd edn, Holt, Rinehart and Winston, 1969). *Industrialization and Society* edited by B. F. Hoselitz and W. E. Moore (The Hague: UNESCO-Mouton, 1963) is an often-quoted collection of conference papers on the sociological aspects of economic development, while other useful collections include:

Consumer Behavior and the Behavioral Sciences: Theories and Applications edited by S. H. Britt (Wiley, 1966).

Education, Economy and Society edited by A. H. Halsey and others (Free Press, 1961).

Industrial Conflict edited by A. Kornhauser and others (McGraw-Hill, 1954).

INDEX

Note: This is predominantly a subject index. Subjects of statistics sources noted in Chapter 10 have been indexed in detail, and the page references are in italics. Other subjects have been indexed as fully as limited space would permit. No authors or monograph titles have been included, and periodical and other serial titles are indexed only when an appreciable description of them is in the text.

Traffic, *159, 167*
Translations, 43, 66
Transport, *128, 130, 136, 154, 159–160, 161, 162, 163, 166–167, 169, 170*; see also Aviation, Railways, Road transport, Shipping costs, *137, 159, 160*
Transport, Ministry of, 133
Transportation, Department of, 95
Treasury
UK, 84–86, 134, 289
US, 92
Trustee savings banks, *151*
Twentieth Century Fund, 97, 182

UNESCO, 115–116
Unemployment, *144, 145–146, 161, 164, 169, 170, 172*
Unit trusts, *152*
United Nations, 109–116, 179, 229
agencies, 113–116
Department of Economic and Social Affairs, 111–113
economic commissions, 112–113
Statistical Office, 110–111, 179
United Nations Conference on Trade and Development, 70, 113, 179
United Nations Documents Index, 110
United Nations Educational Scientific and Cultural Organisation, 115–116
United Nations Industrial Development Organisation, 113
United States Government Research and Development Reports, 73
Universal Decimal Classification, 18–19
Universities-National Bureau Committee for Economic Research, 179

Unpublished material, 67–74, 258–260

Vacancies unfilled, *146, 169*
Varnish, *138*
Vegetables, *144*
Vital statistics, see Population

Wage bill, *137*
Wage drift, *148*
Wage rates, *144, 146, 148*
Wages, *136, 140, 155, 160, 169, 170, 172, 173*; see also Earnings, Salaries
Wales, 88, *161*
Watches and clocks, *138*
Wealth, *154*
Welsh Office, 88, 134
Western Economic Journal, 61
Wheat, *144, 174*
'White papers', 79
Wholesale prices, see Prices, wholesale
Wholesale trade, *139, 160, 165*
Who's Who, 46
Wine, *144*
Wool, *174*
Work in progress, *139*
Working papers, 68–70, 288
World Bank, 71, 116–117

Yale Economic Essays, 61–62
Yale University, 6
Yields
agricultural, *143, 165, 174*
financial, *152, 153*
Yorkshire Bulletin of Economic and Social Research, 59–60